ERIC BELL

Remembering

THE AUTOBIOGRAPHY
BEFORE, DURING AND AFTER THIN LIZZY

Typeset by Louis Rozier
Layout by SPiderKaT for CFZ Communications

This edition published in Great Britain by Gonzo Multimedia

c/o Brooks City,
6th Floor New Baltic House
65 Fenchurch Street,
London EC3M 4BE
Fax: +44 (0)191 5121104
Tel: +44 (0) 191 5849144
International Numbers:
Germany: Freephone 08000 825 699

of the **Edge** productions

ISBN: 978-1-908728-97-5

This book is dedicated to the memory of my dear wife Rhona.

To my dear friend and manager Andy Quinn, for all the work he
has done to make this book possible.

And to Enrique Torron Abad, better known as Quique.
My Spanish friend, who has stuck by me for so many years.

My sincere thanks to the both of you.

All the best
Eric

Preface

I am a musician, not a magician.

But that night, 800 people watch my old Fender guitar as it hangs suspended 15 feet in the air, before crashing down on to the stage in Queen's University, Belfast on New Year's Eve, 1973. Then, to finish my magic act, I make my two 4 x 12 cabinets and amp disappear, as I kick them viciously off the stage. But this is no act, rather a final statement, a cry for help fuelled by drugs, alcohol and sheer exhaustion. I have had enough.

I stagger down some steps at the side and crawl under the stage where there are some rubber mats, and I can hear Phil and Brian still playing as I slowly pass out. Then someone pulls roughly at my shoulder, shouting, "Get back on that fucking stage! Can you not hear the boys trying their best?"

I look up and slowly focus on the face of Frank, Thin Lizzy's personal roadie, and say, "Forget it, I've left the band!"

"All right," says Frank, "but for frig's sake finish the gig!" I mumble if he gets me three bottles of Guinness I will go back on. He says, "You'd better" and storms off. I fall back into a stupor to be woken again, this time by three guys. "That was incredible," says one, thinking my destruction on stage was part of the show. One of them is holding a large bottle of lemonade and as I am as dry as a desert, I ask him for a drink. He hands the bottle to me and I start gulping it down. I realise too late it's straight whisky as the effect hits me on both sides of the temples. By this time Frank is back with the Guinness. I nearly throw up as he hands them to me but the show must go on…

CHAPTER 1

I can remember the very first thought or awareness I ever had at the start of my life. I was in a berth on a huge ship sailing one dark night from Heysham to Belfast with my Aunt Irene, who must have been around 23 years old. I was around six months old. We were laying on a top bunk bed and a leather handle hung down from the ceiling. I was looking out of the porthole, and on one of the buildings near the harbor, was a huge peacock lit up with coloured lights that went off and on. I was watching its reflection bobbing up and down in the water at the docks. It was a real magic night. Peter Pan could have been out peering down way up on the rooftops.

I now know that I was leaving my real mother (I think her name was Dorissss) and being brought back to Belfast to be adopted by the Bell family. Irene Bell and Harold Bell, son and daughter of Mrs Ada Bell. They lived in a small house, 32 Jocelyn Avenue, Belfast 6. Also living there was Ivy, the other daughter, and later on, John McKinley, a lodger. This was 1947.

I had no idea I was adopted until I was 11 years old and Mrs Bell (who I thought was my mother) died. It was in the early hours of the morning when my Uncle Harold came into the bedroom and told me that she had passed away. Then he told me she hadn't been my mother. The shock was so great I decided not to talk again for six months to anyone except my best friend, Billy Moore. I had been moody anyway before this happened but now a real melancholy filled me. I felt totally different from everybody and the chip on my shoulder grew and grew. When I asked about my real parents, my Aunt Ivy and especially my Uncle Harold became quite angry and told me they didn't know anything about them. Years later, when I saw my birth certificate, the name Green was stroked out and Bell written underneath. I also found out later that the Bell family were related in some way to my real parents, which made the whole thing feel a bit better. To this day, I have still never met my mother or father.

Life in the early 1950s was a different planet compared to life today. On Sunday evenings, the Bell family would sit in the parlour, which looked out on the street. Mrs Bell and Ivy and Irene would watch as people came home from church, and would comment on their clothes. "I see Mrs Robb has a new hat. Do you think it suits her?"

In the parlour one Sunday evening, I must have been around five years old,

Uncle Harold was talking about something, and at one point mentioned skyscrapers. I was on a big armchair beside a window and, having a vivid imagination, looked up at the sky, and in my mind's eye saw two men standing at the top of two very long ladders scraping cobwebs from beneath the clouds. Skyscrapers! Who needs drugs?

In these days, as there was no home entertainment – no TV, no videos, nothing but the big old-fashioned wireless – there were a lot more people about on the street, and there were huge queues outside the cinemas and local dance halls and lots of people in the city centre, looking in shop windows. The fashion at this time was either men in dark overcoats and caps, or the younger men dressed as Teddy Boys. Hair breamed back in a Tony Curtis style, large drape coats with wide shoulders, string ties and big thick-soled brothel creepers or blue suede shoes. They would hang around in gangs of five or six, and some would be out looking for trouble.

When I was around 13, nearly everywhere I went there would appear three or four boys around my age or a bit older. In a park, on the other side of the street, or hanging around the front of the cinema. And they would always have to shout at you, and you would either start running or wait till they approached you. They would then push you beside a wall and search your pockets, curse at you, ask you were you a Catholic or a Protestant. If there had been more home entertainment, I don't think this would have happened so much. There were certain streets in Belfast that I tried to avoid. Rough areas that had gangs of kids hanging around.

Every Saturday morning, my uncle Harold would send me out to get him the newspaper and to leave in the pools. I usually walked the long way to the shop, but this morning I decided to take my chances and try the short cut through Frankfort Street, which I never felt safe in. I got to the shop alright, and handed in the pools and got the paper. Then, as I looked out the window, oh no! I saw a gang of about seven snotty-nosed kids. I asked the man in the shop could he let me out through his back door, but he wasn't interested. There was nothing I could do and, with my heart beating three times faster, I walked out of the shop.

Sitting on a large guider (a soap-box with pram wheels on the back, small ball-bearing wheels on the front and a rope to steer) was a tomboy type girl of about 13 years of age. The rest of the gang crowded around her and she saw me and said to them, "I want him for my King" – and I was surrounded. I pushed one of the guys that had hold of my arm and started running. It was about seven minutes running speed to my house and they chased me the whole way home. So, now they knew where I lived, and as I looked out my bedroom window, I could see them and the girl – their Queen – waving her arms in the air. I started thinking, my imagination running away on me, "God, I'm going to end up having to marry that girl and become her King."

The next fashion to hit Belfast after the Teddy Boys had had their day was guys on motorbikes wearing leather jackets and pointy-toed winklepicker shoes. The guy that lived next door to me was hanging about with some of these kids. A few of them would be working on their bikes and revving the engines and, as they were a few years older than me, I just stayed clear. I think this trend started when they showed the American movie *The Wild One with Marlon Brando as the brooding leader of a motorbike gang.*

The first time I saw or held a guitar was in Davie Lyttle's house. There was a framed photo of him sitting on top of a cabinet. He was in a great rock and roll pose with a black acoustic guitar slung on his shoulder.

"Is that guitar yours?" I asked. "No, it's my dad's," he replied. After ten minutes of begging, he went upstairs and next minute walked back into the room with this huge black acoustic guitar. He let me hold it and I remember the smell of the wood and the feel and sound of the strings, which were enormous. I couldn't play guitar at this point, but I felt something deeply about the instrument.

So, I got a job at the local paper and sweet shop delivering papers and a month later bought my own acoustic guitar. I didn't even know how to tune it let alone play it. One day, I went into Matchetts music shop in Belfast city centre. The two men who worked there said I could tune my guitar with a set of pitch pipes, six little tubes that you blew in, and each pipe would sound the note that you had to tune the six strings of the guitar to. They also had a small, thin book that had diagrams of basic guitar chords. Look out!

Now I had the guitar in tune, I started learning and remembering a few chords. Then the ache in my fingertips started, pain that lasted for a few weeks. Someone had told me to hold my fingers in a bowl of cold salted water and this seemed to help, but everywhere I went, I was aware of my fingers throbbing.

Around this time, skiffle music was becoming the big attraction, made famous by one of my favourite singers, Mr Lonnie Donegan. He turned thousands of guys on to form their own skiffle groups. The instruments were very makeshift. If you couldn't afford a set of drums, you could get a washboard and play it with thimbles on your fingertips, and you could use a large wooden tea chest with a brush pole attached, and a length of thick string to take the place of a bass fiddle. Plus there were a few guys strumming on acoustic guitars. The impact Mr Donegan created was extraordinary. He turned on John Lennon and the Beatles, Eric Clapton, Jimmy Page, Keith Richard and hundreds of other very famous musicians.

It was a whole new world opening up for me. At the bus stop where I waited to go to work was a small shop that sold electric goods. In the window was a huge photo of Lonnie Donegan singing in front of a huge old-fashioned microphone. He seemed to be in a recording studio and I would think it must be amazing to do this for your living. That was the job I wanted.

Quite a few small music clubs started appearing in Belfast City – Clark's, Betty Staffs, The Jazz Club, and later on, the famous Maritime Hotel. It seemed every boy and girl in Belfast around the age of 16 would go to these clubs and dance to records, and every now and then, there would be a live group playing on a little stage. One night, I noticed one of the guitarists playing his acoustic and the sound he made was amazing. He had a small steel object under the guitar strings with a wire coming from it that was plugged into a sort of speaker. The one thing I tried to do in those days was to ask any guitar player questions. A lot of them would be big-headed gits and ignore me, but now and again some would be very helpful. This guitarist told me the steel object was a pick-up. If you couldn't afford an electric guitar, you could fit one of these to your acoustic. I bought one and they fitted it to my guitar in the shop.

I was round at my friend Billy's house one evening and his parents had gone out somewhere. His dad had a Bush reel-to-reel tape recorder and we used to listen to the latest pop records. I had my guitar with me and, after a while, we had the idea of trying to plug my guitar with its pick-up somehow into the tape recorder. It worked. The sound and tone was amazing – and the volume! And then… silence. I had blown the tiny speaker in his dad's recorder. It's at moments like this, especially when you're young, that you start to imagine all sorts of things. I might end up in jail or Billy's dad might get really upset and knock me around the head. But, thank God, he was pretty OK about it.

A few months later, a turning point happened in my young life – one of those moments. I was sitting on the windowsill outside my front door; it was a summer evening and I started to become aware of this fabulous sound coming down the street. A girl of about 18 was walking by on the other side of the street holding a portable radio by the handle and the sound was Apache by The Shadows. As she slowly walked away the sound of that electric guitar echoed off the brick houses, back and forth. I was never the same again.

I hadn't got my own record player so I went to some of my school friends' houses after school to listen to records. I went back to Davie Lyttle's house one day and he had a few singles and one or two EPs (extended records, usually having four tracks to listen to). One of these EPs was The Shadows, which had a fabulous photo of Hank Marvin and the boys in colour. Davie was really into Jet Harris, the bass player with The Shadows – the way he played the bass guitar but also the way he looked. Jet looked really cool in these days, a bit like James Dean, and he had his hair dyed blonde. Davie and I used to do the Shadows walk and pose in front of the mirror to The Shadows' records. Then, one day, Davie said he was going to dye his hair blonde and I bet him he wouldn't. It ended up with the both of us saying we were going to dye our hair that night and, at school the next day, see who had had the nerve to do it. When I got back home I told my Aunt Ivy about the bet. Ivy was a real character, sometimes, and told me to go the chemist and buy a small bottle of hydrogen peroxide. She rubbed some into my hair that night before bedtime. I had forgotten all about it by the next morning when she woke me for school. "Oh my God, look at your hair!" I got a real shock when I saw myself in the mirror. My hair was really blonde, nearly white. I dreaded going to school that morning, all of my school mates whistling at me and calling out, "Hello, Blondie!"

I actually told Jet Harris this story when I had the good fortune to be at lunch with him in 1999, at an award given to him by Fender Guitars. He wrote a couple of autographs for me and one of them was for Davie Lyttle saying, "Best Wishes to Davie from Jet Harris. Still a blonde?"

I was completely knocked out by the sound of The Shadows. How could four young guys create such a beautiful sound? I made up my mind there and then to get some Shadows records and try and learn Hank's beautiful melodies and Bruce Welch's fabulous rhythm guitar parts. You had to have the guitar really in tune and play Hank's melodies very accurately as he played with a very clear tone. This was before the guitar would be played with a distorted sound. I bought the shadows first LP again with a fabulous photo on the front showing Hank's Stratocaster and Bruce's telecaster and Jet Harris with a Fender Precision bass guitar. The other thing I noticed about The Shadows was their strange sense of humour. One of the tracks on the album was called *Theme from a Filleted Place, which could mean a sunlit forest or a prepared fish. Very droll.*

But another change was just around the corner. The Beatles.

One day my best friend, Billy Moore, came up to me in the street and was raving about some group called The Beatles. "They don't play instrumentals, they sing and play. They are amazing and are going to be the next biggest thing." And wasn't he right? The Beatles wrote a lot of their own songs and the guitar chords they used were a different ball game from what went on before. It took me quite a while to make the change from the beloved Shadows (who I still love) to The Beatles and all the groups that followed – Searchers, Swinging Blue Jeans, Gerry and the Pacemakers, etc. I bought one of their songbooks and was amazed and baffled by the chord diagrams. Diminished chords, augmented chords, minor 6th chords, major 7th chords. I really had to work on chords for quite a while to learn and sing some of their songs. In one of the early groups I played with, The Deltones, we played a lot of Beatles stuff and I loved the sound we created with these new chords.

Then, slowly, things started to change again with the Rolling Stones. A lot of groups appeared who were playing rhythm and blues songs. The Yardbirds, The Animals, The Pretty Things. I would still go to the music clubs in Belfast and there were a lot of groups now playing live. One of these groups started playing blues numbers one night and I watched the guitarist... he was bending the strings on his guitar, getting this amazing raw exciting sound. God Almighty, I thought, he must have fingers of steel. I hadn't a clue about this style of playing. One day in Crymbles music shop, where about 20 local musicians would meet up every Saturday, I saw a few guys who I knew played guitar. They had been playing a lot longer than me and I went over and started talking. I mentioned seeing the guitarist I saw bending strings. They started to explain how to do it.

You had to buy a banjo string and take off the first string of your guitar and put the banjo string in its place, then take of the second string and put the first string in its place and so on. So, armed with this secret, I bought a banjo string and that night changed all the strings. I had some blues records and started trying to learn the standard blues phrases. It took me forever, a completely different way of playing than Hank. At this moment in time, there was no such thing as light gauge strings. And you had to use the banjo string system until light gauge strings hit the music shops. The other thing that was happening was the volume that the groups played at now. Much, much louder as you had to crank your amplifier way up to try and get the sustained tone of the blues. Again, this was way before effects pedals appeared.

I thought I had heard everything until one day I was walking around the amazing Smithfield Market. It was a place that had shops and stalls and lots of things for sale under a huge glass roof. Sadly, it was bombed during The Troubles. I'm walking past the shops and turn a corner and all of a sudden I hear this music. It's coming out of two little speakers mounted outside a tiny record shop. I just stood and listened to the most amazing, impossible guitar playing I'd ever heard in my life. It completely blew me away, and I needed to know who it was. Inside the tiny shop, a woman of about 60 was perched up on a stool. "Who is that playing?" I asked. She told me it was a Romany gypsy guitarist called Django Reinhardt. She showed me the record sleeve and told me that he could only use two fingers on most of his playing as he had been badly burned by a fire in his caravan. I couldn't believe a character like Django was a real person. I bought two of his albums on the ace of clubs label, named the *Hot Club of France. The music was unreal, with Django swapping licks and ideas with an amazing violin player called Stephane Grappelli.*

I seemed to get interested in music around eight years old, listening to the huge wooden wireless out of which came lots of classical music. I would lie on the old green couch we had and the music would carry me off daydreaming about autumn days, fields, clouds, hedgerows, a sort of a *Wind in the Willows or Tales of the Riverbank. It really triggered my childhood imagination and I'd picture myself flying round the room up near the ceiling. Then, aged about 11, I'd go to some of my friends' houses after school. One of my school friends Alan M had some Buddy Holly albums that had just been recorded and played them while I was in the house. I remember the photos on the LP covers, but at that point, I wasn't that affected by the music.*

Changes were happening now, one being the transistor radio. I remember the first one I saw. David H, a friend who lived around the corner from Jocelyn Avenue, borrowed or stole a transistor from his older sister. It was red and about the size of a pack of playing cards. I thought it was a trick from a joke shop – some kind of sorcery! I couldn't believe it. He sold it to me for £5, which my Uncle Harold gave me. It really was like finding a giant diamond the way the rest of the family crowded around it. But a few hours later, David H's father knocked on my front door and demanded it back. He gave Harold a £5 note and took his son David back home by the arm. I was heartbroken but Harold said he would get me another one (which he did and which I still have and it still works!) It was such a godsend, I could listen to it in bed, flicking through all the radio stations until I heard the sound of a guitar, any guitar. My family must have seen me become interested because, that

Christmas, one of my presents was a small plastic guitar. It was excellent – six strings all different colours, real accurate frets and, for what it was, sounded great. I learned the Harry Lime theme on the first string. It took me a few days and I played it to everyone who came near me. "Yes, very good, keep at it."

We had a small black and white TV by now, and one of the shows I watched without fail had Bert Weedon on every week. He was one of the biggest guitarists in those days and had a spot on the show. He had this huge blackboard with a diagram of a guitar chord drawn on it and spent time showing how to play it. I would sit there with my guitar, a pen and paper, draw the chord and then try to play it along with Bert. I'll never forget the sound of that very first chord. It was magic to me. I was creating this sound myself. I think it was a C.

It's 1960 now and I'm 13 years old. I go to Orangefield Boys Secondary School in Belfast. So different from primary school. Every Christmas we would have a party and the teacher would ask if anybody could do anything – sing, dance, tell jokes, etc. Around this time, I was really into Lonnie Donegan since I heard him on the radio, and then later, on the TV. He was the very first I remember who really let himself go, that really exciting sound that was so infectious. Anyway, myself and Davie Lyttle were both into Donegan and decided to sing one of his songs, *Tom Dooley, at the Christmas party. At this point, I wasn't good enough or confident enough to play the guitar for this song, but another boy, I think his name was Tom Patterson, said he would back us. Within the next few days, he brought in his guitar, it was electric, a Futurama, and a small amplifier. My eyes stood out on stalks as he took it out of its case, plugged it in and started to play. He played a few chords and Davie and I started to sing. I begged Tom for about two hours to let me see his guitar, but he just put it away and said he'd see us on the night of the school party.*

On that night I found myself standing on this stage in the assembly hall. It felt the size of a football pitch. Davie was on the other side about 20 feet away and Tom Patterson in the middle with the electric guitar. It was my first time on stage performing music and I was petrified. We somehow got through it and I asked some of my mates later what we were like. They said it looked like Davie and myself were in a walking race, standing on the spot and walking.

CHAPTER 2

My Uncle Harold saw me taking an interest in something and, after a few weeks, found me a guitar teacher. The teacher only taught classical guitar and to play this you had to learn to read music. I hadn't the patience as I just wanted to play electric guitar in a Shadows rock and roll way, so I had one lesson and never went back. By this time, I eventually talked Harold into buying a record player and, when he wasn't listening to The Bachelors or Karl Denver singles, I would listen to The Shadows and The Spotnicks (a three-guitar and drum group from Sweden, like The Shadows but with their own sound. They also dressed up as spacemen wearing helmets and using dry ice on stage. Weird.) It felt natural to sit by the record player and try to copy the chords first that Bruce Welsh, the fabulous rhythm guitearist with The Shadows played, then try and copy Hank Marvin's licks. All of this took a long, long time and lots of effort but, eventually, I ended up being able to play (very roughly) *Apache and Quartermasters Stores.* This was how I got into my first group.

At school one day, at dinnertime, I was having a friendly fight with a classmate, Rodney H. One of Rodney's friends from a different class came over, thought it was a serious fight and stepped in. When this was all explained to him, he said, "Are you still all right to rehearse tonight, Rodney?" I then found out that Rodney played drums in a group and his friend played rhythm guitar. They rehearsed in the rhythm guitarist's house once a week, the house being a large house outside the Castlereagh Estate, nearly in the country. I told Rodney I was really into music as well and talked him into letting me come to their rehearsal.

So I went to Rodney's house that night and the two of us got the bus to the terminus where it stopped. Then we had a half-mile walk up this steep hill until we got to Fergie's house (that was the rhythm guitarist's name). The door opened and we were led into this really big sitting room and on the plush carpet was a red drum kit, three small amplifiers and three electric guitars!

Eventually, the other guys arrived and after some tea and cakes they took up their instruments and started playing. I just couldn't believe it. They sounded just like The Shadows. They played all instrumentals – Shadows, Ventures, Tornadoes, etc. Then they took a small break. I asked the guitarist if I could see his guitar, which he had made himself. It was based on a Vox Stroller, I think, and it looked and sounded perfect. As usual, he said no, then when the rehearsal was finished and we had more tea and cake, he let me play it through the amp. As I started to get used to it, I noticed the group standing around me up close. What a surprise I got the next day at school when Rodney asked me if I would like to join the group. They were called the Jaguars or something like that. I said I thought they already had a lead guitarist and he said the rest of the group (except the guitarist, obviously) had a meeting later last night and thought I would make the group sound better. So, I joined my first group.

I had to borrow an electric guitar and an amp and Rodney lent me some records, which I had to learn. Then I started rehearsing with them. Around this time, my best friend Billy Moore came with me. He wanted to be a drummer and I think could have been a good one, but for whatever reason mostly ended up hanging around and acting as a roadie sometimes.

I had a few guitar catalogues that I got from Matchetts, one of the very few guitar shops in Belfast city centre. Looking back, there were loads of really good guitars in that book. I liked the look of one called 'The Futurama' and wrote away, sending the deposit which was about three pounds. The guitar cost £30. I got a reply in a few days telling me they were out of stock with Futuramas but had some Rapier 22s which were pretty popular. They cost 22 guineas. A few weeks later I was laying in bed on Saturday morning listening to Saturday Club, a fabulous music programme where all the groups played live, when my Aunt Ivy knocked on my bedroom door and carried in a large cardboard box. At last! Here it was! I opened the box and inside was a guitar all wrapped up in paper, no case. But, when I took the paper off, I fell in love straight away. It was red and white, had two pickups, a selector switch and a tremolo arm. It was an excellent guitar for the money. But after the excitement, I suddenly realised I needed an amplifier, and a guitar lead and strap. Will it ever end? When I told my Uncle he said, "What? Why do you need an amplifier, I thought you plugged the guitar straight into the wall!"

We went to Matchetts and I tried an 8-watt Selmer. In the shop it sounded deafening but when I tried it at the rehearsals, I couldn't even hear it when the whole group played together. Harold went mad when I told him I needed a bigger amp. I couldn't blame him. Anyway, a few weeks later would see me with a 14-watt Selmer.

I was still learning from records and one was called *Saturday Night at the Duckpond* or *Theme from 'Swan Lake'* by the Cougars, I think. It became our strongest number. We had our very first gig coming up soon at the local youth club church hall thing and we changed our name to The Atlantics. Top of the bill was a local band called *The Headhunters*. We heard them practice in their garage on Saturday afternoons and they sounded brilliant. The gig arrived and we were quietly petrified. We went on and started with Saturday Night at the Duckpond and went down pretty well. After we had finished, the guitarist from The Headhunters came over and said when he had heard us start off he was surprised how good it sounded. Then they went on and blew everyone away, very professional, very confident and great players.

We did another few gigs and one of them nearly ended my career. On a Sunday afternoon, we played in a cricket pavilion for another youth club. But during the second or third number, I broke a guitar string, then a minute later, broke another string. I just stood there wondering what to do. Then I overheard one bloke at the front of the stage say to another, "You'd think he would learn to play before he got up on a stage." That was it. I unplugged my guitar and walked off into the small kitchen at the back. I was shaking and really depressed. The rest of the group came in, deciding to take a break now instead of later. When it was time to go on again they nearly had to carry me back on stage. By that time I had put two new strings on my guitar. That was the only problem I saw about the Rapier 22 guitar. The top of the bridge was very sharp and when you used the tremolo arm, it slowly started sawing through the strings. Anyway, I recovered from my first attack of stage fright.

Things carried on for a while with The Atlantics doing another few gigs, and one of them was a nurses' dance. I couldn't believe it when I spotted one of the art teachers from my school standing in the crowd having a drink. He also took weight lifting classes after school, which I attended every so often. I can't remember his name but I remember the man. We were told in Assembly Hall one morning that he had drowned while on a canoe trip during the summer holidays.

Looking back, it was so primitive but we had great fun. We had to sing now and we sang through our guitar amps as we hadn't got a PA. In fact, I didn't know what a PA was until much later. Ahead of me loomed one of the biggest changes of my life. Leaving school for good and joining the real world – the 9 to 5.

CHAPTER 3

Everyone around this time was wondering what I was going to work at, including me. Being a born romantic, I wanted to be a vet, then a newspaper reporter, but I didn't have any qualifications (just a borderline in the 11 plus). My Uncle Harold was a gifted motor mechanic, so I thought I might try that. He was dead against this and said they were grease monkeys, two a penny, and it was a dirty thankless job, going nowhere fast. I still had a few months to think about it but I had no idea what to do apart from cars.

I remember the last day at school. We all met in the Assembly Hall and had a few lectures from the Headmaster telling us not to let the name of the school down and then wishing us all the best. I couldn't really believe that day, walking through the school gates for the very last time and throwing some of my school books high up into the air. Billy was in the same boat as myself; his dad was a heating engineer and got Billy a start in one of the firms in Belfast. So, reluctantly, my Uncle went to a garage and begged the boss, who he didn't like, to give me a job.

So, about a week later I arrived at this enormous garage near Ormean Avenue in the city centre, AS Baird's, who worked on Humber, Singer and Hillman cars. I was given a brand new pair of overalls and introduced to a young man called Tommy – I would be his apprentice. I stood out from everyone else in my new overalls so everyone (about 100 youths and men) knew it was my first day. They gave me a warm welcome. First, they wired up the steel bench to a car battery and when I went to lift some spanners that were on the bench, I got the shock of my life. Later, as I was walking past the carwash, a young man hosing down a car let me have a soaking, as he bounced the water off the car roof onto me – what a start.

Tommy had asked me to get a small jack, as we were about to work on the brake linings on this car. I saw the jack and, not thinking like a '9 to 5 person', got on it like a scooter the way a child would, and started scooting across the huge garage floor, when I heard this really angry shout. "What the effing hell do you think this is? A bloody playground?" It was the foreman standing there in his white coat. He gave me quite a lecture, and then stormed off. This was my first day. Welcome to the real world!

Tommy was really good to work for. He let me help him with all the interesting jobs that had to be done on the cars, which kept me happy, as most apprentices end up doing all the dirty boring work, like changing tyres, and cleaning oil sumps and batteries. But I found it very hard to mix with the other workers. They talked about football and horse racing and betting, and joked with each other. I just couldn't relate to any of this. I was now going to night class once a week to learn metalwork and welding, and I was still very interested in cars up to this point in time. That's where I was the night they announced on the radio we had in the workshop, that JF Kennedy had been shot.

I was still practising guitar when I could, and one night The Atlantics had a gig about 30 miles outside Belfast. We hired a van and driver and when we arrived at the gig, we found out there were another two groups as well as ourselves. We went on first. I met this girl and after I had played she came out to the van with me. As luck would have it, the driver was still there, having a rest. After a few minutes, he reached down under his seat and handed me a bottle of wine. This wine was cheap to buy, Mundies Full Strength Red Ruby Wine. One minute I was reasonably normal, then the effect of the wine hit me and I was off my head, shouting at the top of my voice in my own crazy world. Later, I would start getting a taste for this cheap plonk.

One night when I came home from work, I was having my dinner when there was a knock at the front door. My Aunt Ivy answered it and told me there were a few young men who wanted to talk to me. I left my dinner and went to see who it was. I brought them into the parlour and they told me they were out of a group called The Deltones. They also told me they were playing about twice a week and were making a bit of a name for themselves on the local circuit. They were looking for a new lead guitarist, as the one they had was thinking of managing the group instead of playing. I then found out they had their own VW van, with windows, and fitted out with old sofas. And there was a Vox AC 30 amplifier for me to play through, if things worked out. They then gave me a list of songs to learn, mostly from the pop charts at that time.

A few nights later, they called around in the VW, which was very impressive, and drove me to Dougie Knight's rehearsal rooms. When we eventually started to play, I noticed this kid sitting behind the drums, he was about 11 years old. It must be the drummer's brother or cousin or something, I thought. But, it turned out he was the drummer! As it turned out, he sounded great and so did the rest of the group. Eventually, I started singing harmony along with Don "Bo" McCleary, the singer. The other guys were Eddie "Mousey" Willis on rhythm guitar and keyboards, "Pim" Jim Campbell on bass guitar and Davy Johnson, the kid on drums. We played a lot of Beatles songs, plus songs from the charts.

There were some really good groups around Belfast at this time, especially when the 'blues boom' arrived: The Alleycats, The Mad Lads, Just Five, The Method and a lot more besides. But, getting back to The Deltones. I had been with them now for about three months and we were playing the club circuit in and around Belfast. The clubs we played were Betty Staff's, The Jazz Club, Clark's and others I can't recall in Bangor, Holywood, and Newry. We played one night at an open-air show in the brass band pavilion on the beach in Newcastle (about 35 miles from Belfast). It was like something out of *Dad's Army*, with an ancient piano player, a comedian, an opera singer... and The Deltones. We went down really well with the audience of all types – children, babies, parents, older people and dogs. I ended up having a few beers with some guys my own age and staying in Newcastle after I'd finished playing. That night, we slept in a double-decker bus in a station until about 7:30am when some man who was checking around the buses told us to clear off.

Around this time, something happened that kind of changed the course of my life. One night Tommy and myself had to work overtime in the garage. There were only the two of us in the huge upstairs floor, apart from Mr Galway, the boss, who was in his office. After a while, Mr Galway locked the office, came over to us and asked Tommy to finish off and please bring his car downstairs. So, as Tommy got in the boss's car (a Humber Super Snipe estate that looked about 40ft long), I went into the men's room to clean the oil from my hands. A few minutes later, I heard this loud crushing, whining sound. Rushing from the men's room I saw a scene very much like something from a cartoon. Mr Galway was standing beside the ramp looking like a bullfrog ready to explode. Tommy was standing beside him, looking like he didn't know whether to laugh or cry. Sitting on the ramp was the Humber, looking as if it had been through a crushing machine. It was such a large car, Tommy mustn't have realised about a foot of it hung over the end of the ramp. So, as the ramp started to take the car downstairs, it caught on the upstairs concrete floor. This was on a Friday night, the end of the working week. When I got back to the garage on Monday morning, I couldn't find Tommy anywhere. Then I was told he had been fired. The foreman came over to me and asked why I was hanging around doing nothing (he was a real Mr Personality) then took me to a large fat bald man and said, "You're working with him now", and walked away. The man, called Clements or something, was nice enough but wouldn't let me help him the way Tommy had. It became very boring, and I started losing interest quickly in the 9 to 5 way of life.

One day, I was working taking off a door panel inside a car with the radio playing, when this amazing record came on. When it finished, the DJ said it was *Route 66,* a track off the Rolling Stones' first album. It completely blew me away, just the sheer excitement and energy from it. I think that's when it hit me what I really wanted to work at – I wanted to be a professional musician. The seed was now sown and it grew and grew until a few weeks later, the inner voice said, "Why don't you leave this job and do what you really want to do?" Before I knew what I was doing, I was standing inside Mr Galway's office asking for my cards. He didn't seem that surprised, and in fact, looked rather pleased as he handed me my cards and a small, light wage packet. And that was that!

I remember going home in a sort of daze, really glad about what I had done, yet at the same time feeling very lost and not belonging to anything. When I got home, my aunt Ivy was in the small kitchen we called the scullery, preparing the dinner for the workers coming home. "You're home early, everything all right?" she said, putting the big black pan on the gas ring. I mumbled something, but Ivy could sometimes read me like a book. She looked over at me. "There is something wrong, isn't there?. Oh my God, you've left your job, haven't you? My Jesus, just you wait till your Uncle Harold gets home!" She went crazy, and didn't stop for about half an hour.

Not having a trade in those days was like being branded as an outcast from society. My Uncle came home and basically gave up on me. My leaving AS Baird's garage devastated my family, and they didn't really speak to me for about three months. Anyway, that night, not eating anything, I went up to my bedroom. Now it was just me and my guitar against the rest of the world. Later, Ivy brought me up a cup of tea and asked me what I was going to do with myself now. "I'm going to make my living playing the guitar," I said. "You can get that bloody nonsense out of your head, my lad. You're going out in the morning to get yourself some sort of a job. You're not hanging around here all day!"

After she left, I lay down on the bed and just stared at the ceiling. After an hour of very painful soul searching I said to myself, "Right mate, it's shit or get off the pot time. If you want this bloody guitar thing to happen, you better start working at it for real." I made a vow to myself that I would practise two or three hours every night and 15 minutes in the morning before I went out to work.

Next morning, I was woken up by Ivy, and after a quick breakfast, went into the city centre to the dole office to get some sort of job. Now that I had no trade anymore, I was what was called a general labourer, or someone who does the dirty work. I asked the man behind the desk if he had any jobs that came under the heading of a plumber's helper, as some of my mates told me it was a real easy job. The man handed me a card with the name and address of the place I had to apply to. This was to become one of many strange jobs I was going to experience in the future.

Instead of being a plumber's helper, I ended up being a lamp-lighter (one of the last in Belfast). This was when they still had the old green gas lamp posts lined up and down the streets. That first morning I was sent out with a little man who looked very like the cartoon character Mr Magoo, with his bike, which had a little ladder attached to it. I followed him reluctantly to the first lamp. Taking the ladder off his bike, he told me to watch what he was doing. He climbed up the ladder and opened one of the four small glass windows at the top of the lamppost, and with a rag, cleaned the insides of the glass, and then the outside. Then he fiddled inside the lamp for a minute or so and climbed down. And off we walked to the next lamp. "Right, up you go," he said, "and make sure you clean the corners of the glass." Having climbed up the ladder, I opened the glass door that was on hinges, and started cleaning the four glass windows on the inside with the rag Mr Magoo had given me. A few seconds later, I nearly fell off the ladder. The rag I was using was soaked in paraffin and had touched the small gas jet flame that was inside where I had been cleaning. It burst into flames for a few seconds, then turned into a piece of charred black cloth, and pieces of this floated down on top of Magoo. We just looked at each other. This job was to last two weeks before I left. Some of the other jobs I had were working in Falls Mills, The Belfast Ropeworks, a pickle factory, a shirt factory (three times) and Stewart's mobile cash stores. I was also briefly a window cleaner and a builder's helper (which didn't really start at all).

In Belfast, there was something in the air, something about to happen. I started to notice some guys with really long hair every now and again. People, especially old women, would stop walking and point at them, and these guys would be wearing blue denim shirts, black knitted ties, leather waistcoats, bell-bottom jeans and donkey jackets. When I played with The Deltones, Billy and I would go back to those clubs on our own and become part of the "in-crowd" and meet new people, and some girls as well. The atmosphere in the club scene had a great feeling, it made you feel part of something big that was happening.

We went to the Maritime Club where an R&B band called Them, who were causing quite a stir in Belfast, were playing. They had been playing there for a few weeks and there was a queue of people right down the street and up the stairs trying to get in to see what was going on. We eventually got in the building, and were standing in the queue on the stairs leading into the hall. I remember hearing this really loud, raw sound with very strong rhythms. It seemed to draw you towards it. We ended up at the very back of a basic hall with a stage. We were standing on chairs to see over the heads of the crowd that packed the place. Them looked larger than life and the music sounded raw, electric, pulsing with energy. Van Morrison, the singer, his hair nearly to his shoulders and wearing a striped long-sleeved sweatshirt, spat and shouted the blues. He looked smashed on drink, threw his shoes into the audience, and fell on top of the drum kit. They were really exciting.

The guitarist, Billy Harrison, played on a huge semi-acoustic Hoyer guitar. On my Saturday adventures into the city centre, I spotted a Hoyer in Matchetts music shop and put a deposit down for it. It was a lovely guitar but I couldn't get a cutting sound from it. I eventually sweet-talked my Uncle into putting a deposit down and helping me pay for a Gibson 330. I think this guitar cost £200, which was a lot of money in those days. Again, my family and friends thought I was completely mad. It was perfect, the neck was perfect, the tones were perfect, but underneath I also longed for a Fender Stratocaster. That came later. The only problem I found with the 330 was, when I turned up the volume, it started feeding back (which was great, but not all the time). I stuck black tape over the f-holes, and this helped quite a bit, but after a few gigs I started walking six paces away from the Vox AC 30 and found I could control the feedback and also use it when I wanted.

I was starting to get a taste for Mundies wine (well, a liking of the effects of it anyway). It was 10 shillings a bottle and I bought it from the off licence. This was the type of stuff the winos and down and outs drank, the real hard stuff. As you weren't allowed to bring alcohol into the clubs, Billy and I would go down the nearest alley to the club to drink it before we went in. Poor Billy would try everything to talk me out of drinking it but I always ended up coming out of the alley like Mr. Hyde. In its own way, this stuff was as strong as LSD. Before it really took effect, we would go to the club, get in and then –blast off! It made me feel that I didn't really care about the 9 to 5 world, that somehow things would work for me in other ways. But, the next day, I would feel shaky and disoriented, in a sort of trance (commonly known as a hangover!).

At this time, I was working in the Belfast Ropeworks. It was like one of the workhouses out of a Dickens novel. I felt really depressed working there. The job was hard manual labour. I had met a girl and we had been seeing each other for only a few weeks and I carried her photo in my work shirt. Every now and again I'd take her photo out, look at it and get back to work.

One of the many jobs I had was working in the Belfast Ropeworks. My very first day, I stood outside these massive black, wooden doors with a crowd of people all waiting to get in. Then, the doors were opened and I followed the crowd into the building. It was just like a film set that you would see in a Charles Dickens movie. Ropes of all sizes were everywhere you looked and I just stood there, looking around me and wondering what to do. Then this worried looking man came over to me. "Right, this is your first day so I'll show you what you have to do." We walked over to a corner of this enormous room, and I didn't know what to make of it all. There was a railway buffer sunk into the ground and sitting beside it was a small cast iron train with casters and wheels and levers. This train, I found out, stood on railway tracks and travelled very slowly until it reached the other buffer at the other end of the enormous room, which was quarter of a mile long. The man explained that the little train had an iron disc with 12 hooks that were placed in the disc just like the numbers on the face of a clock. When the train started its journey, the disc would turn slowly. Looped over each hook was a small rope and, as the disc turned, the 12 small ropes would be plaited into a huge rope, the type they use to tie ships to their moorings.

I had to walk behind the train with the revolving disc and, every 20 yards or so, was a concrete post with a square cut out. I had to pick up a very heavy wooden pallet with 12 pins and push the end of the pallet into the square in the concrete post. Doing this would keep the 12 small ropes from being tangled, as each one was separated by a pin. When I eventually reached the end of the room, there was an iron post fixed into the ground. I had to take the 12 small ropes, each one having a loop of rope, and place them over the iron post. Then a minute or so later, a warning bell would ring. I would stand far away from the iron post, and the huge rope was stretched, quivering like the string of a giant bow. If you'd stood too close it could have been lethal. The people at the other end of the room then pulled the huge rope back to where they were. I then stood on a small platform on the train and took the brake off, and the train would make its way back to where it had started. But, sometimes, because this train was ancient, it didn't slow down when I applied the brake. When this happened, I had to reach for a rope that was overhead and pull on this, which would ring a bell, warning the people working beside the railway buffer to get out of the way. Now, I knew what the buffers were for, as the train would crash into them and stop.

I had been working in the Ropeworks now for about three months, quite a long time for me, but this was going to change. On this day, I'm standing on the train and apply the brake, which doesn't work. So I reach up to pull on the overhead rope, but hold it too long, and the rope burns right into my hand. I get off the train before it crashes into the buffers. The sound of the crash was heard by one of the managers, whose office was nearby. He came out and was walking towards me looking not very pleased. But I didn't care, I was looking at the burn the rope had left on my hand. "What do you think you are doing, Bell? This is the third or fourth time this has happened. It's not good enough." "It's not all my fault," I said. "That frigging train is ancient, and look at my hand. I'm a guitar player and I'm supposed to be playing tomorrow night." I got really annoyed, and he told me to go to the first aid room and see the nurse, who put cream on the burn and then bandaged up my hand. And, as you may have guessed, I was unemployed once more. I did manage to play a little at the gig next night, which was all I was worried about.

Another weird job… As I was out of work yet again, I went over to the dole a day or so later. In those days of the 60s, there were loads of jobs available and, if you were a general labourer as I was, they would send you anywhere. So, the job they handed me, printed on a little card, was a pickle factory. Here we go again. I found out what bus would take me to the factory, got off and was given directions by the bus conductor. I couldn't believe it. When I had been going to Orangefield Boy's Secondary School, there was a large old house standing in a field and it was said to have been haunted. I had the feeling that the house was now the pickle factory. It was. The manager brought me into his office, which was freezing, and I noticed an electric fire with one bar lit. "OK, follow me," he said, and walked down a few hallways until we came to a bench with a few pieces of machinery fixed to it. "Right, this is part of your job. Some girls will carry trays of pickles and beetroot to you, and you place lids on top of the jars and pull down this handle, which attaches the lid. Try not to break any."

So, he leaves me and I just stand there, and it is freezing. Then, a few women appear with the trays, say hello and leave. Right, I thought, better get on with it, knowing in my heart that I didn't want to be here too long. What a future. But, again, these objects I was working with were out of The Ark. I would put a lid on a jar and pull the lever, but every now and again, the glass jar would shatter and there would be pickles and beetroot and vinegar and broken glass everywhere. I started to develop a phobia each time I pulled the lever, waiting for the glass to shatter. I don't know how many I broke, and the boss wasn't very pleased.

He told me there was another job for me to do and walked me through the large, freezing house until we came to a grey coloured concrete room. The room was bare except for about six large steel vats that sat around the walls. At the bottom of each vat was a trapdoor. "Right," he started to explain, "what happens is, these vats will be full of beetroot and will be slowly cooking all night. Your job is, when you arrive in the morning, you will open the trapdoors and all the beetroot juice and skins will pour out. You will notice a grating in the middle of the floor. You take this pole with a hook on the end and clear away the skins to let the juice pour through. The juice can get pretty deep, so you will have to wear waders." And he showed me a giant pair of water boots that fishermen sometimes wear. I just stood there in disbelief. The next morning, I went to the room where the beetroot had been cooking all night. The smell was overpowering, especially at that time of the morning. I put on the waders and started opening the small trapdoors at the bottom of the steel vats. I wasn't prepared for the amount of juice and skins that came gushing out and, when all the trapdoors had been opened, I was standing in this purple lake just above my knees. God Almighty! I just want to be a guitarist.

A few weeks later, the boss came out of his office and asked me to come in. I knew what was going to happen and saw the brown envelope that he was holding in his hand – my wage packet. He told me he had to let me go, as I wasn't suitable. I just hadn't got the mindset to stay in any of the jobs I was offered by the dole. How people do it, year after year, is just beyond me. It reminds me of stopping people in the street from going to work. "Excuse me, but what do you work at?" "I work in a bank," might be the answer. "OK, but what would you really like to do?" In my experience, about four out of six people haven't found out what they really want. I sort of knew right away what I wanted. But, the sacrifices you have to make and the risks you have to take, and with no promise of getting anywhere at the end of it. A lot of people want security and a home and a settled life, and I don't blame them. But, it wasn't for me, which is why I got fired from so many jobs. They could all tell I just wasn't interested.

CHAPTER 4

Another major turning point! I walked home from the Ropeworks as usual after work, it was very dark, and it was cold and raining. It was great getting home. Our house was small, the front room tiny. We had no central heating, but there was a huge blazing fire in the grate and a huge, hot dinner from Ivy for the working class hero. Later on that night, there was a knock at the front door. "Some people to see you, Eric."

I went to look and saw seven guys standing there. They told me they were The Bluebeats Showband. I wasn't really interested in showbands and was just half listening to what was being said, until someone mentioned they were based in Glasgow. Then I found out they were professional, full-time musicians. "Yes, you see, our guitarist, Jack, he's a really good player, but he has to sit some very important exams and so on. So, we heard you were a good guitarist…"

I told my aunt who they were and that I was going out for a while. We ended up in the Spanish Rooms pub in the city centre, where they sold Scrumpy, a very strong cider, which was cloudy with small pieces of apple and cork floating in it, at one shilling a pint (five new pence). I had two, and half way through a profound conversation, forget what I was talking about. By the time they drove me home, I was asking Harold and Ivy if I could join The Bluebeats and live in Glasgow?

"What? Forget it, Eric, you're going to no bloody Glasgow!" Harold said. I pleaded and pleaded and said the only thing I was interested in was making my living as a guitarist. After about two hours, Ivy said, "Why don't we let him do it, Harold? There's nothing to keep him in Belfast. It's not like he has a really important job to keep." Eventually, my Uncle said I could go, but there were conditions. That I stayed away from drink and drugs, and that I write home every few weeks.

I told the boss at my job I was leaving. I was leaving for Glasgow on a boat in a van in four days time. My dream had come true. I remember the very first gig in Carlisle. The hall was so big we actually drove the minibus into the hall from the back doors right up to the front of the stage. Also, it was Hogmanay Night. The guitarist, Jack (he was a great player), stood on stage beside me and showed me the intros and chord changes from the songs, and I would watch and try to remember it all. This was the way I was brought into the band to replace Jack, who would be leaving the band and going back to Belfast in a few days. The hall was packed, about 1,500 people all pissed and having a wild Hogmanay Night. After the gig we went back to someone's house and there was enough drink for five showbands. This was my first night as a pro musician. Somehow, we got back to Glasgow and ended up outside a large boarding house somewhere in Paisley Road West. I found out this was where the band lived, in one large room with eight bunk beds. I was shown to the bottom bunk of bed No. 2. We all lived, or rather were based, in this room for roughly one and a half years.

We played all over Scotland, mostly Irish Ballrooms and dance halls. These were huge places, holding up to 2,000 people, and most of the time they were pretty packed. Some of the places we played were pretty remote – hotels in the middle of nowhere – and while we were playing that night, the snow would be falling outside. As soon as the dance ended, most people would make their way home, leaving a few still up at the bar. When I got up for breakfast the next morning, I couldn't believe the snow – everything was covered, it looked beautiful and I can still see it. When these snowfalls happened and we were playing in these remote places, we had to stay over for a day or two as we couldn't get through the snow. It all looked like a Christmas card. I felt really happy those mornings, snowed in and eating a huge fried breakfast with the band. I felt like I belonged.

One of the gigs we played was the Town Hall in Carlisle. We were playing support for the Spencer Davis Group, who were very popular at this time. There were about 2,000 teenagers at the show. The lead singer-guitarist, Steve Winwood, was about 18 years old or so. He was a great player and singer, and looked great as well, wearing a pair of chequered hipsters, trousers that were worn on the hips rather than the waist. He was playing a Fender Stratocaster and it seemed he broke a string every song. A roadie would appear with a guitar and take the one with the broken string and one song later, the same thing would happen, and so on. At one point, their manager strolled over to where we were standing in the wings, and told us that Steve was getting fed up with being a pop star and wanted to be known as a serious musician. He told us to watch Steve, and the way he teased the young girls. He would push the mike stand just within reach and as they made to grab it, would move it back again. When we got back to Glasgow a few days later, Hugo, the sax player, took me to some boutique, and we ended up buying a pair of chequered hipsters each.

Another gig I remember was when we played support for Billy J Kramer and the Dakotas, another famous group from the 60s. One of my guitar heroes then was Mick Green, who had been guitarist with Johnny Kidd and the Pirates. He had recently joined the Dakotas. Anyway, after the Bluebeats had played, we came off stage and were walking down the corridor to our changing room, when a door opened and Billy J and the Dakotas started walking towards us, to the stage. I saw Mick Green, stopped him and said, "Did you play the solo on a song called *Ecstasy?*" *(no, this was way before that drug!)* *'Yes mate, that was me." I started raving about how much I enjoyed his solo, when he said, "Sorry mate, but I do have to go on stage now." I felt a right prat, I forgot he was getting ready to play. (I asked Mick at a party a few years ago if he remembered that night, but he didn't seem to recall it.)*

One of my first encounters with a young Scottish lass was when the Bluebeats were playing in a place called Galashiels. It was at the end of a gig and the band were having tea and sandwiches at a table near the bottom of the ballroom. I went up on stage to pack away my guitar lead and amp, then looked down at the empty dancehall and saw a young girl about 17 standing just a few feet away. I said hello and we started talking – about ten minutes later, we were out in the van. We sat down, talked a little. I got close to her and started to kiss her, but she seemed cold and uninterested. Then I remembered something some guy had told me, one of the lines he used which worked for him. I tried it.

"You know, I think Irish girls are much more passionate and warm than Scottish girls, the ones I've met anyway." "Is that right?" she said, and stood up and started to rearrange the seats in the van. She then lay down and said, "Come here." After I lay down beside her, three minutes of heaven passed, it was beautiful. It was only the second time I'd made love so far in my young life. She ended up coming back to Glasgow with me (and the other seven guys) in the van. We made love again twice in the back of the van, which was dark and had a little pair of curtains hiding us from the others. When we got back much later to our boarding house, everyone was tired, we had some tea, and the lights were turned off. I forget the girl's name now, so I'll call her Mary. Yes, we made love again in my bed. But this time, when I had come, Mary was becoming more and more excited and wanted me to carry on but I couldn't … I was totally exhausted! It sounds weird now, but I told her to get into the lead singer's bed, which she did, and by the sounds in the night, everyone was very pleased with the new arrangements. I felt a quick pang of jealousy, which lasted about five seconds, then I slowly stretched out in bed and thought, "I wish all my friends could see me now", smiled, and had a great sleep. Mary stayed around on the arm of the singer for a few days, and then we dropped her off near her town as we were playing somewhere roughly in the area.

The Bluebeats Showband would grind to a halt every few weeks when gigs were few – three or four nights off in a row and very little money. I was being paid five pounds a week wages. Back around 1966, that could last for a while if you were careful. I wasn't drinking very much in those days, so what I had went mostly on fags and food. Our room was facing a pub called Three Coins in a Fountain, and we would hang around there, killing time and seeing how long a glass of beer could last. We would go for a walk sometimes to the city centre, but didn't do this too often. There were serious gangs in Glasgow then, one of the best known called The Tongs, and I always felt a bit uneasy with the eight of us walking in a group along the pavement (looking like a gang ourselves).

It was out of boredom and lack of money that the infamous 'Wanking Race' was born. This had started before I had joined the band, so they were all used to it. The idea was anyone who wanted to take part had to pay two shillings. This money was put to one side, then we all got in our beds, with hands outside the covers. You could look at a naked lady book, which someone would hold in front of you for ten seconds for inspiration (this cost an extra two pence), then he would go over to the light switch and shout, "Lights out!" and this would start the race. There would be the groaning of bedsprings, and the groaning of us lot, until someone would shout, "Lights!" The guy at the switch would turn the lights back on and the winner of the race would leap out of bed, spilling his seed on the carpet, then take all the money, which would amount to around 12 shillings, quite a sum for someone with no money.

It sounds strange now, but back then I don't remember anyone having a bath or going to a launderette and we seemed to always wear the same clothes. It was rather primitive in the early 60s compared to these days.

CHAPTER 5

One of the strangest nights I had with the Bluebeats was when we played in London in one of the Irish ballrooms, somewhere near Kilburn. We were playing a slow set and I was trying out an old showband trick. There were couples waltzing around and as the girl faced me, I would give her the eye and a smile, then when her partner was facing me, I looked away, then smiled at the girl when she came round again. This would go on for a few songs if the girl was interested. When we finished playing that night, the bar was still open for another hour or so upstairs. I went up and walked around and spotted the girl I had been smiling at. She was sitting beside another girl and there didn't seem to be any boyfriend. So I went to the bar and ordered a bottle of beer. I was very lucky in a way as the effect of one beer on me was pretty strong. After the beer had changed me into Steve McQueen, I went over to where the two girls were sitting. I looked at the girl I had been smiling at and asked if she and her friend would like something to drink. She said yes and then the other girl got up, smiled and said goodbye. After a few drinks I asked the girl if I could walk her home? She said yes and we went downstairs to the cloakroom. She got her coat and we walked out into the street.

We walked for 20 minutes or so and passed a group of youths, mostly blokes, standing at the corner of her street. They shouted out something to the girl (I'll call her Margaret) which I didn't make out, and we kept on walking down this long dark avenue until we came to where Margaret lived. It was now about 1.45am. When we got to the front door, it was very dark with a sort of overgrown garden and a few small trees. We went into the house. She didn't turn any lights on and we went upstairs in darkness into her bedroom. The curtains were slightly open but she still didn't turn on any lights. She went away and came back a few minutes later, took my hands and we sat on her bed.

The whole thing started to feel a bit weird and I started to imagine things like she was on the game or a killer. She reached under the bed and brought out a bottle of cheap wine and we took turns at having a few swigs each, the effect hitting me pretty quickly. Anyway, I started to put my arms around her and she just sat there without moving, as if in a trance. Then, suddenly, something hit the window, something small like a stone. She jumped up and looked out into the street and said, "Oh shit, it's my brother! Quick, hide in the bathroom and lock yourself in and don't come out for five minutes. I might have to go out with him." I jumped up and followed her to the bathroom, with the house still in darkness. Before I shut the bathroom door, she warned me to keep quiet and to let myself out when I hear the front door shutting. I stood in the darkness in the bathroom feeling very nervous, not knowing what was happening. Then I heard sounds on the stairs, either her going down to the front door or someone coming up. I heard a few voices and then a door slamming.

I stayed where I was for another five minutes or so, listening really hard for any noises. Then, very slowly, I opened the door, everything still in darkness. I just wanted to get out of this house as quickly as possible. I slowly made my way down the stairs, expecting something to happen at any moment. I reached the front door and very slowly opened it, shut it behind me very quietly, and started walking back towards the Irish Ballroom. You can imagine how I felt when I got there and saw it was all locked up, the van and band were gone and there was nobody there. To make matters worse, I didn't know where we were staying that night, what hotel or B&B we were booked into. And I had about £3 in my pocket. Great! The only thing I knew was that we were playing the Gresham Ballroom on the Holloway Road the next night, or rather tonight. It was around 2:45am now – what to do? I was starting to feel miserable now, very cold, hungry, and most of all, very stupid. Then an idea came to me. I remembered someone mentioning about not having a place to stay one night, and they called into a local police station and were allowed to stay the night. I found one after a little while, plucked up the nerve, and walked in. I told my story to the cop behind the desk, who listened half-heartedly then said, "Sorry mate, but this isn't a hotel, can't help you." Another myth shattered.

So, I walked back to the ballroom again as I didn't know what else to do, but at least it was on a main road with street lights and lots of shop windows were lit, which made me feel safer, as I was only around 17 years old. In the entrance outside the ballroom was one of those machines that took passport photos, so I went inside and sat on the swivel seat and pulled the little curtain across. It was very cold now and I just sat there killing time. I must have dozed off because I was rudely awoken by a policeman shining a torch in my face. "You can't sleep there, mate, you'll have to move along!" I told him briefly what had happened, but he was just doing his rounds and couldn't help. After this, I just walked up the main street, feeling very stiff and cold, trying to get warm again.

Eventually, I spotted a greasy spoon type transport café. Luxury! I went in, ordered a giant mug of tea and chips and bread and butter, and sat over this for as long as I could. I had been so cold, I felt my eyes steaming up as I thawed out. I felt the owners of the café were starting to look over at where I was sitting, so I got up and went out into the street again. This is what being down and out must feel like all the time I thought, wondering how they survived. I found another café, had another tea and thought what to do now, as it was only around 5.00am. I decided to try and get a bus that would take me close to Holloway Road, where the Bluebeats were playing that night. Soon, the sky started getting lighter and a few people and more cars started to appear as the day began. I got a bus to Holloway Road and, eventually, after asking a few questions, found the Gresham Ballroom. All I had to do now was kill more time until around 7.00pm, when the band would arrive with the gear.

I passed a couple of hours slowly and then spotted a cinema. It was Saturday morning and it was getting ready to open. I remember the film they were showing, *The Yellow Rolls-Royce. I wasn't very interested in the film, I just wanted to get warm and have a sleep for a while. So I paid my money and went in. It was a huge cinema (before they started dividing them into six boxes) with plush red seats and an enormous shimmering yellow curtain in front of the screen. I was the first person in the place so I picked my seat carefully, right in the centre about 18 rows from the front. At last I could relax. I was just settling down when I heard someone from my left pushing past the seats in the row I was in, coming closer and closer. I froze and waited. I mean, the cinema was empty apart from six people. I couldn't believe it. He sat down on the seat next to mine and started twitching around, then he put his arm slowly around the back of my seat. I thought, "Here we go." My heart was beating faster and faster. I had a little pen-knife on a key chain in my jacket pocket so I turned around and in a very broad Belfast accent said, "If you don't fuck off I'll stick this knife in your throat!" He leaned away saying, "I don't know what you're talking about, I don't know what you're talking about,", and got up and walked off. It took me quite a while to settle down again, but I was shattered and dozed off for a bit. The rest of the time after I came out of the cinema was in yet another café, then at last I made my way to the Gresham Ballroom.*

When I got there, the boys were just unloading the band equipment. They sort of treated me like a hero, calling me Alfie after the character Michael Caine had played in the movie. I told them what had happened and they thought it all as strange as I did. We played that night and sounded dreadful. We sounded weak and bored, and about three months later, the Bluebeats finally ground to a halt. We got the boat back to Belfast and all went our separate ways.

When I got home, my Aunt Ivy opened the front door, saw me and nearly fainted. "Oh my God, look at the state of you! Why didn't you come round the back?" (so the neighbours wouldn't see me). I must have looked pretty rough, not eating very well and still wearing basically the same clothes I had left in nearly a year and a half ago. After I had been home for a while, Ivy made me a giant Ulster fry and then I said I was going to bed for a few hours as I was exhausted. Before going upstairs though, she asked me the dreaded question about what I was going to do now that the Bluebeats were no more. "Probably practise on the guitar," I said. "I'm a professional musician now." She frowned at me. "Forget it. There's no way you're sitting around here playing that bloody thing all day. First thing tomorrow morning, you're going out to get some sort of a job. Try the shirt factory, maybe they will take you back." And they did.

I was back in the shirt factory for two weeks now, and all that time in Scotland felt as if it had been a dream, as if it had never happened. One of the good things about working in the shirt factory was the boss, Charlie Faulkner. He was a man about 70 or so and great to work for, though he made you work.

There was this big room with about 30 girls and women, all sitting at sewing machines working away, and three males – myself, the boss and another guy who was the cutter. He cut the shapes for the shirts from the cloth that had been laid down on a long table. Every now and again, Mr. Faulkner would call me over to his tiny office and hand me a pile of pound notes. Some to put on a horse running in a race that day and the rest to buy a large bottle of whiskey. So, out I would go, back the horse for him and get the booze. When I got back, he would take the whiskey and pour a measure into paper cups that were sitting on a large tray. Then, he would go over to a huge switch on the wall that was beside his office and turn it off. All the sewing machines would slowly whine to a halt, and the forewoman and I would go round and hand each of the workers a cup of whiskey. Out the fags would come and the women would have a natter until the boss would turn the switch back on again. "Right girls, back to work."

I called around to see John, the bass player from the Bluebeats, to see if there was any news about the band reforming, but his mother told me he had joined the Merchant Navy. I kept in touch with a few of the other guys from the band for a while, but we drifted apart, most of them lived in a different part of Belfast than I did. I struck up my friendship with my old mate Billy Moore again, who lived in the next street, and we would go to some of the clubs in town to watch some groups, which made me want to play again. I was still obsessed with music and the guitar, but around this time, gigs and playing were a bit on the lean side. A few months passed by and I still worked in the shirt factory during the day and stayed in most nights of the week practising and listening to music, seeing some friends now and again. But even they were falling by the wayside, as I would tell them I couldn't come out because I had to work on my music.

I was over in Crymbles music shop in the town centre some weeks later, and some guy from England was there talking to Michael, one of the salesmen, about a PA amp. Then the English guy started asking about musicians, as he was looking for a guitarist for some band he had in Leeds. Michael called me over and I soon found out the English guy was called Briley and he managed an Irish Showband called the Shannon Showband, who were based in Headingly, Leeds. We started talking and a half hour later, I had a gig in Leeds. I went back home delighted and very excited to tell Ivy. Here we go again. Within a week, I had told Mr Faulkner from the shirt factory I was off again, and he wished me all the best, smiling at me with half-pity and half-envy.

Briley picked me up from the boat and we drove through the night until we reached Leeds. Then down some old fashioned cobbled streets until we pulled up outside the house where I would be staying. It was a big old house and four of the musicians lived there, not counting Briley or me. I couldn't believe it the next day when I got up. One of the sax players was Ray Elliot, a gifted musician from Belfast, who could play sax, flute, piano and vibes and was a great jazz and blues player. He had been in Them (the second one), the famous group from Belfast. He had just recently been back from touring America and was now in an Irish Showband based in Leeds – what a funny business.

I got to meet the rest of the band the next day at a rehearsal. They were a very mixed bunch of people, every one seeming to be totally different from everyone else. The songs were mostly Irish and C&W, with a few pop songs thrown in. We didn't sound very together. We had this huge see-through plastic bag that our stage gear was bundled into, red polo necks along with dark trousers. One night, I thought it was very funny. We were booked to play in a Working Man's Club just outside Leeds. We arrived late and rushed into the changing room, the huge plastic bag sitting in the middle of the floor. Everyone dived in at once and most of us had the wrong size polo necks and trousers on – we looked pretty strange. We rushed onto the stage and the place was packed with very serious, poker-faced people staring up at us (we are determined not to enjoy ourselves types).

Anyway, we all walked slowly into the changing room, then back out onto the stage, I think it was the quickest we ever packed up.

The Shannon played an average three nights a week – Irish Ballrooms, Working Men's Clubs and the odd Cabaret Hall. Looking back, I don't know how we lived. I can't actually remember getting paid. It was like I had a roof over my head, I got fed and sometimes got bought fags and beer by the manager. On the nights we didn't play, sometimes about four of us would meet at the room where the trumpet player lived and he would be drinking his whiskey and cursing the band, saying it was shit and there was no money and it was going nowhere and he was going to leave. This went on for quite a while, until one day he did leave. I started to get very bored with the music and the whole situation and would start to jam some blues on stage at the sound checks with Ray Elliot from the band. The manager, Briley, didn't like this at all. He wanted an Irish band, even at sound checks.

At one point, a few weeks later, I felt I wanted to go back home for a week or so and my Uncle Harold bought me a return ticket to Belfast. It was great seeing family and friends, and then, all too quickly, it was time to fly back. When I got back to the house in Leeds, Briley was very nervous and I sensed something in the air. Then he told me, because I had been playing blues licks in songs like *Danny Boy* on stage, I had been replaced as guitarist in the band. There was a new bass player as well, as Kevin, who was a part-time school teacher, was finding it hard to make time for the band. I went mad to say the least and asked Briley why he hadn't told me this before I had flown home to Belfast, as I then could have stayed there instead of flying back to Leeds and no job. He wasn't really interested and said I had to find somewhere else to live soon.

I met the two new guys who were to replace Kevin and myself. They were very pleasant and told me they had been in Engelbert Humperdink's backing band until he started to get famous, then they were dropped. Briley then asked me to stay in the band for a few weeks until the new guitarist had learned the songs, the idea being that he would stand beside me on stage and learn the songs (in the same way I had learned the songs in the Bluebeats). I didn't want to do it, but it meant I would eat and be allowed to stay in the house, for a short while anyway.

The Shannon Showband seemed to be slowly falling apart. Hugo, the lead singer, was having lots of arguments with Briely. Hugo was from Belfast and his parents had a house in the next street from the house I stayed in. A week or so passed and Briely had heard some big Irish labourer called Frank singing in a local pub. He brought Frank down to our next rehearsal and we found he had a very pleasant voice for the type of music the Shannon was playing. But, before anything else had happened, Hugo told Briely to stuff his band and left. Around this time I was getting ready to leave too, and thinking of moving back to Belfast, not having much choice. Then Hugo approached me and said he was going to form a small group of his own and that he knew quite a lot of pubs and clubs and was sure to get work. He said I could live in his house and that there was a spare bed in the attic where he slept. So, later that day, I moved into Hugo's house.

Hugo was a very cool type with dark brown hair, and wore a black leather waistcoat, brown cord trousers and black cowboy boots. He was a very good singer and entertainer, and we would work on songs for the new group on acoustic guitars, usually around 1.00am in the morning. And before we went to sleep, he would always put on an album on his tiny portable record player and I'd go to sleep to the sounds of Bob Dylan, Marty Robbins and Johnny Cash. Hugo would play a gig every now and again at some of the nightclubs in and around Leeds, and sometimes I'd go along, either to watch or just play guitar on a couple of songs. There were always lots of classy young ladies around, and Hugo knew quite a few, but when I started to talk to them they would politely disappear. "You're a bit young for them," Hugo would say.

Another big change was looming. One afternoon I saw Hugo getting all dressed up and thought he must have a gig somewhere. I thought I would like to go along but he told me he wasn't playing anywhere but was going to a party and if I wanted I could come along. We arrived at this beautiful big old-fashioned house made from that sandstone that is so popular around Leeds. Hugo rang the bell and we were led into a large sitting room with about 12 students sitting on chairs and lying about the floor. I sat down thinking it was a bit early for a party, as it was only around 4.00pm, and also noticed there was no sign of beer or bottles of spirits. Then, I looked over at this guy sitting at a table beside three large windows. He was holding a safety pin with a small black lump on the point and he was heating this gently with a lighter then crumbling it into a hand rolled cigarette. As I sat there, feeling pretty strange to say the least, a few minutes later someone came over and handed me a huge fat cigarette saying, "Want a drag man?" The words from my Uncle Harold came into my head, "And don't be getting mixed up with any drink or drugs!" "No thanks," I said and he smiled, shrugged and walked away, passing it around the room to the rest of the students.

After about 20 minutes, I started to get bored, while everyone else was giggling and laughing. It doesn't seem to be doing them much harm, I thought. A few minutes later, the guy came over to me again, "Sure you wouldn't like a smoke, man?" I looked at him with the funny cigarette. "How do you smoke it?" I asked and after he had explained, I proceeded to smoke about half of it. It smelt sweet and made me think of the opium dens in China for some reason, not that I've ever been there. He left me then and I just sat there in a dream. I didn't think that I felt any different – I didn't know what was supposed to happen anyway. Then the guy came back over to me and asked me how I felt. "I don't feel any different," I answered. "That's the third time you've said that," he said, and then something seemed to click in my mind and I just started laughing and couldn't stop for quite a while. I felt like I was in a play with everyone acting a part and I lost all sense of time.

But the thing that had the biggest effect on me was when someone put on the Beatles' *Sgt. Pepper's* album. I was drawn into the very speakers and running around Ringo's cymbals, and the guitars sounded as if they had voices. It was like hearing a completely different kind of music – lots of messages and hidden meanings, like the Beatles knew everything in the Universe, and were sharing it through their music. Then someone played Are You Experienced? by the Jimi Hendrix Experience… and that was it, Earth calling Eric!

I don't know how long I was in the large room, as I said time didn't seem to mean anything. "We're going into town, Eric," said Hugo, and somehow five of us ended up out in the street waiting for a bus. It really was the Magical Mystery Tour as I stood there stoned out of my head. Everyone knows I feel like this, I thought, even animals, as a small dog went by on its way, smiling at me. Eventually, the bus arrived and I followed the rest of the guys upstairs. The bus was rocking from side to side and the feeling of the drug seemed to be getting stronger and I fell into a seat. Then the bus conductor came upstairs for the fares. We were all sitting in separate seats and he stood beside me. "Fares please." I slowly realised everything wasn't free, I had to pay for my Mystery Tour. Starting to panic, I put my hand in my pocket and pulled out a fistful of loose change. It didn't mean anything to me and I handed the lot to the conductor, who looked at me as if I was stupid, gave me my ticket and some coins back, and got his other fares.

We got off in Leeds city centre and walked about a bit, although I can't remember that much about it. I do remember one day some weeks later, going to some market with Hugo, and we each bought a second-hand fur coat (the ones that old ladies used to wear). We put on the coats, rolled our trousers up to our knees, and walked through some of the large department stores, being stared at and pointed at by everyone we passed and loving every minute of it.

Hugo still had the idea of forming our own group and we were looking through one of the entertainments papers for musicians when we spotted an ad saying, "Bass player available, transport and good gear, ready for work." I phoned the number and spoke to the guy who told me his name was Corbett. As a joke, I asked him if he was related to Harry Corbett, who had a very famous glove puppet bear and dog called 'Sooty and Sweep'. "Yes, he's my father," came the reply. Anyway, the guy's name was Matthew Corbett and, as Hugo or myself didn't drive, he said that he would drive over to us. We waited for him and then we saw a little van stop outside the house with 'The Sooty and Sweep Show' painted on the side in really bright colours. We looked at each other and went out to meet him. He was a really nice guy and he drove us over to his parents' house, Hugo in the front seat with Matthew, while I was in the back with all these puppets. It was amazing, and one of those moments when you wish some of your friends were with you or could see you. When we arrived, he took us into his father's office and on one wall was an enormous framed photograph of Sooty and on the facing wall was one of Sweep. Harry wasn't there. I would have loved to have met him.

Years later, Matthew Corbett took over *The Sooty Show* from his father and, in fact, I used to watch it with my son Erik, as it was on children's TV every week. It was excellent, and Matthew wrote all the music as well for the show. He was a great bass player, but for one reason or another, we never got to work together.

I went to Leeds University one night with Hugo and a few students. There were a few bands playing and I was really knocked out with some of the musicians, some great folk guitarists and banjo players. One of the guys who played electric blues guitar came over to the house one day and plugged his guitar into the Burns amp Hugo owned. He turned it and the volume on his guitar right up and started playing around with sustain and feedback. "Wow, let me try that," I said. I'm still trying.

The old sex life in Leeds was basically non-existent. I did ask some girl out for a drink one night, and was amazed when she said she would buy the next round. They never did in Belfast.

At some point, Hugo landed a gig in a place called the Melbourne Hotel. We had a piano player, drummer, Hugo on rhythm guitar and lead vocals, and myself on lead guitar and vocals. I sat down on a chair to play this gig. It was a very light cabaret-type music, but at least I was playing, earning a bit of money and a sort of social life as well. I can't remember what happened, but about a few months later I was back in Belfast. Shirt factory, here I come!

I'd been back now for a few weeks, and one Saturday afternoon I got the bus to Belfast city centre and made my way to Crymbles music shop. Every Saturday, about 40 or so musicians would be standing around in Crymbles, not buying anything but talking about gigs, who left who's band, what musicians were available, etc. It was the best place to be to hear all the latest local news about the Belfast Music scene.

This particular Saturday, I was talking away to about five guys at once, when the door of the shop opened and in walked Van Morrison. Slowly, the talking got quieter and stopped altogether as Van walked past us and made his way upstairs to the first floor. Van was a living legend in Belfast. It was he who had started the first R&B club (The Maritime Hotel) in Ireland. Then his group, Them, had been signed up by Decca records. Then he had two hit records in the top 20 charts, *Baby Please Don't Go and Here Comes The Night. Them had appeared on television on the two biggest music shows of the day, Ready Steady Go and Top of the Pops, and they had played tours in the UK, Europe and America. And now, Them had broken up, each member going their own way.*

In Crymbles, the talking had started up again, when Van appeared coming down the stairs with one of the guys who worked in the shop. He seemed to be pointing roughly where I was standing. Van then walked over to me and asked if we could have a talk. As the guys I had been talking to stared open mouthed, Van and myself stood outside the shop.

"Are you Eric Bell?" he asked. I said I was. "Hi, I'm Van Morrison." I just looked at him and said I knew who he was.

"Are you doing anything tonight?" he said. I told him I wasn't doing much. "Do you know where Hyndford Street is?" "Yeah," I replied. It was about a 15 minutes walk from my house. He asked me if I could call up to his place about 8pm and to bring my guitar, and off he went.

I went back into Crymbles and lots of the guys came over to me, asking me what Van said. "You're in the Big Time now, Beller," somebody said. I walked on cloud nine to the bus stop, got the bus home and ran into the house. "Guess what? I met Van Morrison in town today. I'm going up to his house tonight!" My Aunt Ivy and Uncle Harold were from a different generation, but both of them were happy for me.

At 8pm that night, I knocked on Van's front door feeling very shaky. Van's Mom came to the door and I walked into the small front room, very like a lot of the working class houses then in Belfast. Van's Mom and Dad, plus a large dog, were going out for a while, leaving myself and Van in the front room. I noticed this amazing reel-to-reel tape recorder sitting on a small table. It had lots of knobs and dials and meters on it, and as Van switched it on, he said, "Can you get your guitar out? I just want you to play along to a few songs, the first one is in G." I plugged my guitar into a little amp that was beside me, and the first song started. It was just Van on his own singing to an acoustic guitar, which sounded great.

As I was sitting there playing with ideas that came into my head, he sat opposite me smoking a cigarette and muttered, "Yeah, that's nice" every now and then. This audition, which was what it was, went on for another 45 minutes or so. Then we finished and packed up. As I was putting my guitar away, Van said he was going to a party in the city centre and did I want to go. I was really knocked out that he asked me and we got a bus into town. It was a great feeling being with someone who was famous and people recognising him. It sort of rubbed off on yourself and made you think, maybe this could happen to me someday. We walked through the town until we came close to some buildings near the Albert clock. We walked down an alleyway near some shops, found a door that led up to a flight of stairs and entered a large room lit by lots of candles. Van said hello to some girls and left me standing there with my guitar. Everyone seemed very sophisticated and cool, and after ten minutes or so I left. Some fuckin' party, I thought.

I saw Van again in a couple of days, and he lent me Them's first two albums, which were marked showing the songs I had to learn. He told me he had booked a rehearsal room at Dougie Knights, a place in town where bands had the choice of three or four large rooms to rehearse in. I did my homework on the songs, and the night came to go to the rehearsal. When I got there, there was a bass player and a drummer. It was Mike Brown on the bass and Joe Hanretty on drums. I knew them to see as they were out of a very popular Belfast R&B group called The Alleycats. We started talking about what might happen playing in Van's latest band, which was called Van Morrison and Them Again, when Van walked in. He immediately went over to the PA, turned the vocal mike on and said, "Yeah, can we try Gloria?" (a very popular song which Van had written as a B-side to one of his hit records).

So, Mike, Joe and myself started the song, waiting for Van to start singing. About what seemed like two minutes had passed and he still hadn't sang, then he came snarling and spitting the words in his own style. "Wait a minute, wait a minute," he said, and the whole thing ground to a halt. Van came over to me. "What are you doing?" he asked.

"You're supposed to shout 'Gloria', not fucking whisper it." I just looked at him, wondering what to do. My first reaction was to tell him to stuff his band, but I thought about it and decided to go along with it for a while. The thing was, Van was very intense about his music, and I was used to playing with musicians where there was a bit of humour to lighten it. But not with Van. Anyway, we carried on rehearsing, and by the end had about 15 songs to try out at our first gig.

The venue was the Square One Club in the city centre. I made my way there and saw this huge crowd of people queuing outside. I had to push and battle my way to the front of the queue and then there was another queue on the stairs leading up to the club. It was only because I had a guitar case in my hand that people started realising that I must be one of the band and let me pass. I walked into the hall where we were playing and the other guys were there and we made our way to the dressing room. "Wow," I said to myself, thinking about the crowd of people I had just pushed through. What an atmosphere it'll be tonight.

It really did feel like a very important gig. In the changing room was a large table filled with bottles of beer and a few bottles of spirits. Then, the door opened and in walked some guys from the local press and a photographer. We were due on stage in about 45 minutes, when the door opened again and I recognised Alan Henderson, the original bass player with Them.. I saw him and Van walking over to the corner of the room and having what looked like a serious talk. Then, a few minutes later, Van came over to where Mike, Joe and myself were. "Ah, listen," he said. "It's like this. There's going to be two bass players on stage tonight." He looked round at Alan. "This is Alan Henderson, he thought of the name Them, he owns the rights to it, and he says if he can't play tonight he'll pull the gig." What a night!

It was time to go on and we walked out on stage. The place was packed to the rafters and the audience was right up to the front of the stage, so close to the band that two girls started untying my shoelaces and then tying them together. There wasn't much room on the small stage, and I tried to see the funny side of it. I looked at the list of songs on the top of my amp and started preparing to go into the first song, *Baby Please Don't Go.* Van looked at Joe the drummer and then across to me. "Start a blues in E." "But, what about the list?" I said. "Fuck the list, start a blues in E." So, before I knew what was happening, Joe counted the band into a slow blues and away we went. After this, some people started shouting for Gloria and Here Comes The Night, wanting to hear the hits and the well known songs. But it didn't happen. Van just made things up, words and little riffs on the guitar and, after a while, most of the audience started getting into what we were trying to do. After the gig, we all got taxis home. I was buzzing like mad, forgetting for a while that I had to get up in the morning – back to reality and the shirt factory.

The second gig I remember was upstairs in Sammy Hueston's Jazz Club, which again was packed. I think we played some of the better known songs that night, and everyone was happy. About a week later, at the weekend, we had a gig in Carrickfergus Town Hall. We were driven there by a friend of Van's. The hall we were to play in that night was enormous and so was the stage. It was a massive building with lots of rooms and Mike, Joe and myself picked one for our dressing room. But, there was no sign of Van or his friend. I got my guitar out and started tuning up and getting myself into that mood, preparing to walk out on stage.

The time flew by and a few men walked in and asked if everything was alright, and told us we were on in 15 minutes. Then Van appeared. He was dressed in a suit with flowers stitched all over it, and draped over his shoulders was a small blue cape. He must have bought these when he was in America. So, we started walking down these enormous corridors, which let on to the huge wooden stage, and we took up our positions. As I said, this was a very large venue and the 60 or so people down at the back of the hall looked like a very small crowd. They didn't come up to the front of the stage so there wasn't much of an atmosphere like there had been at the other gigs we'd played. The sound as well was echoing off the walls and all the spaces in the building.

At one point, as we were playing the slow blues number, Van, who would give hand signals from time to time to let us know whether to play loud or soft, signalled for us to take the volume down. He walked over to his amp, picked up a large book and walked back to the mic. I looked over to see what he was going to do, and I noticed the book he held was upside down. Putting the book under his arm, he said in a very clear strong voice, "To wank or not to wank, that is the question," and he said it again in the very same way. Then he said, "Hands up all the wankers in the hall." Among the 60 or so people standing at the back of the hall were a few Teddy Boys, drape coats, crepe sole shoes, greased back hair. When Van had said what he said, it sparked them off and they started whooping and shouting and skimming coins at us, which was incredibly dangerous. The guy who was running the gig came on stage and announced that if they didn't stop, Van and the boys would stop playing. I don't know what happened, but we walked off stage, went back to the dressing room and just sat there. Then, the guy came in and told us not to go outside for a while, as the Teddy Boys were looking for trouble. So, we hung about backstage for a while and were then told everything had settled down outside and we got in the car and were driven home.

The last gig I played with Van Morrison was at the Students' Ball in Queen's University in Belfast. On the day of the gig, we got there in the afternoon and there were a few student's larking about. I noticed the stage was covered with different colours of paint and still a bit wet, so when we were setting up our equipment, our shoes would be sticking to the stage. After doing a rough sound check, we split up and would see each other later on that night in the dressing room. We were to play around 9:30pm so I started getting ready, tuning my guitar and making sure the guitar leads were working, etc.

It was around 8:30pm by now, and I'm looking over at the cans of beer and bottles of spirits. I really didn't enjoy playing with too much alcohol in me, as my playing could get a bit sloppy. So, I just had a few beers and a small whiskey. But, after a few drinks you can sometimes feel you could handle a few more. Time passed quickly and before I knew it we were going to play in ten minutes. My head was spinning a bit as we walked on stage in front of a large crowd of students. We started up and about four numbers in, Mike Brown, the bass player, walked over. "Hey Eric, Van says can you turn down a bit, it's a bit loud." I looked over at Van and turned down the volume of my guitar, and at that point, Van, who was also playing electric guitar, turned up. Probably because I had had one drink too many, I thought to myself, "Fuck this," and turned the volume back up again. I didn't really know how loud I had played that night, but the vibe on stage wasn't great.

We carried on and seemed to have gone down well enough with the crowd who were all out of their heads anyway. Towards the end of the night, everyone had gone, leaving the four of us sitting on chairs, waiting for taxis to take us home. I wasn't feeling that great because of the drink and, after thinking about it for a while, walked over to where Van was sitting. "Ah, listen, Van, I'm leaving the group." He just looked at me for a moment, put his hand in his pocket and said, "There's your money, man." And, that's all that was said.

A week later, I was lazing in bed, as it was Saturday morning and no work to go to, when my Aunt Ivy rapped on my door and, bringing in a cup of tea, handed me *City Week,* which was a local paper that had a few pages about the music scene in and around Belfast. "There!" she said, "I hope you're proud of yourself." She left and I looked at the page: "At the Queen's University Students' Ball last night, the band playing was Van Morrison and Them Again. The night was partly ruined as guitarist, Eric Bell, was trying to outshine Van Morrison with sheer volume."

I remember about a few days afterwards, I called around to see a guitarist friend of mine called Eddie Campbell. I knocked on the door and was told to come in. I got the shock of my life as, sitting on a chair in Eddie's front room, was Van Morrison. "Fuck me," I thought. "He doesn't waste any time."

Thinking back to those days now, I can't help but admire Van. As I said earlier, Van had achieved so much when he came back to Belfast around that time I met him at Crymbles music shop. But no one seemed to give a shit. He did everything himself – find musicians, organise rehearsals, pay for the rehearsal room, and probably got the gigs as well. It was no surprise to me when a short while later he packed up and left for America.

So, I was on the loose again and thought about what I was going to do next. As not many people I knew in those days had house telephones, you just had to call around to their house and hope they were in. I decided to call round to see an old bass player friend of mine, Sammy Cooke, who was always forming bands. He lived on the outskirts of Belfast, so one rainy night I got the bus, then walked the half mile to Sammy's house. He was in, thank God, and we talked about old times and my days in Leeds. "I've formed a blues band called Shades of Blue," Sammy told me. "Our guitar player, Gary Moore, just left a few weeks ago, he's moved to Dublin to join a group called Skid Row." I knew Gary for a few years, and lots of times when playing Belfast in our various groups, we had watched each other play. Great! I was in a group, and a blues group at that, no more showband stuff. Shades of Blue were Sammy Cooke, bass and vocals, Eddie Willis on rhythm guitar and keyboards, Stuart, whose last name I can't remember, on drums, and myself on lead guitar and vocals. We rehearsed for a while and played the usual clubs around Belfast and just beyond.

One night I will never forget. We were playing in the Jazz Club, a very popular place right in the city centre. It was pretty packed that night and people were up dancing to records before we would come on to play, which was in around an hour's time. As I was making my way through the dancers to the loo, an old friend of mine, Eric Knight, who looked like Brian Jones from the Rolling Stones, said, "Hi Eric, would you like a smoke?" He showed me a cigarette, but twice as thick, which he had in the palm of his hand. I hadn't smoked much hash since Leeds. "Great," I said. Then Eric said he had smoked enough and I could have it all. So, I got to the loo, found an empty cubicle, went in and locked the door. Blast off! I don't know what was in it, but in a little while I had left the planet completely. I remember sitting there and reading all the graffiti written on the toilet door. I had no idea how long I was spaced out, when suddenly I heard, "Eric, Eric!" I jumped up and then thought I had just heard my name in my own head. Then someone was banging on the door shouting, "Eric, are you in there? We're on!"

Slowly, I realised what was happening. I eventually got the door open and Sammy was staring at me as if I had just stepped out of a UFO. "Oh no, for fuck's sake, what have you been taking?" I felt really weak and very shaky as we started walking towards the stage. Everything was in slow motion as I got my guitar, which was a beautiful Gibson 330, and put it on. Everyone in the band was getting ready to start playing when I heard this really loud noise, like feedback. I sensed that the guys in the band and most of the audience were looking at me, as I started to hallucinate. Over the top of the stage was a fluorescent tube light, one of those purple lights that show off people's dandruff and capped teeth. It was shining on my guitar and making the tone and volume controls glow with an eerie white light. The real problem was, I was seeing about ten controls instead of the usual four, and I was trying to find where the real volume control was to stop the feedback. The rest of the band had enough and went into the first song without me. I eventually found the real control, turned it down and joined in on the song. But the effect of what I had smoked grew stronger, and to this day I can't believe what happened. When I put my hand on the guitar neck, it bent and then straightened back up again. I took my hand off. I kept telling myself this wasn't really happening, but it did no good. After the third or fourth song, the band had had enough, and so had I. I took my guitar off, left it on the stage and walked off. Unfortunately, there was no changing room so I went over to the side of the stage and lay down on a pile of coats that some of the audience had left there. I stayed there until the gig finished, then got a bollocking from the rest of the band, saying that if anything like this ever happened again, I was out.

We played the well-worn circuit again and again until one night we were playing in the famous Maritime Hotel, doing support for top Dublin group, The Movement. At the end of the night I was on stage packing up my amp, when the singer from The Movement, John Farrell, came over. We started talking and then he asked me if I knew a guitarist called Eric Bell. I said that was my name and he told me the band had been trying to get in touch with me to maybe join them. I asked quickly if they still want me to join, but John said that tonight was in fact their last gig. There was one of the new type showbands being formed in Dublin and John was going to be lead vocalist and they would be looking for musicians to audition. He asked me for my address and said he would write and let me know the details as soon as he found out what was happening. A few weeks passed and I heard nothing from him. Then, as I was getting ready to leave for work a couple of days later, an envelope dropped on the floor by the front door. Yes! It was for me! I opened it and inside (it looked like a sheet of toilet paper) was a very brief note from John Farrell. It said the auditions were being held in Dublin in a few days' time, and if I wanted a lift to Dublin, I was to meet two guys outside the Athletic Stores on Thursday morning at 12:30pm. Another day off work!

I asked Ivy if it was alright to take the day off work, and she said it was fine – she never seemed to mind me trying to get somewhere in the music business, as long as I had a job of some sort to bring home some money in the meantime. I packed my guitar and got the bus into town to meet the two guys. As I approached the stores I saw them both dressed to kill and looking like movie stars to me. They had these very stylish suits on and their hair was perfect (and lacquered) and they looked tanned. I learnt later that most of the young showbands used 'Tanfastic', tan from a bottle. I don't know what they thought when they saw me. My hair was really long and scruffy and I was wearing a donkey jacket and jeans. They spoke in strong Dublin accents and told me their names. Shay played keyboards and sang and Jim played bass and also sang.

We walked round to an office where we would meet one of the managers of the band – there were two, one based in Belfast and the other in Dublin. The Belfast manager was called Jim Aiken, and he was driving us down to Dublin as he had a meeting with Jim Hand, the other manager. We got into Jim's Jaguar Mark 2, and a few hours later we were in Dublin, driving down O'Connell Street, one of the widest streets in Europe. I'd only been in Dublin once before and that was just for the day. There was a great vibe from the place – green and cream telephone boxes and huge black phones with press A and B buttons, green and cream buses, and all of the street names were written in English at the top and Gaelic at the bottom.

We arrived at Desmond Dominic's School of Speech and Drama building, where the auditions were being held. There were crowds of musicians standing on the steps, others going in and coming out of the front door, and some hanging around in the street. "We must be too late, they must have found someone by now out of all this lot," I thought. But we got out of the Jaguar and went into the building. I was shown into a huge room where a seven-piece band was setting up. No messing. I was pointed to a Vox AC 30 amplifier, so I plugged my guitar in and fiddled about a bit to get a sound. We tried a few standards, like *Roll Over Beethoven,* but I think I must have freaked everybody out with the volume I was playing at, as one by one, they stood with their hands covering their ears. As I had been playing with a loud blues band in Belfast, I couldn't really blame them. We tried a few more songs at a lower volume, which included the evergreen Danny Boy, and then I was asked to sing. One of the songs I picked to sing was Respect by Otis Redding. It was a great feeling to hear the brass section coming in as I sang. After a few more songs I was told to wait outside. The other manager, Jim Hand, asked me if I could stay in Dublin that night, as there would be a meeting tomorrow to decide on the musicians and who was getting the job. I said I could stay but hadn't much money with me. He then handed me a 20 pound note which was about three times the size of an English one. I stood speechless as £20 was a hell of a lot of money in those days. He then asked a guy called Dougie, who was also from Belfast, to get me a B&B for the night.

I knew Dougie a little as he was the drummer from a very popular group from Belfast called the Mad Lads, who had a resident spot in the Maritime Hotel. So, Dougie took me and my guitar to a B&B just off O'Connell Street, paid the bill for me that night, and said he would call for me the next morning. We had to go to some office to find out who had landed a job in the showband. After he left, I went out to a local café and got something to eat, and went back to my room. I remember sitting on the bed thinking things through for a while, and then I got on my knees and prayed. I felt I really needed a break and I wanted this job, so I prayed and prayed, asking God would He please help me to get it.

Next morning, Dougie called for me and we both went to a place called the Corn Exchange Buildings where Jim Hand had his office. There was a type of waiting room outside the office and about seven guys were sitting there, and every now and then one of them would be called into the office and come out after 20 minutes or so saying, "Yes, I've got the job!" and he would sit down as the next guy was called in. Eventually, I was called into the office and the two Jims were sitting there. "Well, Eric, how are ye? Sit down." They started telling me how much time and effort and money they were going to put into The Dreams. And they certainly didn't want or need anybody to rock the boat on them. I was also told The Dreams would be on a good wage and we would eat in the best hotels before each show. We would also be playing, on average, six nights a week with Monday off.

"So, the job's yours if you want it." "Thank you, God, thank you!" I said to myself. "There's just one other thing," said Jim. "You take drugs, don't you?" "Well," I said, trying not to show shock and surprise at how they found out. "I smoke a bit of hash now and again." They looked at each other and Jim A said he didn't think it was addictive. Then they told me they would like to take a chance with me, but I must understand that if I was caught even once smoking hash, I would be fired immediately. I was also informed that two members of the band would be keeping an eye on me from time to time. These were the conditions, take it or leave it. I took it.

Next day, I went back to Belfast and told my family the news. I think they were proud of me and the fact that I was on a good steady wage – I was to make more money playing music than I had made at the shirt factory. I called up to see Sammy and told him my news and that I'd be moving to Dublin in a couple of days. I also called round to the shirt factory and told Mr Faulkner I'd be leaving yet again, and that was the last time I saw him or the job.

When I got back to Dublin, Dougie had found a place where we were to share. It was in Manor Street, about ten minutes walk from one of the quays where the River Liffey flowed. In those days there was a cattle market nearby, and every Monday morning about 500 cattle trotted past our house. They were on the pavement, on the road, cars stopping to let them pass. Looking back, it was a great flat. It was owned by a Mrs Logan and her husband, a very Irish couple, and they had three daughters. Dougie and I had a large bedroom, a smaller bedroom and a large sitting room, and shared a bathroom with a few nurses upstairs. No, nothing happened with any of them – the daughters were too young and the nurses were too smart!

The Dreams had another meeting at Jim's office and we were told to go to a certain tailor to get measured for band suits. We were to have two suits each, wearing one while the other went to the dry cleaners. The two Jims had everything organised and were very professional. They bought us a new Transit van (one of the large ones) fitted with windows and aeroplane seats. They bought us amps and other equipment and they got us our very first gigs in Liverpool. "If you're going to make mistakes, make them in England first lads, before the people in Ireland hear you." And we certainly did. The first gig was terrible, it didn't sound like a band at all. Just seven guys who had never met before, walking onto a stage and playing a song they weren't sure of. When we had finished we walked into the changing room and, one by one, we threw our jackets violently onto the floor. Shay, the band leader, responsible as he was, jumped in. "Pick them fuckin' jackets up. Jim's still paying for them!" We all started laughing and hung the jackets up.

We played another one or two gigs, Irish ballrooms around Liverpool, and started to sound like a good band. Then we sailed back to Dublin and Dougie the drummer and myself started to settle in in our flat. By this time, the publicity machine had started. Photos of The Dreams and write-ups and files on each member of the band started to appear everywhere, in papers, posters and mags all over Dublin. I thought the two Jims were excellent managers, and the greatest stroke they pulled was to get The Tremeloes (a very famous English pop group at the time) to write a song for The Dreams to record as their first single. Jim Hand also acted as an agent and brought over English groups like Mungo Jerry, Marmalade and The Tremeloes to tour Ireland. So, Jim and The Dreams were invited to the hotel where The Tremolos were staying, and in one of their hotel rooms they started to work on the song that was to be our début single. It was called *I Will See You There. On the B-side of the single, we recorded one of Shay's songs, called A Boy Needs A Girl.*

It was my first time in a proper professional recording studio and I found it all very interesting and exciting (though I wished I had been playing blues music). Anyway, it all turned out pretty good and the single was released in a storm of publicity and we started to tour around Ireland. We drew great crowds nearly everywhere we played, which was probably every ballroom in Ireland. Some of these ballrooms were really standing in the middle of nowhere. We would drive through some very small country town, then would see nothing for about 20 miles, apart from fields, turn a corner and there would be a huge ballroom. But the most amazing thing was, where did the crowds of people come from? Anyway, somehow on the night there would be 1,000 people or more dancing the night away.

Our new record reached No.1 in the Irish charts for a few weeks, and my life became playing every night except Monday nights, when I would either stay in and listen to music, rest and look at the fire, as we had no TV, or go out to a trendy ballroom called the TV club. We were told when The Dreams started not to be seen at this place, I think to give the impression that we even worked on Monday nights. It was very like that in the showband scene, very competitive. So, apart from Monday night, the rest of the week would be… meet each day outside a store called McBernies, where our van and driver would be waiting, and then leave for the gig. Then when we arrived at the town where we were to play that night, the driver would find the best hotel and we would order our evening meal and have a drink or two. We'd then get to the gig, get changed into our suits and go on and play for two hours or more.

Dublin in those days, around 1968, was magic to me. I got to meet lots of musicians, both from showbands and groups. They were like two different tribes, the guys from the showbands would look like movie stars, very well dressed, driving flash cars around Dublin with flash-looking women beside them. They even had their own way of talking, calling everyone 'Head' and they would sometimes put the word 'egg' into their speech. "Look at that chick over there," would become, "Leegook at theegat cheegik over theegar." And when this was spoken very fast, they could have a private conversation in company. The group musicians were not flash, more laid back (as Philip [Lynott] would say, "Suffering for their art, man") and they hadn't much money. But they were mostly very good musicians. Sometimes, the group musicians would be approached by someone from the showband scene who would offer them a job in a showband for very good money. If the guy took the job, he was branded a traitor by the group scene. It was all very serious stuff.

Dublin was the type of city where you could go out on your own at night with nothing planned, go into one of the many pubs and end up at some party with lots of friendly people. I had a sort of routine that I really enjoyed when I had the time. If The Dreams weren't playing too far away, I would go to the Luna Chinese Restaurant every Sunday afternoon for a salmon curry. It must have been the only place in the world that served it, as I've never spotted it anywhere else on my travels here and there with various bands. I'd go to Nearys bar at midday sometimes for a pint of Guinness, brown bread and oysters, or sit in Bewley's café on Grafton Street beside the beautiful stained windows, smelling and drinking real coffee, watching the many characters of the city come and go.

One night, I was playing with The Dreams somewhere up North and we all went out for a drink at the local pub. I must have had one too many. When we got back to the hall, there was a group playing on stage (our support). We had to walk on stage and walk behind them to get to the changing room, and that's when I noticed their guitarist was playing a white Fender Stratocaster. They had stopped playing to let us pass, and as I walked past their guitarist I asked him if he would be interested in swapping his Fender for a Gibson 330. So, at the end of the night he came into our changing room and asked if I was serious about the swap. I said I was so we went out onto the stage, he with my Gibson and me with his Fender, plugged into our amps and played a bit and then swapped guitars there and then. That was how I got my first Fender

Stratocaster.

A week or so later, something was going to happen to The Dreams to break up the monotony of driving all over Ireland six nights a week. We were flying to Hamburg, Germany to mime to our single on a TV pop show! I'd flown once before, from Belfast to Leeds, but I'd never flown to a foreign country before, in fact I'd never been to a foreign country before. I remember the morning we left, standing on the tarmac queuing up to board this huge plane with the steps leading up at the back where the tail was. Then we were off. Later, we were served an excellent lunch and a drink or two, and I felt on top of the world (and being paid as well).

When we arrived at Hamburg, we were met by some agent or other and then driven to our hotel. About four members of The Dreams had been in Hamburg before with a band called The Debonair. They were telling me and everyone else that you could buy a really sharp suit for five pounds in the stores there. We went to one of the stores later on to look around. It was like a huge supermarket. We never found the suits but this guy kept shouting and pointing at me, until I realised he wanted me to put out my cigarette. It was the first time I had been told I couldn't smoke in a shop. We then went back to our hotel, had a rest and, as we were not working until the next day, Jim, our manager, said he would take us out for a meal and a look around the city of Hamburg. After our meal and a few very strong German beers, we ended up in the Red Light district. The part we were in was like an outdoor car park with small brick walls standing about ten feet apart from each other. At the top of each wall was a spotlight and at the front of each wall were ladies of various sizes and various ages. We all split up and I ended up talking to a girl of about 18 years old. I must have been pretty drunk, not realising how long I'd been talking to her. I thought we were getting on really well when she suddenly said, "If you just want to talk, you must pay me for my time!" This woke me up a bit and I said my goodbyes and slowly met up with the rest of the band. Jim then suggested we all go and see the famous Star Club where The Beatles had lived and played before they were living legends. When we got there, it felt like a very rough area with lots of drunks and down and outs spoiling for a fight. We had another few beers and got taxis back to the hotel and passed out.

Next morning I woke with a terrible hangover, thanks to the German beer, and felt like I had only had two hours sleep, which was probably true. When everyone was up, after lots of wake-up calls, we met downstairs for coffee. "Anyone seen Jim?" was the question, as the guys from the TV studio would be here quite soon. It was incredible leaving this time in the morning, something like 8.45am. Eventually, a few of us went to look for Jim, the first place being his hotel room. We knocked but no answer, then opened his door which wasn't locked, and there he was, fully clothed with his shoes still on. Lots of shaking and lots of coffee later, we had him on his feet and it was time to leave for the studios with the two over-efficient Germans. It was hard work travelling at their pace as we were all hungover and very untogether.

When we arrived, we were shown into the dressing room and then the make-up room, with each of us holding a precious cup of strong coffee. We were ushered into a TV studio where seven small rostrums stood, and each one of us got up and stood under huge coloured spotlights, which were slowly roasting us. We stood around for a very long time, and then through the speakers came the intro of *I Will See You There*. We started miming, which I think is really weird. Jim, our manager, was standing in the corner and watching everything going on. There didn't seem to be any problems, and then, all of a sudden, there was a bit of a commotion and everything ground to a halt. The floor manager came over to me and put his fingers in the corners of his mouth and pulled. "Why aren't you smiling?" he said in a harsh German accent. I was going to say, "Because I have a fucking hangover and am slowly dying under these bloody lights," but I changed my mind. I couldn't believe it – they must have stopped the show six times or so because, every time the cameras were on me, I wasn't smiling. So I said I would smile as soon as they played the song again, and I would keep smiling until it ended. This was what it was like being in a pop showband."You vill look happy, ya?" Next day we flew back to Dublin.

As I mentioned earlier, Monday was our night off, and though we had been told not to be seen hanging about the TV club, that's were most of us ended up. They sold horrible cheap wine and sherry in paper cups, but it did the trick. About half of the musicians in Dublin (both showband and group members) would be there, picking up girls, slagging each other and being sick in the loo. It was great fun if you'd had a few drinks, as I found out. One night, for some reason I decided not to have anything to drink and ended up in the TV club sober as a judge. All these musicians and other people I knew came staggering over and started talking a load of crap and it was all one big bore. I then realised the truth – never go to the TV club sober!

CHAPTER 6

A few months passed, and Jim Hand took two weeks off and went somewhere in Greece for a holiday. When he came back to Dublin, he was raving about this song that he had heard being played that was becoming very popular in Greece. It was called *The Cassachock* and was a type of Greek dance. And he wanted The Dreams to record it for our next single. So, a few days later, we were all sitting in Jim's office listening to a recording of it. It had lots of mandolins and other Greek stringed instruments on it, reminding me of some other song I had heard, Zorba The Greek, I think it was called.

Two weeks later, we were booked into a studio in the TV Club to record *The Cassachock*. When I got there, I noticed this guy sitting down with this large mandolin type instrument, playing the parts of the music that I had thought I was going to play. Then I was told I would be playing rhythm guitar on the record (if it was needed). I took all of this rather badly, as I wanted to play lead guitar on it, instead of some session guy twanging away on some mandolin. I hung around for a while, got bored, then left the studio and went to the nearest pub. When I got back, it was all over... even to this day I can't remember if I played on the record or not.

Jim hired some dancer who worked out some steps for a dance for *The Cassachock,* then the dancer spent some time teaching the band to dance it. I certainly didn't want to be part of it, so I made my excuse that I couldn't dance and play the guitar at the same time. The record was then released and two female dancers were flown over from London to dance the Cassachock on stage with us. Of course, when the girls arrived, everyone in the band was trying their best to impress them and get into their knickers. It was all very funny.

A tour was set up to promote the record, and we started working our way around Ireland again. *The Cassachock* was stirring up a lot of interest in The Dreams again, but meanwhile I was getting more depressed. I heard about the group Skid Row, the one that Gary Moore had joined, and on one of my Monday nights off, I decided to go see them. They played in a real old cellar place called The Five Club, which I think was in Harcourt Street. I stood in a darkened doorway on the other side of the street facing the club and smoked a little one-skinner joint, then went over to the club and paid in before the smoke took effect. As I was walking downstairs, I heard this incredible music and thought it must be a record being played, but no, it was Skid Row. I made my way to the front of the stage and was completely blown away by their playing and their sound. Gary was on guitar playing amazing stuff, as was the bass player, 'Brush' Shiels, and drummer, Noel Bridgeman. I just stood there in my green mohair suit beside all these long-haired hippies, my jaw on the ground, wondering what I was doing playing with a showband.

After a while, Gary spotted me in the audience, and when they took their break, we started talking. I ended up later that night borrowing Gary's Telecaster and jamming a few blues with Brush and Noel. It felt so good and really strengthened my resolve to form my own group. It must have looked strange to see a guy playing blues in the Five Club wearing a shiny mohair suit and showband hairstyle. After the gig, when I got back to Manor Street, I knew I had to leave The Dreams, but I realised I must now start saving as much as possible before I left. I decided to stay for two months.

On one of my Monday nights off, I ended up very drunk and got a taxi back to the flat. The people in the house were all asleep and I eventually worked out how to open the front door. I don't know why, but I got the idea in my head that the house was haunted. At the top of the stairs was a religious statue bathed in an eerie red glow from a red bulb behind it. As I stumbled up the stairs, I kept looking at it like it was the first time I had ever seen it. It certainly added to the creepy feeling I was experiencing. I opened the door to my sitting room but didn't turn on any lights, and staggered into the small extra bedroom we had. The street lamp outside the window lit the room up a little and I walked over to where an enormous old-fashioned wardrobe stood. I opened the door to the wardrobe, looked in and said, "If there's any fuckin' ghosts in there, fuck you, I don't care!" and, pushing and wrestling with coat hangers, I climbed inside. I lay down on the bottom for a while, then just started laughing, the whole thing being ridiculous. And being so drunk, it took me ten minutes to stand up and get out again.

My friend Kathy came up to the flat quite a lot now, and she had made good friends with Mrs Logan. Kathy had heard me mentioning that Julian Bream, the fabulous classical guitarist, was playing in Liberty Hall in Dublin quite soon, and as she knew I loved all types of music, she told me she had bought two tickets. It was a great surprise and a few nights later we went along to Liberty Hall. The place was packed and we were lucky as we had seats downstairs about 15 rows from the front. It was funny seeing Julian Bream live for the first time. He strode on stage like a wrestler holding his guitar by the neck like an axe, nothing like what I had pictured. But when he sat down and started playing, he was amazing. To fill a hall holding about 400 people with just a nylon-strung guitar and no microphone and project each note is a sign of real talent. He had played about four pieces of music when something broke the mood. Two young ladies had arrived late and were being shown to their seats. He kept on playing for a while, but the noise and distraction eventually became too much and he just stopped playing and glared down at the two ladies until they had found their seats and sat down. Then he glared for another extra few seconds and carried on. He was fabulous, and at the end of the concert, was given four encores, the crowd not wanting him to leave.

I was still playing away with The Dreams, and still planning when to leave them, but something happened on one of my Monday nights off that I hadn't planned for. I had gone into town early that Monday and ended up in one of the city's many pubs with a few musician friends, and we were having a few drinks and the time passed quickly. I hadn't had much to eat that morning and it was now around 6.00pm and the drink had really hit me. So much that it took me quite a while to realise that I was now on my own. My mates probably had mentioned that they were leaving but I was seeing everything now in a distant blur. I decided maybe I should get something to eat, so I made my way unsteadily round to the Coffee Inn, as it was just in the next street to where I was. (This was to be one of Thin Lizzy's favourite hang-outs in the future). They served mostly Italian food, very cheap, and the spaghetti sauce was the best I've ever tasted.

I don't know how long I must have sat slumped over my meal, but now I was back in The Bailey, the pub I had been in earlier on, and couldn't remember walking back or even if I had paid for my meal. All I knew was that I didn't want to go back to the flat yet, so I decided to go to the Crystal Ballroom, which was only a few minutes walk away. I was pretty drunk by now and, as I walked through the entrance of the Crystal, I sensed the four doormen looking at me. I kept talking to myself to walk straight and to act normal as I made my way to the ticket office where I slurred to the man inside that I played with John Farrell and The Dreams Showband. (If you mentioned this, lots of times the venues would let you in without paying). The guy inside thought I was too drunk to come into the ballroom, but I kept telling him I was just going to drink black coffee and sit quietly upstairs in the bar. He gave up and let me in.

When I got upstairs, I aimed myself at the bar and asked for a large black coffee. As I stood there swaying, two guys I knew came over and we started talking about something. Next thing, the mug of coffee that I held slipped from my hands and smashed to the floor, and a few seconds later, one of the doormen was standing beside me. "Someone wants to see you at the front door, come on," he said. I knew enough to know that they said this to get you down to the door, then they would ask you to leave. "If it's about the broken mug, I'll pay for it," I said. "Never mind about that, come on, someone wants to see you," he said, and took my arm and brought me downstairs. When we got there, one of the other doormen came over to me. "Did you pay in tonight?" he asked. "No," I slurred. "I'm out of John Farrell and The Dreams." "I don't give a fuck who you're out of, everybody has to pay in here. You're too drunk anyway, get out!" and he started pushing me around. I, of course, because of the drink, thought I was John Wayne and pushed back. The next thing I remember before hitting the ground was as if someone had hit me with an actual brick in the face.

When I came to, I was lying outside on the pavement with this incredible pain in my head. I got up with the help of a parked car and then saw my face in one of the car's mirrors and really got a bad shock. My face was cut and covered with blood. I started crying and lost my temper and staggered over to the entrance of the Crystal Ballroom again and saw the doorman who had hit me. "Look at my fuckin' face, you fuckin' animal!" I shouted. "I'll wait for you some night and stick a knife in your fuckin' back!" He warned me to shut up and go home or I'd get the same again. I knew I could do nothing and came out into the street again and spotted a policeman. I went up to him, told him what had happened and he came down to the Crystal with me and took a statement. Of course, nothing happened to the moron who hit me but the policeman told another one of the doormen to take me to the nearest hospital as it looked like my eye might need stitches.

Ten minutes later, I was helped down a long corridor in Mercers hospital by some white-coated doctor who kept telling me to keep quiet as I was shouting and cursing about what I was going to do to the guy who had hit me. The doctor then examined my face and said I would need three stitches in my left eye and he would freeze it before sewing it up if I wanted, but thought I was drunk enough not to feel it, and went ahead. He was right, I was so out of it I didn't feel a thing. But when he took the stitches out again a few weeks later (without freezing it) I nearly passed out with the pain. Next day, I was called in to Jim's office in Corn Exchange Buildings. I arrived wearing dark glasses. He asked me what had happened and I told him my story. He didn't seem to believe me, and he told me that someone had seen the whole thing as it had happened and phoned him up and told him a different version of the story. "Anyway, Eric," said Jim. "I'm sorry to lose you but I'm putting you on two weeks notice. I'm going to Spain for two weeks and when I come back, we'll replace you then with a new guitarist." And that was that. So, I spent the next ten days or so playing in dark glasses and was called Roy Orbison by nearly everyone I met. When Jim came back from his holiday, he seemed to have forgotten about replacing me in the band and things settled down to normal again.

I continued playing with The Dreams and, a few weeks later, met a young lady one night when we played in Cork. She was called Eleanor and we became very close. She told me she was moving from Cork up to Dublin to study some course her father had suggested, which made things a lot easier for the both of us. It was then I decided to leave The Dreams, as I'd saved up a bit of money by then. So, a few days later, I went to Jim's office to tell him I was leaving.

"Well, Eric," said Jim, "so, you're going to form a group? How many musicians have you got?" "I haven't got any at the moment," I answered. "And how are you going to get around? Any transport?" "No," I said. "And have you got any gigs lined up and a manager or an agent?" Again, I said I hadn't. "Right," said Jim, "Have you got an amplifier?" "No," I said. "I think you're making a big mistake here, Eric. You've got a very steady job with The Dreams, plenty of money, you could buy yourself a house. There's lots of work coming in…"

The one thing Jim had said that had really got to me was the fact that I hadn't even got my own amplifier. But my mind was made up and we both agreed that I would stay with the band for two weeks until a replacement was found. A few days later, as we were travelling to the gig, all the guys in The Dreams kept asking me was I really leaving the band, and what was I going to do, and did I have any musicians yet? And the more I thought about it all, the more I realised what a risk I was about to take. The two weeks passed and a new guitarist was found. Jim called me up to the office and we said our last farewells – and he gave me the amplifier as a going away present. At least now I had my own amp.

CHAPTER 7

Everyone I knew thought I was mad. I was in The Dreams, one of the top young showbands in Ireland. The money was good, I liked all the guys in the band and they were all good players. But, I was living a sort of Jekyll and Hyde existence. On my nights off I would lay stoned on hash listening to Hendrix, Cream, The Beatles, and next night I would be out playing *Simple Simon Says* on some stage in some Irish ballroom with The Dreams. I thought it over for months and then decided to leave and form a three-piece group.

Luckily, I had saved up some of my wages in the Building Society that I intended to live on until I met a bass player and drummer to form my new group. So I started going into town and made my way around the pubs and clubs where the rock and blues musicians hung out. I would see some guys all sitting at a table in one of the pubs, and just knowing that they were in a group, I would walk over and introduce myself and what band I had been in. As I still had the showband hairstyle, and probably the showband manner, they looked at me like I was some kind of weirdo. "Do you know of any bass players and drummers that would be into forming a three-piece band?" I would ask. They would look at each other and shrug and blink and shake their heads and after a few moments I would say thanks and walk away. This type of thing went on for a few weeks at least and I started to realise maybe I had been stupid to leave such a steady gig with The Dreams.

My money was going down fast. This girl Kathy who I had met in The Dreams really helped me out. She bought me food and cooked it, bought coal and made a fire and cleaned the flat. She fancied me a little bit but we were just good friends as far as I was concerned. We would sit at night (now I wasn't playing) in front of the fire and drink cheap sherry. I would get depressed as the group I hoped for was nowhere in sight. But Kathy told me that I had talent and should keep believing in myself. A few nights later was to be the start of my dream coming true.

That night I went to the Bailey, a very popular pub just off Grafton Street. I went up to the bar and ordered a half of Guinness as I really had to watch my money now. I didn't see any musician types to approach that night and was thinking of going back to the flat, when Eric Wrixon walked in. I knew Eric a little as he was from Belfast too and had been keyboard player with the original Them when they were the resident group in the Maritime Hotel. Eric was with another young showband, Terry and the Trixons, who were also very popular around Ireland. We started talking and he told me he was leaving the Trixons in a few weeks as he had had enough and wanted to play music again, or just go off and travel somewhere. So we ended up going to the Countdown Club where we knew the owner and could get in for nothing. Once we got in, we headed for the bar where they sold cheap sherry and wine, Eric buying, as he was still working. At one point in our conversation, Eric asked me if I had ever tried acid or LSD. I said I hadn't and he took out a really tiny tablet and said if I wanted to try it, to bite it in half and just let it melt on my tongue. I didn't really think much about it, bit it in half and handed him back the other half, which he took. After a little while, I started to think this acid stuff wasn't that great, when the band that was playing that night came out on stage. Eric and myself sat down on the floor facing the stage like everybody else, to watch and listen to the band. In those days of 1968, people sat in the lotus position and smoked dope and listened to the music.

The band was called Orphanage and were Joe Stanton (lead guitar), Pat Quigley (bass guitar), Brian Downey (drums) and Philip Lynott (singer). I had never heard of them before. I remember one of the songs they played, Bob Dylan's *It Takes A Lot To Laugh It Takes A Train To Cry.* They were very good. Philip was dressed in a long white African type robe and moving very gracefully and singing great. Next thing, this large gust of wind nearly blew me over as some guy walked past wearing bell bottom jeans (I was still sitting on the floor). The acid was working. But the one thing that kept playing in my mind for quite a while was Brian Downey's drums, especially the sound of the snare drum. Then another thought kept playing, "I must get Brian for my new group. I must get him to play drums."

When Orphanage took their break, I noticed only Philip and Brian went into the changing room. I got this idea to go over and speak to them; they must know lots of musicians. I told Eric I was going to speak to some guys and went over to the changing room and knocked on the door. "Come in," said a deep, soft-spoken Dublin voice. I went in and introduced myself and met Philip and Brian for the very first time. I thought the acid had worn off by now and, yes, it had been very pleasant. I didn't know it came in waves, so halfway through asking them about bass players and drummers, I just started laughing and walking round the room. They both looked at me and then each other, and then me again. A few minutes later I told them it was my first trip and it was getting strong. This seemed to bring us closer together. We swapped various phone numbers and Philip asked me what pub I drank in. "You want to try the Zodiac off Grafton Street," he said. "That's where the group musos drink." I mumbled my thanks and was just opening the door when I heard Phil say, "Do you fancy forming a group with Eric, Brian?" Brian thought for a moment, and then said no. But Phil asked him again, saying Orphanage had played the circuit and it would be good to play with other musicians, fresh ideas, etc. Brian then shrugged and said, "Whatever you want to do, Phil. I don't mind." I could see they were very close friends.

Philip stood beside me at the door and said they would form a band with me if he (Philip) could play the bass guitar and we try to work on some of his own songs. He told me he was in fact taking bass lessons with Brush Shiels (bass player with Skid Row). Then he said he could call up to my flat with a tape of some of his songs, if I could borrow a reel-to-reel tape recorder. So we arranged it on a piece of paper so I would remember, as I was still tripping on the acid. I came out of the changing room and eventually saw Eric and told him what had happened. He then became interested in joining the band as well and I didn't have the heart to tell him I wanted a three-piece band, so we were now going to have a four-piece band. Later that night, we ended up going to another club called Just Charlie's, where I thought I was in a cartoon and then met the Devil! After this, we ended up in Eric Wrixon's flat where we discussed life for about three hours and decided it was a big joke. I found out he was actually doing some male modelling in *Spotlight*, a popular mag of the times. After that we walked to a place called Kelly's Corner and stood at the end of the road at 7.30 am to tell the workers going off to work not to bother as it was all a joke! Luckily, we didn't actually stop anyone.

A few nights later, Philip called up to the flat in Manor Street with a tape of his songs. I didn't know what to expect when we got the tape running and was very pleasantly surprised when the first song started. I think it was *Dublin* and another called *Chatting Today.* He asked me what I thought and I told him I thought they were excellent. I also felt my guitar playing could work really well with them. So, this was my first real meeting with Phil. He came across as very gentle, full of energy and seemed to give out a true determination. He dressed really well and very stylish and was wearing a sort of detective raincoat that night. We arranged a first rehearsal, again on loads of pieces of paper filled with addresses, phone numbers, times, etc.

Our first rehearsal took place about three days later in the cellar under a sort of music shop, I think. We had to set up our borrowed equipment of amps away over in the corner of the room, which was the only area of the room that was dry. We had to walk over to it across a plank as the rest of the cellar was about one inch deep with water. The very first thing we tried was a slow blues in the key of C. I had to show Philip where he was on the bass a few times, but his sheer enthusiasm and natural feel shone through. There was something there between us and it felt right. I couldn't believe I could play anything I wanted and nobody was getting on my back all the time. Anyway, we stayed until someone threw us out and we ended up in some pub to have a talk. The first thing we needed was a good place to rehearse, and the second thing was having music to rehearse when we got there. So, we decided to bring our albums down when we met again, which was in a week's time.

I think it was Phil who stroked a tennis pavilion for us to rehearse at a cheap rate. The problem was, it was about three miles outside Dublin and the hall was minus zero! I can still see Philip really struggling up the stairs on the bus with an enormous homemade bass guitar case, and then getting back down again when we got off. The hall was damp and very cold and I played with a scarf pulled right up to my eyes. I felt I was getting mild electric shocks from the guitar strings as they felt so cold. Our different taste in music was very noticeable when we checked out each other's albums. Phil was into Dylan, The Band, Hendrix, Bob Marley, Spirit. Brian was into blues and a few jazz things. I had these weird records of the Sputniks, Marty Robbins, Nat King Cole Trio, Segovia, while Eric Wrixon was into Jimmy Smith and soul type stuff. This had so much to do with the style Thin Lizzy was to develop along the way. One of the first tunes I remember us learning was a Deep Purple thing called *Wring That Neck*. It was an instrumental with the organ and guitar playing in unison and lots of jamming and very solid bass and drums.

We started to sound better and better, but were really pissed off with the travelling and the dampness of the pavilion. We decided to rehearse at Desmond Dominic's place (where I had auditioned for The Dreams). It was a million times better. It was right in the city and was warm, with lovely big wooden rooms with huge mirrors on the walls, as it was also used as a ballet school. I was loving it all; my hair was growing longer, I was wearing what I wanted, but most of all I was playing what I wanted. And we all got on.

I remember one of the rehearsals being very funny. We were having this jam and were really into it, all stoned on this amazing hash. I could hardly see the rest of the group through the smoke, when the door suddenly opened. "Right, boys," came this very loud theatrical voice, followed by a very loud clap of the hands as Desmond Dominic walked in. He then bent down and turned the power off. It all happened so quickly that we were still playing but with no amps or PA. Then, one by one, we stopped playing and the whole thing slowly ground to a halt. I thought it was so funny, very like a comedy sketch. We just stood there as if in a trance, and realised the rehearsal was over.

At one of these rehearsals, a young guy about 16 came in and started talking to Phil. I think he had a mike for sale or something. He was called Terry O'Neil. He started hanging around and then told us he had got us a few gigs for pretty good money. And he was only 16! The first gig we played was at some hall near the River Liffey. We played support for Purple Pussycat, a group that had the only other black front man and singer in Dublin, Mr Dave Murphy. We seemed to go down quite well and caused a bit of interest with the way we played and looked.

Sometimes we had acoustic rehearsals to save money, and would arrive at Phil's flat in Donnybrooke, Philip and myself playing acoustic guitars, Brian drumming on his knees, and Eric Wrixon listening and rolling joints. We would try and put in some serious work, mostly on Phil's songs at these rehearsals. It was all very creative stuff and when I came up with an idea, Phil would smile and it would become an important part of the song. But other times, Phil would ask me for an idea to join one part of a song to another, and I would play everything I knew and it still wouldn't work. Then I would really have to think and try things I'd never played before. This could go on for most of the rehearsal.

At this point in time, my money was starting to dwindle away and Phil asked me if I would like to play a few acoustic gigs with him in some of the folk music pubs in the city. "You'll probably make a fiver and a few pints of Guinness." So, a few nights later, Philip and myself would be sitting in the middle of a crowd of about 30 people, playing anything from Simon and Garfunkel to the Rolling Stones to an instrumental by gypsy guitarist Django Reinhardt. At one of these gigs, a Swedish jazz musician and his wife spoke to us at the break. They loved Django and invited us to a party out at Howth, a beautiful fishing town. "But first we must stop off at our house," the lady said. Their house was way up on top of a grassy cliff overlooking the sea.

I seem to remember something had upset them. I think someone had smashed one of their windows and had tried to break in but hadn't had any success. Anyway, after this had been sorted out they drove us to the party at Barney McKenna's house, the banjo player from the Dubliners. The house was packed with about 20 people, but Barney wasn't there – he was out fishing. This was around one o'clock in the morning. Phil and myself had a few drinks and sat down on a sofa, and at that point, the front door opened and Barney came in. He had had a few pints and was wearing a huge white Arran sweater, jeans tucked into water boots, and a few fish on a line slung over his shoulder – what an entrance!

"Ah, Jasus Barney, how are ye? Get the oul banjo out!" After a while, Barney sat down on a chair in the middle of the room, eyes closed, and started playing these amazing jigs and reels. Meanwhile, Philip and myself were rolling small joints (one-skinners we called them), which were easier to smoke without being too noticeable. Then Phil went over to where Barney was sitting. Barney had said he wanted a cigarette, and while he kept playing, eyes shut, Phil lit up the one-skinner and put it between Barney's lips. He kept on playing the banjo with the joint burning away in his mouth. About ten minutes later, he stopped playing and shifted his chair about two inches backwards and then one inch forwards and then started playing again. This happened a few times. Philip and myself were cracking up on the sofa. I've seen people doing this in various parties and places, shifting their chairs very slightly backwards and forwards.

CHAPTER 8

As you may guess, it was a totally different lifestyle being in a group rather than The Dreams showband. Phil would take me around all the popular pubs and clubs in Dublin and introduce me as his new guitarist. He seemed to know everyone. He would also keep driving me onwards. "Eric, you should be practising really hard and working on your guitar playing, you could really make a great reputation for yourself." Phil himself was putting the hours in on the bass and improving all the time.

I remember we went to the cinema to see *Woodstock,* the classic music festival movie, and also the *Monterrey Pop Festival.* When The Who or Jimi Hendrix were playing, Phil would say, "Look at the shapes he's throwing, Eric," (meaning the way the guy was moving) or, "Wow, look what he's wearing." He was really very aware of these things as well as the music. In those days, he was great company and exciting to be with.

Now to how the name Thin Lizzy came about .We were rehearsing one afternoon in the Countdown club. It must have been our third or fourth rehearsal and, as we were packing up, someone asked what was the name of the group going to be. So we started on various film titles, then book titles, album titles, and this led us into comics and all the famous characters.... Desperate Dan, Dennis the Menace, Minnie the Minx. Then I remembered a female robot maid called 'Tin Lizzie' from the *Dandy* comic. I mentioned this but none of the guys were interested, so we carried on thinking of names. While this was going on, I had a crazy idea, but sometimes crazy ideas work. Because I came from Belfast, the Dublin accent sounded a lot different to me. Dubliners left out the letter H in some of their speech. My idea was to change the name Tin Lizzie to Thin Lizzie, so people in Dublin would have to make an extra effort to say the name correctly, which might help the name stick in their memory. I think because it was so bizarre an idea, they eventually went for it. It must have been a bloody good name really because, even to this day, it's up there with the best of them.

We had now played about four gigs under the name Thin Lizzie and were building up a steady following. We had a great image for the time. I remember looking over at Eric Wrixon, bent over the keyboards, wearing a buckskin jacket, a joint in one hand and a bottle of whiskey and a glass beside him; Philip 'throwing shapes' that would become his trademark in later years; and Brian's amazing drumming. We were still rehearsing as much as we could and, at one of these rehearsals in the Countdown Club, Phil had got hold of some really strong smoke. We started working on the song, *Saga Of The Ageing Orphan,* and at one point, I saw the entire stage with all of us on it, gently lift and slowly start to float around the empty club while we were playing. Later on, something even funnier happened. We were still working on the arrangement of Ageing, still very stoned, when one of the cleaning ladies who came in during the day started tidying up around the club. Then to our amazement, she walked up onto the stage while we were still playing and started sweeping up, as if we weren't there, and even lifted Brian Downey's hi-hat to sweep under it! I find it hard to believe now, but that's what happened, and every time I hear Ageing, these memories come flooding back.

Terry O'Neil was still getting us some gigs, and one of these was to play at a party at the Gallaghers' house. The Gallaghers were tobacco people and they were very rich. We arrived outside this magnificent house sitting in its own grounds and were shown into the room where we were booked to play that night. We sat up our gear in one corner of the room, as ladies in evening dress and men in dinner jackets drifted in and out. Then someone came over to us and asked if we could start playing and to please watch the volume. I had forgotten my guitar strap so I had to sit down to play that night. We started off and kept the volume down and everything was going smoothly until the guy who was supposed to mix our sound came over. He said that if any of us wanted any drinks that he would get them as he hadn't much else to do that night. So, we all ordered a few pints of beer and as the night wore on ordered more beer and then we got on to the spirits. This was when I started gradually turning up the volume on my guitar until Philip leaned over and asked me to turn down a bit as people were starting to complain. I was enjoying myself, experimenting on my playing and slowly getting drunk, not realising how loud I had become. Ten minutes or so later, after Phil started to get more annoyed with the volume, I put my guitar down and said, "All right, get yourself another guitar player," and walked out of the room and into the enormous garden outside.

There were tables and chairs set up all around the garden so I went over to one and sat down as I was feeling more drunk than I had thought. A split second later, a waiter was standing beside me. "Would you like anything to drink, sir?" he asked. "Ah, yes please, could I have a whiskey and blackcurrant and a vodka and tonic for my girlfriend?" and slurred that she was in the ladies' room. He went away and a short while later came back with the drinks. Well, that was that. The Jekyll and Hyde experiment was about to start again. After lowering the whiskey and a little of the vodka, I eventually willed myself to stand up and staggered in a zigzag line towards the house, looking for action and a bit of fun. I walked past the room where Phil, Brian and Eric Wrixon were still playing away and ended up at the bottom of this enormous marble staircase.

All of these lovely ladies in evening dress were walking up and down the stairs and I would stop and tell them how pretty they were. They looked at me like I was some old wino and, after a while of this, I just shrugged it off and ended up at the top of the house, where I found the toilet. I opened the door, went in, locked the door, sat down and lit a cigarette. I don't know how long I was there, it could have been ten minutes or half an hour. Then people started to knock on the door to use the toilet, and every now and then I would shout for them to fuck off. It was after this that Mrs Gallagher herself and a few bouncers arrived on the scene. She knocked on the door and said, "Who's in there? Open this door at once!" Something told me I had better respond, so I got myself up, opened the door about two inches and peered out. Mrs Gallagher took one look at me and turned to the bouncers. "Get this object out of there at once!" They pushed the door open and then took hold of my arms to take me downstairs. "Listen," I slurred, "I used to earn £35 a week with The Dreams showband," thinking, because it was a lot of money to me, that she might be impressed.

I was then taken downstairs and they got the van open that was parked nearby and I lay down in the back and was violently sick.

A few gigs and a few weeks later, Phil started to talk about the idea of us all living together so we could really work on the music. At this time in the music business, there were lots of groups living in a sort of commune set-up. It did sound like a good idea. We talked about it a bit more, and a week or so later, I met Phil in the city centre in Dublin. He smiled that smile as he jangled the keys in front of me. "Wait till you see the place Eric, it's amazing, it's in Clontarf." Clontarf was a few miles out of the city, very close to the sea, where the more well to do people lived. (The idea being that this would help keep us from hanging around the city wasting time that we could put towards our music.) Well, that was the idea. We went out to see the place. It was out of town, about half an hour on the bus, and just a minute's walk from the beach and two minutes walk from Clontarf Castle. Our new address was Castle Avenue and we had the top floor in this huge house. A flight of stairs ended at a large bedroom, then there was a bathroom, then up another six steps or so on the right was a sunroom that jutted out from the side of the house and was made mostly of glass, apart from the floor. On the left was a huge kitchen and further on was an enormous sitting room. So, Phil and I left our old flats and eventually moved in.

At the start, I shared the bedroom with Philip and it really was magical times. We would wake up in the mornings, make tea, then back to our beds, and Phil would roll a huge spliff and we'd listen to *Astral Weeks* by Van Morrison. A few days later Eric Wrixon moved in and he lived in the sun room. He said he had a real piano and he wanted to move it into the sun room where he could practise all day. So, a week later, Eric, Phil, Brian, myself and a few others struggled up the stairs, round the corner and up the other stairs with this very heavy piano and placed it in the sun room beside Eric's sleeping bag. From what I can remember it was very out of tune and was played on for a week before the novelty wore off and the pubs in the city beckoned.

Philip had just recently met a young lady called Gail, who was from the North of Ireland, and she moved in with him, and my girlfriend Eleanor, from Cork, moved in with me. One day when we were drinking in the Bailey, Phil and I met this hippy-type character called Pete Eustace who was from England. He moved in as well and became the group's sound engineer. And later on, Larry Mooney, who managed groups, moved into Castle Avenue as well. Brian Downey didn't move in, but might as well have done as he was up in the flat every day. My friend Kathy from the Manor Street days was a frequent visitor also, and helped us get the place looking good. We also would put people up for a week or so to help them out and then they would move on.

Castle Avenue was starting to develop quite a reputation as Philip and myself were to find out. One day in the Bailey, we were approached by two bullet-headed Americans who told us they had heard we had a place where they might stay for a few days. Philip took one look at them and said sorry, but there was no room at the moment. Then, one of them opened up the back of a camera he had and inside was an enormous slab of black hash wrapped up in cling film. "We haven't much money, but you're welcome to some of this," he said. So, that was that, and they ended up staying for a week. They told us they were GIs and had just returned from Vietnam.

CHAPTER 9

Eric Wrixon had met some guy who owned a pub somewhere around Dublin, and they had been talking one day when Eric spotted a Hammond organ sitting in a corner. Somehow, he managed to talk the owner into parting with it, and when he arrived back to Castle Avenue, he was very excited and told us he now was the proud owner of a baby Hammond organ. We didn't believe him at first, as these organs are very expensive, but some days later at one of our gigs, Eric arrived in a van and said, "Could you give me a hand lads, it's really heavy." It took eight of us to lift it and place it on stage. Apart from the weight, it sounded amazing, as only a real Hammond can. But it was not to last, and the guy who Eric had got it from now wanted his baby back. He must have found out how much they were really worth.

We recorded one of Phil's songs called *The Farmer*, which reminds me of The Band, who Phil was very much into. Then, we recorded I Need You, complete with a brass section. I thought *The Farmer* was a strange choice of song to record, but looking back, maybe it had been a good song for that time.(around April 1970). Anyway, only about 500 copies were pressed and, apart from a few airplays, nothing much happened about it. It was around this time that Eric Wrixon was to leave Thin Lizzy.

At one of our rehearsals in Parnell Square, Terry O'Neil called a meeting and said, although the group was going down well at gigs, after expenses there was never that much money left to share out. And this worried myself and Philip as the rent for our new flat had to be paid. "So, I think either the group goes three-piece or splits up," suggested Terry. After a long discussion, Eric Wrixon said, "When do you want me to leave?" Although Eric left, he still stayed on living at Castle Avenue and could be seen at the end of most nights studying an enormous map of the world. About a month or so later, he had made his mind up to either move to Sweden or Germany as he had some musician friends out there.

Now a three-piece, Phil, myself and Brian rehearsed as often as we could and now had lots of acoustic rehearsals at the flat, as this saved a lot of money being paid out on electric sessions. Phil and myself on acoustic guitars and Brian drumming on his knees. At night, I would be sitting on the sofa playing on my guitar and Phil would walk past and sometimes, when he heard something I was playing, would ask me, "Is that yours, Eric?" meaning was it an idea I had made up myself, rather than copied from someone's record. At moments like this, we would get together for a while, and this is how a lot of the songs would be written. Philip had a real talent for hearing something in its raw state, taking it much further and creating a great song out of it.

Brian Downey was also very important in the forming of the songs. Some drummers just hear a song, and without very much thought, start banging away in a boring four to the bar beat that has been heard a million times before. But Brian, to me, was a very natural drummer, and approached the drums as a musical instrument and added greatly to the structure of the finished song. He had lots of favourite drummers – Mitch Mitchell from the Jimi Hendrix Experience, Ansley Dumbar from John Mayall's Bluesbreakers, Ginger Baker from Cream. When I first met Brian, I found him very easy going and he became one of my best friends. We were pretty close right up to the time when I left the band. Another Influence on Brian's drumming was a Dublin drummer called Jimmy Doyle. Around the time we became a three-piece group, Thin Lizzy were rehearsing in the Countdown Club one day, when these two guys walked in and sat down facing us and listened until we had finished rehearsing. As we walked over to them, one of the guys asked Brian about some beat Brian had just been playing. They started talking and the guy introduced himself as Jimmy Doyle. He then took a pair of drumsticks from his coat pocket and started drumming on top of one of the small tables that sat in the club. Brian just looked and went, "Wow, what was that?" Brian ended up going to Jimmy Doyle for lessons, as did Noel Bridgeman, drummer from Skid Row. Jimmy played rock drumming when he wanted but could also play dance band music, which used bossa nova rhythms, and more jazzy stuff, and Brian would work through these different styles.

This was interesting because, when Lizzy moved to London about a year or so later, we rehearsed every week in a room over a pub in Euston and sometimes we would become really stuck for things to play. When Phil had an idea for a song, he would play it through a couple of times to Brian and myself, then we would start working on it. And sometimes it would be really difficult to come up with ideas. When this happened to Brian, Phil would say, "Hey, Brian, play some of the stuff you got from Jimmy Doyle." "Nah, it wouldn't work, Phil, it's a different feel," Brian would answer. "Just try it, Brian," Phil would insist. So Brian would start to play these crazy rhythms and Phil would ask him to change little bits of it and then start playing the bass over it. They were a very strong rhythm section and knew each other's styles inside out and, in the early days especially, were a real pleasure to work with.

I sometimes think Brian Downey, without knowing it at the time, helped save my life. One beautiful summer's morning, I woke up in the flat and had it all to myself. My girlfriend, Eleanor, had gone off to Cork to visit her family, Philip's girlfriend, Gail, had also gone to her family for a while and Phil had gone into town early. I wondered what I would do and, after a cup of tea and toast, decided I might take some of the LSD that we had stashed. I know it sounds like all we did with our lives was take drugs, but it really was the times that we were living in – most of the musicians I knew did the same. So, I found the stash and thought what the hell, I'll take a full tab of acid instead of a half, as it was a really beautiful sunny day, just the type of day for a great trip. After I had taken it, I went over to our very mixed record collection to find some suitable sounds to enjoy. I felt like listening to Hendrix's album *Electric Ladyland* and left it out to play in about 40 minutes time when the drug should be starting to kick in. I slowly started walking around the flat looking at things, taking my time, and went into the sun room. It really was just like a little greenhouse, so I went up to the huge front room again and put *Electric Ladyland* on the turntable and the sounds of Jimi Hendrix came swirling out of the speakers. After a while, I could see the sounds, like long grey wispy streams of smoke floating through the rooms of the flat.

I was really enjoying everything with its new experiences, and soon I ended up in Phil's bedroom where his bass guitar and my guitar were laying on top of his bed. "Oh, right," I thought, "it's time for the guitars to start walking soon." Then I made my way over to the large window and stood looking out. After a while, I saw two colours outside the window, blue from the sky sat on top and green for the garden sat below. The two colours started slowly forming into a curtain, which seemed to hang down outside the window. I kept looking at it and became convinced that if I opened the window, I could then grab onto this blue and green curtain and climb down on it to the ground. I don't know how long I stood there, but soon the tips of my fingers were pressing on the window pane and I could feel the glass bending, as if it were made of cling film, under my finger tips.

Suddenly, I heard this noise like a very loud gong and then heard it echoing right round the flat. I just stood there, not knowing what was happening, and then it sounded again, echoing around the rooms. I slowly realised it was the front doorbell. I got a bit worried to say the least about answering the door in the state I was in, then it sounded again. Right, I thought, better answer it. The one thing I found very hard about being on acid were the moments when it seemed to be totally over and you think, wow, that was incredible, but it's worn off now – only it hasn't. So, feeling back to normal, I made my way to the top of the stairs and looked down.

"Oh, Jesus," I said, looking at what seemed to be some sort of special effects from a sci-fi movie. The bottom of the stairs were about a half a mile down and the wallpaper at either side seemed to be breathing in and out. I started the journey down and felt very small, and then I was fighting my way through a jungle as the gong sounded again. I reached the front door, opened it and there was Brian Downey, the Friendly Ranger himself. Because of the acid, Brian looked exaggerated, really cool and worldly. "Hi, man, how you doing?" Then he looked at me more closely. "You're tripping, aren't you?". I said something, but my mouth felt like plastic, and he came in and we went up the stairs, which looked back to normal. We walked into the large sitting room and Brian went over to the record player and put another album on. We sat down on the couch and he took out a packet of cigarettes, rolling papers and a small reddish lump. "Wait till you try this, it's red leb, really strong," and gave me a really cool grin. After it was rolled and smoked a bit, he passed it over to me. I took a few puffs and it tasted and smelt like earth, and when I breathed out, the smoke came out of my throat instead of my mouth – it was very strong dope.

After a while, Brian got up and went into the kitchen, probably getting the munchies from smoking. He came back into the room and said, "Hey Eric, try this," and handed me a carrot, which was very misshapen, looking a bit like a deformed hand. I looked at it and smelt it and wanted to taste it, so I took a bite. Right at that very moment, Brian shouted, "No, don't bite it, it's a hand!" I looked at it and saw the torn flesh and tasted the blood. I spat it out and threw the carrot at him then, shuddering, picked up the closest thing to me, which was an electric fire, and threw that at him as well. "For fucks sake, man, stop!" yelled Brian. "It's only a joke." "Some frigging joke!" I said. "Don't you understand, I'm tripping?"

Eventually, the effects of the acid started to weaken, and Brian and I walked to the bus stop and got the bus into town, where we met Phil, spent the rest of the evening there and then caught the last bus back to Clontarf. One of the reasons I mention the LSD trip is that I understand now how young people kill themselves by believing that they can fly, etc. I had a similar experience at the window when I was convinced there was a curtain outside, and believe to this day that Brian ringing the doorbell when he did probably saved my life.

Thin Lizzy now started playing more and more gigs outside Dublin and started building up quite a large following, and soon we saw the same people turning up at our shows. I still had the same white Stratocaster that I had swapped for my Gibson and it was slowly falling apart. This was pointed out to me one night by one of our managers, Ted Carroll. "Eric, that guitar of yours is becoming embarrassing. I think it's about time you got a new guitar." At this point in time, there were no Fender Strats in the Dublin music shops, so when we had a gig outside Dublin, we would leave earlier and stop at any music shop we saw in any of the towns we were driving through and I would go in. But no one had a Fender Stratocaster. We ended up having to get one sent over from London (this is the same one I play on stage today).

I remember the day it arrived. We had been offered a lunchtime gig in the Abbey Theatre. It was an idea of the actors there, to bring people into the theatre during their lunch break to give them a taste of what live acting was about, to break down the invisible wall between the actor and the public. It was on the first or second day at the Abbey that my new guitar arrived. I remember that there was no case with it, it was just wrapped up in see-through paper in this huge cardboard box. And when I took it out and started playing it, I didn't like it. It took me about six months of constant playing until I felt comfortable with it. The gig Lizzy had at the Abbey was pretty strange. We set our gear up behind the stage curtain and sat down. The audience couldn't see us and we made up a lot of the music on the spot for the actors as they acted out their parts on stage.

One of the plays they put on was about students living together at college and, in one of the scenes, they were pretending to smoke a few joints. As none of the actors knew how to roll a cigarette, they asked Philip would he mind rolling a couple for them. Phil, the loveable rogue that he was, rolled three or four, and put some hash in one of them. He handed them to the actors, who then went out on stage and the play started. A while later, the real joint was lit, and by the time they realised, a few of the actors were pretty stoned. But, as they were all really likeable people, they took it all very well and we all had a bit of a laugh about it. Unfortunately, the gig at the Abbey Theatre lasted only a few weeks, a real pity I thought, as it was a great idea.

When Thin Lizzy wasn't playing, Phil and myself still kept an open house at Castle Avenue, and there would be loads of people calling up every night and lots of our musician friends would arrive around two o'clock in the morning after having played some gig in Dublin. Fashions and trends come and go, especially in the music business, and one of the trends around 1970 was looking for hidden meanings in song lyrics and on the covers of record albums. This was all linked with drugs, and bands like The Beatles were the forerunners. So, in our flat, there would be loads of us sitting all over the floor, searching LP covers and playing bits of lyrics over and over again. One of the strangest was the rumour that Paul McCartney was dead and a lookalike had taken his place in The Beatles. This all started from the cover of The Beatles' album, *Abbey Road,* where they are all walking across a zebra crossing and Paul is barefoot. In certain religions, this is linked with death.

Getting back to Thin Lizzy, I think the biggest break we had in those early days was when Frank Rodgers, who worked for Decca Records in London, came over to Dublin to check out some of the musical talent that was around. Frank, who was Irish and brother of the singer Clodagh Rodgers, ended up coming to see Ditch Cassidy, a great soul singer and showman. Ditch was going to do his thing for Frank at Zhivago's nightclub in the afternoon and, at the very last moment, asked Thin Lizzy to back him for his audition, as his own band couldn't make it for some reason. We all got there around three in the afternoon, and Ditch was out front singing, with Phil, Brian and myself backing him. When we had finished, we started to pack up our gear when Brian Tuite, another manager who had an interest in Lizzy, came over to us and said could we meet him in the pub around the corner in 15 minutes? Anything for a free drink! Fifteen minutes later, our careers were about to change. Brian Tuite walked into the pub with Frank Rodgers but no Ditch. Frank had liked Ditch, but wanted to sign us up for Decca Records and record an album in London. We just couldn't believe it. We had only been together as a group for around ten months!

CHAPTER 10

Around the start of January 1971, Thin Lizzy was on a boat bound for London to record our first album. We were sitting at a table in the bar having a beer when Phil suddenly said, "Look, I think that's John Peel standing up at the bar over there." John Peel was one of the most famous DJs at the time, working for Radio 1. After a few minutes staring over at him, we all agreed it was indeed John Peel. Then Phil, always a great man to use an opportunity, said, "Right, I'm going over to introduce myself and ask him will it be alright to keep in touch. He could really help us, you know."

Brian and myself weren't too sure about it all, but Phil was in one of those moods. "All he can say is no," and pushed his chair back, stood up and walked over to the bar. About five minutes later, he came back rubbing his hands together. "Great, he seems a really nice guy. I think he liked my nerve and he said to keep in touch." What a contact, and we hadn't even reached London yet.

When we did reach London, it was early evening and getting dark. We were taken by taxi with Brian Tuite to a place in the Marble Arch area called Sussex Gardens, a very long street filled with cheap hotels, B&Bs and hookers. Phil, Brian and myself shared a room that had three bunk beds, and though we were exhausted, we were much too excited to sleep. We still couldn't believe it was happening. Next morning, we had to be up by 8:00am.,have breakfast and make our way to the nearest tube station carrying guitars, bags and accessories. It was all strange and completely new to us, and eventually we found the right tube that would take us to West Hampstead where Decca Studios was. I seem to remember when the tube train came rushing up to the platform, Philip put his hand out to stop it as you would for a bus. "Only off the boat, lads?"

We arrived at Decca Studios. I thought it was a beautiful building, small and with lots of designs and details that early buildings sometimes have. We walked in and had a look around, then a large man with a black beard walked over and held out his hand. "Hi, I'm your producer," he said in a broad American accent. "My name's Scott English." (Scott had written the huge hit, *Hi Ho Silver Lining* for Jeff Beck and Mandy for Barry Manilow). We introduced ourselves. The three of us were very nervous and Phil whispered to me, "I wonder would Scott mind if I rolled a joint?" Then he pulled out this tiny piece of hash and said, "Ah, Scott, is it alright to smoke in here ?"

"Sure, man," said Scott and pulled open a drawer and took out a huge bag of grass. "Here, just help yourselves."

A half hour later, we were setting up in the studio and Phil was really winding me up by telling me that this was the very studio where Eric Clapton had recorded that stunning album with John Mayall's Bluesbreakers. "Yeah, Clapton was probably standing about there, Eric," said Phil, pointing to a spot a few feet away. After a short while, we were ready to go and started to tune up and hit a few drums. "Right, you guys, let's put one down," said Scott. "What?" said Phil "Jaysus, man, we're only tuning up." Soon, we did start recording one or two tracks but I don't think Brian liked the drum sound in the studio and we spent hours and hours doctoring and fixing and taping his drum kit. I found the recording really enjoyable and couldn't get over the fact that I could basically play anything I wanted and it was being recorded, yet a year or so earlier, in The Dreams, I was afraid of playing a different note.

Next day, Brian Downey and myself took a break from the studio and went round the corner to a café to get a tea and to sit in a different environment for a while. And there, sitting two seats away from us, was the Irish songwriter Gilbert O'Sullivan. He was dressed in his schoolboy clothes, which was his image in those days, and he really looked like a large kid, his chair tilted back against the wall, and he was drinking a milkshake through a straw. We didn't speak to him, which was a pity as I always thought he was an excellent songwriter. He must have been in recording as well as he was also signed up with Decca.

Back in the studio, we were using acoustic and 12-string guitars, as well as the electric sound, and to me this was the real Thin Lizzy, the one that I was so proud to be in. The studio was by now filled with clouds of smoke and anyone who walked in would have been out of their heads after one or two breaths. Five days later, we had finished recording and we were now getting ready to mix. Brian Tuite had bought a bottle of champagne and beers, and me, Brian and Phil were starting to relax after a period of very intense playing. As we were playing through the tracks, the control room door opened and these five guys walked in. They said they were recording upstairs and could they borrow a guitarist to play one or two solos on a couple of their songs. I think they said he couldn't think of anything to play on them (it does happen). As I was the guitarist, I said I would give it a go, and it seemed a good idea at the time, but when we reached their studio via an old iron fire escape, I wasn't too sure anymore. I realised I was out of it – after all, I was supposed to be relaxing now that Lizzy's album was nearly finished. Anyway, they played the tracks for me to listen to and I just drifted off into the huge speakers, and basically forgot why I was there. It was all a bit embarrassing, but I did end up playing something. I wonder if they;d use it? I think they were called Farm.

We had a night off in London before returning to Dublin and Phil suggested we go to this gig called the Lyceum. We took a taxi there and paid in. It was an amazing old building, like a huge old-fashioned theatre with lots of balconies and little rooms and corridors. London was a very happening place in 1971, and the people at the gig were dressed up in the most amazing hippy -style clothes, so much more flashy than anything you would see in Ireland. As was the thing then, everyone sat on the floor smoking and waiting for the band to come on stage.

The band that night were Wishbone Ash, an excellent melodic rock group with a twin-guitar line up. They came on stage and started right away and sounded very impressive. After about 20 minutes though, Philip turned to me and Brian and said, "I think the musicians in Ireland are just as good as these guys, if you just shut your eyes and just listen. But they look so much more impressive than the Irish bands because of their stage confidence and the clothes. We just can't get clothes like that in Ireland." The twin guitar line up also impressed Phil as he asked me later on what I thought about another guitarist joining Thin Lizzy. I told him I wasn't interested in playing that way and we left it at that. But, years later, he had his way with the line up of Brian Robertson and Scott Gorham, which sounded excellent but, as I said, it really wasn't my thing.

A day later, we were back again in Dublin wondering what was going to happen now. We, and our management, kept in touch with Frank Rodgers and Decca, and we kept on playing a few gigs up and down the country. Our album was finally released a couple of months later in April 1971. There had been a couple of changes though, which we didn't know about. It seems that when Decca A&R men heard it, they weren't too happy with the final mix and got one of their own engineers, Nick Tauber, to remix it. I, for one, got quite a shock when I heard it, as some of the wrong guitar parts had been used and now it was too late to do anything about it. But, after quite a few listens, I just got into the overall mood of the album and started to enjoy it. The album cover was very strange – a fish-eyed lens was used to superimpose a broken down car onto the same car's headlights. What was he taking? And the German cover had an old car driving up the shapely leg of a young lady (everyone must have thought of a Tin Lizzie as an old Ford car).

When the album was in the shops in Ireland, lots of our fans bought it, but as far as the general public was concerned, it wasn't a great seller. But then, another stroke of luck – Kid Jensen, one of the DJs from Radio Luxembourg, had got a copy of our album and was playing a track from it every night on his programme, Jensen's Dimensions, and all of our fans in Ireland heard about this and tuned in. Then Kid announced one night that he was going to play the album in its entirety, he then played it both sides and voted it his album of the year. He also invited us over to Luxembourg to be interviewed live on his programme. So, we flew over and met Kid, who showed us around, and then the night for the interview came. We had brought a very large bottle of champagne over with us for Kid as a present and he opened it before our talk. Now, I find champagne goes straight to my head and, before long, Brian Downey and myself were laying on the floor in the corner of the studio totally zombified. Phil was the one who kept it together and, as Kid started to talk to him, myself and Brian got the giggles and started shouting. They signalled for us to keep it down as it was all going out live, then it was time for Kid to read out the news so we really had to behave. But when he got to a part were he mentioned that there had been a little trouble in Belfast, that was it. I started shouting "Come on, Kid,,that's fighting talk! Come over here till I sort you out!" and Phil sitting beside him, biting his lip to stop laughing.

Next day, we went round to Kid's house for a while, and that evening he took us out to some club in Luxembourg. Lots of the DJs went there after work and we met a few, including Tony Prince. Tony was a very popular DJ and a real live-wire. He had had a few drinks when we saw him, and he told a crowd of us at the club to watch as he went over to a small rostrum, lifted up one end and crawled under it. About five minutes later, a stripper came out to do her thing and, as she made her way to get on the rostrum, it moved, looking like it had crawled across the floor. She screamed and ran off behind the bar, as Tony Prince got out and yelled and laughed and it really was very funny. Then all too soon, we were back in Dublin again.

The fact that we had an album out on a popular record label, and being voted album of the year by Kid Jensen, made more people start to take us seriously. We had a meeting with the management and we all agreed that a move to London would be the next best bet. In 1971, it was one of THE places to be in the music business and also we wanted to see how we would go down with an English audience. So, there we were again, on the boat for England... this time to stay.

Around this time, my girlfriend, Eleanor, was about four months pregnant and we moved into this small room in one of those huge old London houses in Hampstead – 31 Belsize Avenue. It had about 15 rooms, and one of our managers Ted Carroll lived on the ground floor, Gary Moore and his girlfriend, Sylvia, lived in the next room to him, our roadie Frank Murray and his wife, Ferga, had a room upstairs, and another 15 musicians, an actor and two Indian families shared the rest of the house.

Looking back, moving to London was the beginning of the end for me and I had some very bad experiences there. Being so used to Ireland, I found London very cold, impersonal and very fast, with everyone rushing around everywhere, and I seemed to pick up on the tension. I also couldn't believe the mixed cultures. Again, in Ireland about 99% were Irish people, and then I would be on a tube train in London, and there would be Arabs, Germans, Chinese, Black people, all different races in one carriage. And everyone ignoring each other and hiding behind their newspaper. I remember one of the first times I travelled on the tube and, naturally, started to speak to someone. I quickly got the impression that they thought I was some sort of a pervert or mugger or nutter. So, as they say, 'When in Rome'. I found it very difficult to breath in London, especially in the Summer, and I would sense a sort of coal dust smell in the air, something like the smell just outside a tube station.

Eleanor gave birth to our baby boy on 4ᵗʰ July and we named him Robin, that being my middle name. It now became increasingly difficult, as the room we lived in was very small and now had to house three people and all of the stuff that is needed to bring up a baby. It seemed around this time, everyone we knew was having a baby and on long Summer days, there would be a whole troupe of musicians and their girlfriends and babies making their way to Hampstead Heath, which was about a 15 minute walk.

The other thing which I found hard to take sometimes, was the fact that Lizzy was probably the most popular group in Ireland when we left, and now we had to start all over again from the bottom as no one in England knew who we were. "Thin who?"

Ted Carroll eventually found an agent in Acorn Agency, run by Chris Morrison. The office was situated in Dean Street, a very busy part of Soho, right in central London. We still travelled around in our old white Ford Transit, which leaned over to one side but carried five people and tons of equipment. One of the first gigs I remember we played in England was supporting Patto. Mike Patto was the lead singer, and the guitarist, Ollie Halsoll, who was probably the fastest guitarist on Earth. They were, as most bands in England were at the time, very confident and professional, and for a time, I felt very tense and insecure. It all seemed a lot more serious than in Ireland. Another thing which took me a while to get used to was all the English musicians seemed to set up practise amps in the changing rooms and sit there practising away for hours, with the drummer tapping on some table and the singer warbling in the loo. And then we would walk in, looking still like we were just off the boat. We were playing a lot in those early days in London, most times for next to nothing. But, we were told that it would get our name all over the listings and gig guides in the top English music papers.

We did some weird gigs; one of the strangest was playing in a jail for the prisoners. We really couldn't believe it until our van pulled up outside the prison gates, drove into the courtyard and the van was searched (for some reason, I don't think we were). We carried our equipment into the prison chapel and set up on the small red-carpeted platform where the priest would normally stand. Facing us were about 200 empty chairs. Then, someone came over and said they would be bringing in the prisoners in about half an hour. I'll never forget that feeling, standing on that little stage with Phil and Brian as the doors were opened on either side and they all marched in wearing denim shirts and black trousers, accompanied by four guards. They all sat down and the feeling was intense and everything was very quiet as they sat there looking at us. Then, we went into our first song. As I said, it was very weird, there were no women, just this sea of hardened male faces. But, we slowly settled down and, at the end of our set, were given a great reception by the prisoners, who were smiling and more relaxed as they were marched back out of the chapel. We actually ended up playing in another two prisons.

After four months of constant gigging, we started to build up a small following and see some of the same faces turning up to support us. We would be mostly playing tracks from our first album, some blues and a couple of Hendrix and Stones songs. We were still signed to Decca records, who weren't too sure whether to keep us on or not, as our first album hadn't sold in vast amounts. Then someone suggested that we record an EP. We all thought it very strange, as the EP, though very popular in the early 60s, was now completely out of fashion. But, like a lot of ideas that work, we dared to be different and recorded four new songs – *Dublin, Things Ain't Working Out Down On The Farm, Old Moon Madness and the title song, New Day.* It was recorded in another Decca Studio in Tollington Park. I liked the atmosphere on the track Dublin, and thought the cover was excellent, drawn in a cartoon style. A lot of Thin Lizzy fans bought it and it now must be worth a small fortune as a collector's item .(I haven't even got one myself!)

So, we kept on gigging and playing support to bigger acts like Status Quo,

Canned Heat, Medicine Head, and later on played universities with David Bowie and the Spiders from Mars, Tyrannosaurus Rex (before they became T Rex) and, to Phil's delight, Rod Stewart and the Faces.

One day, in the office at Acorn Agency, Chris Morrison called a meeting with us and said that he would like to become our manager and sign us up with a different agent. He was very serious about it all, so we all went for a Chinese meal, met the new agent and, an hour or so later, everything was settled. But, new agency or not, the money Lizzy was going out for was still very low, and now and again we would sail across the Irish Sea and play a two week tour just to fill the coffers. I really looked forward to these tours, as we would be staying in good hotels, pulling good crowds and meeting lots of old friends again. Our spirits would be greatly lifted for a while.

Now, back in London, we were told that we would be recording our second album in a matter of weeks. It was a real shock, we weren't prepared for it as we had been playing so much that time had flown by. The recording was roughly six weeks away, so we started rehearsing in the pub again, but when it was time to record, the amount of music and songs wasn't quite enough. So, we made up songs and ideas in the studio to finish the album. What seems to happen to a lot of bands is, before they record their first album, they are out on the road playing and a lot of their original songs are being played night after night, so that when it's time to record that first album, they are more than ready. A lot of their strongest songs are put on the first album, but when it's time to record the second, they sometimes find they haven't got the material.

The second album was to be called *Shades Of A Blue Orphanage.* This was Philip's idea of taking the name of the blues band I had been in in Belfast, *Shades of Blue,* and *Orphanage,* the band he and Brian had been in. We started recording *Shades at De Lane Lea Studios* in *Wembley,* and it was all very disorganised. We had recorded lots of good stuff on the first album, I thought, and it had been tried and tested on lots of live gigs, but now we were forced to make up and arrange new songs virtually on the spot in the studio. I thought there was some good playing at the time, but again, when I heard the finished record, a lot of my guitar ideas were either not there or mixed down much too low. That was when I swore to myself that the next album we record, I was going to insist more about what I really wanted. Still, for what it was worth, the album was released and our good friend Kid Jensen in Luxembourg voted it No.1 again in his charts on *Jensen's Dimensions.*

I forgot to mention that, during the recording of *Shades*, Ritchie Blackmore, guitarist from Deep Purple, would call down from time to time to talk to Philip. He had been at one of our London gigs and had been very impressed with Phil, and had asked him to play bass in the new group he was forming, as he was leaving Deep Purple. Phil started to hang out with Ritchie and went over to his house and recorded a demo, which he played to Brian and myself. We were sure that Phil was going to leave and go with Ritchie, but it didn't happen for one reason or another.

Thin Lizzy started to tour a lot more in Europe now, especially Germany. On one of our gigs in Hamburg or somewhere, my amplifier broke down just after two songs. A few of Deep Purple's roadies were at the club and came up and asked if I wanted to borrow one of Ritchie's amps. I thought this a really kind gesture and couldn't believe the power of the amp. It was about ten times louder than mine, being all 'souped up' with special valves, etc. I met Ritchie later in the club that night and thanked him, and we had a drunken talk about music and guitars. But, some of the other gigs we had been booked to play were a joke. After one of these gigs, Phil barged into the changing room, threw his bass on the floor and sat down, head between his knees. "What the fuck are we playing places like this for, what's the point? I mean, there's a couple out there, three feet from the stage, sitting at a table, staring into each others eyes, and we're so loud their bottle of wine is shaking all over their table. It's a bloody cabaret club!"

A few nights later, we played this huge hall, which had no stage, the bands setting up on the floor. We went on first, to be followed by a local German group. When we had finished playing, we came back to the changing room and the guy who was running the gig came in. "Very nice, very good, boys," he said in a thick German accent. "I want to give you a gift to take home," and he handed Philip, Brian and myself a large brandy glass each. They were engraved with a coat of arms, and we thanked him, waiting for him to now fill them up with brandy. But he didn't. Still, it was a very nice present, and besides, there were lots of bottles of very strong German beer in the fridge waiting for us. Anyway, he then left us to relax and soon our roadies came in and started rolling the joints and breaking out the beer.

About an hour later, I was out of it. I stood up, staggered to the door and went out into the hall. There were lots of lovely ladies all over the place and I approached some of them but, as usual, I was too messy and too drunk, So I forgot about that and went up to watch the German band playing. They were playing *Hey Joe,* Jimi Hendrix's first single, and after they'd finished the song, I staggered up to the guitarist, who was also the lead vocalist. As there was no stage, it was easy to get to talk to him.

"Excuse me, but is there any chance I can get up and play a slow blues with your band?" I slurred. He looked at me in surprise, then said, "No, everything we play is worked out. Please go away!" Then he looked around at the drummer to count in the next song. I felt really angry at being brushed off like that and went over to the side and stood looking at them. Then I looked at one of their PA speakers that was standing on a table and went over and, before I knew it, I had kicked it and it tumbled over onto the floor. The German band just stopped playing and time stood still. Then, the huge guitarist took off his guitar, and started walking over towards me, looking extremely angry. Luckily for me, at the same time, one of Lizzy's roadies came sprinting down the hall and pushed his way in between me and the guitarist. "I'm really sorry, mate," he explained. "The band's been working too hard, he's really exhausted and drunk and doesn't know what he's doing." It took quite a lot of talking until, finally, the guitarist glared at me then walked away back to his band, as our roadies set the speaker back on the table again.

At this point, I was helped back to the changing room where I collapsed into an armchair. They left me there and, feeling very depressed, I had another beer and a smoke. Then I saw the brandy glasses sitting on the table and picked them up, smashed them against the wall, and then passed out. I don't know how long I'd been out on the chair, when I felt somebody shaking me hard. I opened my eyes and saw Phil standing over me. He looked furious. "Hey, Eric, did you smash those brandy glasses?" My head was really spinning around and, for a few moments, I didn't know what he was talking about. "Oh, those, probably," I said, and started to pass out again. I heard Phil's voice in the distance shouting, "That glass was a present for Gail. We're going back to London in a few days and I won't have anything for her. You're gonna step out of line once too often, Eric!" and he stormed out, slamming the door. I just sat there, too pickled to care.

A while later, Ted Carroll and our roadies came into the changing room. "Right, let's go, we're going back to the hotel." We all walked out into the night to the car and the atmosphere was very tense. We sat in the car for a while in silence, then Phil, who was in the front, turned round to me. "I'm fuckin' warning you, Eric. Don't be fuckin' me around any more!" Brian and I just sat there saying nothing.

About 20 minutes later, we had arrived at our hotel. It was now around 2.30am. We let ourselves in and, as we were walking down the corridor to our rooms, Phil suddenly threw his shoulder bag on the floor, turned round and punched me. Lucky for me, it didn't do much damage as it had just glanced off the side of my face. I just stood there, shocked, then went for him. We ended up rolling about on the carpet, punching and mauling each other until the manageress came out to see what all the noise was about. "Oh, Police, Police, I am going to call the Police!" she shouted, and ran off. Ted and Frank Murray eventually separated us. I was taken to my bedroom and Phil to his, and after a while, the situation calmed down. The police arrived and gave us a good talking to. "Any more trouble and you go to jail," kind of thing, and that was that. The next thing, Brian Downey was telling me was that he was leaving the band as he had had enough.

Next morning, I awoke as usual with a terrible hangover. There was a knock on the door and Phil walked in. (I must mention here that, no matter what we had got up to the night before, next morning Philip would be looking like a million dollars, really healthy looking and dressed to kill. I don't know how he did it.) He came over to me. Myself and Brian were still in our beds. "Hey Eric, I'm really sorry about last night. I was really out of it," and he came over and we shook hands. I apologised for breaking the glasses and for pissing him off and everything felt better. We then had a talk with Brian for quite a while, and he finally decided to stay with the band.

One of the last shows we were to play was cancelled, so this meant we were going back to London a day early. As it was a long journey by boat, I decided I would take the time to do a bit of thinking about my life in general. One of the decisions I made was to try a bit harder to get closer to Eleanor and my baby son, Robin. Thin Lizzy had been working so hard that everything else had taken second place. When we finally arrived at 31 Belsize Avenue, I went straight up to my room and went in, but no Eleanor or Robin. The room looked really neat and tidy and I sat down for ten minutes or so, and then Eleanor walked in. She looked great, all dressed up, wearing makeup and looking better than I'd seen her looking in a while. She was very surprised to see me and I explained to her about the last show being cancelled. I didn't know why, but I felt there was something not quite right.

"Where's Robin?" I asked. "Oh, he's with Maggie," she said. Maggie was a friend who had a room upstairs and sometimes helped out with babysitting. "Listen, Eric, I have to talk to you about something." And then she told me she was having an affair with Ian, a Canadian guy who also had a room in the house. The night ended up with me on my own in our room, and Eleanor and Robin upstairs with Ian... the start of the slippery slope had begun.

The next few days were very strange, seeing the both of them walking down the Avenue, pushing Robin in his buggy. I started feeling everyone in the house was talking about what had happened. I started becoming paranoid. There was a sort of party in Gary's room one day, about 12 people, mostly people that lived in the house, plus a few outsiders. There was some really strong smoke being passed around and, at one point, I went up to the loo. As I was standing there, I started staring at the black rubber ball that was at the end of the toilet chain. There was a small spot of white paint on it and the ball was slowly swinging towards me and away from me. I just kept staring at it and felt as if a strong click had happened inside my head. I've never been hypnotised before, but I feel it must be something like what I was going through at that moment. I started seeing two things happening at the same time – the ball was swinging forwards and away, and also standing completely still. I don't remember how long I stood there, but when I got back to Gary's room, I was really spaced out, and I felt very cold and sick, so I had to leave and be on my own.

CHAPTER 11

I think Ted could see that I didn't want to stay in the house anymore, and I ended up in this horrible room somewhere near West End Lane. It was a small attic room at the top of this huge house owned by an old Polish woman and her husband. I hated it, but took it to be away from the situation at Belsize Avenue.

The room had a sloping ceiling, painted dark blue with lots of small silver stars sticking to it. Now and again, Ted would drop round to give me my wages, which were next to nothing, and I would spend it on a bottle of cheap sherry. I wasn't really interested in eating that much, and the only people I saw were Philip and Gail, who lived in a room about 15 minutes walk from me. Brian and myself would meet in that room once a week for acoustic rehearsals. I would call round at night to see them every now and then. Phil would be working on his clothes, taking the side stitches out of a pair of jeans, then sewing them up again to make them tighter, and adding little sequins and stars onto some of his jackets. He was very interested in clothes, and sometimes I would spend an hour or so waiting for him in the various clothes shops around London, especially in Kensington Market, as he would try on every jacket, shirt and trousers in the shop. Philip was also like this with bass guitars and amplifiers. Any time he had money, he would turn up at the next gig or rehearsal with another new guitar or amp, always on the lookout for that better sound.

I hadn't been to 31 Belsize Avenue for a few weeks now, and one day called round to see Gary and Ted. When I was there, I saw Eleanor and she asked me was it alright to come over to my room the next day as she wanted a serious talk. She didn't know what to do – stay in London and possibly try again with me, or move to Canada with Ian. Next day, she turned up and, after a long talk, she told me she was going to Canada. After she left, I just sat on the bed, numb, staring at the wall. I started to feel very lonely and very frightened and really didn't know what to do. I ended up drinking a bottle of the cheap sherry and doing a lot of smoke, just to blot everything out. Unfortunately, Lizzy wasn't playing very much at this moment in time, and I got more and more depressed and lonely in my attic room. I started thinking

about packing the whole music scene in and moving back to Ireland, but what would I do there, even if I could get myself together to go?

The next day, I decided to go over to Belsize Avenue, maybe hear of a few gigs coming up or whatever, just to get out of this bloody room for a while. When I got there, about 7.00pm, the house was very quiet for once, everyone seemed to have gone out, although Ted and Frank were sitting in Ted's room listening to records. Frank then left and Ted was busy doing his books or something. I sat there for a while drinking tea, then remembered that I had stashed a tab of acid in a little miniature bottle behind some of Ted's records that were lined up on the shelf. I was so bored and down and wanted something to happen. I looked behind some of the records and it was still there. I took it –what a mistake! But, as they say, it was a good idea at the time.

I sat for a while longer and decided to go over to see Brian Downey who had a large room on the corner of West End Lane, which he shared with Pete Eustace, our sound engineer. The acid was just starting to take effect by the time I rang Brian's doorbell. Pete answered, asking me in and telling me that Brian had gone out to the cinema with his girlfriend but I could stay in the room and wait until they came back. I didn't fancy staying there on my own while on acid, so Pete said why didn't I go out with him as he had to go visit someone. I learned later that we were visiting some dealer to score some hash. It was pretty dark and cold and we walked for about 20 minutes before reaching the dealer's house. (If I could go back in time and change things, one of the major changes would be here.)

Pete rang the doorbell and some guy opened the door and led us into a sitting room. I was, at this point, seeing things in a different light. There were three guys sitting on large bean bags that looked just like sacks, the floor was covered with raffia-type mats and a lamp shade hung down very low from the ceiling over the sacks. Two of the guys wore striped T-shirts and one of them was opening chestnuts with a large bladed knife. "I'm in a Chinese junk and these guys are opium dealers," I thought. But, what was very strange was, the guy that had the knife had a small radio beside him and the music coming from it sounded very weird. I started listening to it and couldn't believe it. It was Thin Lizzy, a recording of a live session that we had played on the John Peel Show. It sounded very strange to me, and then the guy looked up at me and turned it off. My ego floated out through the ceiling. Things got worse as the night went on. I remember sitting on the floor out of my fucking head, and these guys asking me all these stupid questions and Pete just sitting there in the wings.

Remembering - Eric Bell

I knew I shouldn't have bothered with the acid as I was in a depressed mood when I had taken it, and now I was becoming very paranoid. The guys who were asking the questions were English and started giving off imagery of British bulldogs and old-time London policemen with large sideburns. It all became very confusing and frightening and I was so out of it, I couldn't even manage to get up and walk out the door, which was only a few feet away. The last thing I remember was some guy knocking on the door and coming in holding a large old-fashioned alarm clock, asking for the right time. He turned into a sort of prophet or Father Time before my eyes, then Death, showing us that time was running out. We eventually left the room and walked back to Brian's place, but even though Brian was home, I didn't stay long. I just wanted to get the last tube home, crawl into my bed and die.

A few gigs came in for us and, one night after a show, we had this very long drive back to London. But, about 50 miles from London, our driver, Charlie, had had enough. He drove the van on to the side of the motorway, switched off the engine, closed his eyes and settled down for a rest. Everyone in the van became quiet. About 20 minutes passed and it started to become very cold. I could see us sitting there for another hour at least and thought, "I'll bloody drive for a while, it's a straight road home and mostly deserted. All I have to do is keep the van pointing forward in a straight line." I turned to Charlie. "Listen, Charlie, if you're not ready to drive yet, can I have the keys? It'll be better than sitting here freezing to death." I climbed into the driving seat.

Philip, who always sat beside the driver because of his long legs, was the only one who looked worried about me driving. "Are you sure you can drive, Eric?" he asked. The truth was, I'd never driven on a road before in my life. The only driving I had done was driving and parking cars around AS Baird's huge garage. After lots of judders and stalls (as if the van was throwing up), I got the van moving smoothly. Everyone settled down again, except Philip, who kept opening his eyes every so often. We had covered about 15 miles, and hadn't passed one car, then Phil spotted a car up ahead. "Eric, I think it's a police car, don't overtake it, stay behind it." I couldn't believe it. It was the only car on the whole motorway, and it had to be the police.

"But Phil," I argued, "if I stay behind them, that will look very suspicious," and, even as we spoke, the police car was slowing down. So, without thinking about signalling or anything like that, I passed them and went back into lane. Nothing happened right away and I thought no more about it, but Phil kept looking in the wing mirror. Then he said, "Here they come, I told you not to fuckin' pass them." Everyone in the van started looking around for places to hide their stash. I shouted at Charlie, who was in the back, to pass me his driving licence. He handed it over as the police car passed us and signalled for me to stop. I did so, but as I wasn't a qualified driver, it took about 20 seconds of juddering and bouncing until the van came to a standstill. They must have thought I wasn't going to stop.

I was very tired and very stoned and thought, "This is it," and pictured myself being put away for a while. Luckily, I had taken a look at Charlie's licence before the two policemen walked over to my window. "Would you mind getting out of the van, sir?" I got out and they asked me for my licence and studied it for a moment. "What's your name, sir?" one of them asked. "Charlie McPherson," I answered. "Charles McPherson?" he asked. "Yes," I said. "Would you spell McPherson for me, sir?" "M-c-p-h-e-r-s-o-n." I spelt out slowly. "Thank you, sir. I don't think you should be driving at the moment, you seem very tired. Can anyone else drive the van?" I said that there was. "Right sir, and what is your nearest police station in London?" "West Hampstead," I replied. He wrote out something, handed it to me and told me to take it to that station when I got back. Then they both walked back to their car. Why they didn't search me, then the lads, and then the entire van, I'll never know. I got back in the van again, handed Charlie back his licence and the ticket, and he got into the driving seat. We waited until the cops drove off, then started on our way back to London. I was very popular for a while! Never a dull moment in the Lizzymobile.

We got a call from our office saying to come in for a meeting. When we got there, Chris Morrison told us he had been approached by someone to see if we would be interested in recording an album of Deep Purple hits. It would be worth around £500, and the money would be very handy to pay debts like phone bills in the office, etc. The album would be by Funky Junction, and there would be no mention of Thin Lizzy. There would even be a picture of 'Funky Junction' on the cover playing live, though the shot is so bad you can't make out anyone's face, which was the general idea. The only snags were, Philip didn't sing like Deep Purple singer Ian Gillan, they had a keyboard player, the fabulous Jon Lord, and we were a three-piece. Philip and Brian then suggested we get Bernard White and Dave 'Mojo' Lennox over from Dublin. Bernard was lead singer and Dave was keyboard player with a Dublin group called Elmer Fudd. "You'll have to fly them over, Chris, put them up in a decent hotel and drop them a few bob," Phil suggested.

A few days later, we were all in De Lane Lea studios together. We were lucky, as we had all played Deep Purple songs in the past. Everything went very smoothly until the end, when we were told that we needed another 15 minutes of music to fill out the album. I had the idea to do a Jimi Hendrix tribute by playing a version of *Danny Boy in something like the style of his Star Spangled Banner*. The rest of the time was taken up by a blues shuffle, I think, and some weird instrumental. The album was released on a cheap label, and sold in supermarkets and Woolworths. I never found out how it sold but, since then, it has been rereleased on CD, and now there is a huge sticker on the cover saying, 'Played by Thin Lizzy'. It's pretty hard to get now and has become a collector's item.

A few more gigs in Germany had come in, but these were good ones. We were booked to play a few festivals, supporting Beck, Bogart and Appice, Family and Nazareth. Jeff Beck is one of my favourite guitarists, and I was really looking forward to hearing him play but, basically, I missed it. We did two gigs with BBA. I remember on the first one, at this huge hall somewhere in Germany, we had just arrived early in the afternoon and were walking up to the stage to check things out. We saw Tim Bogart, bass player with BBA, on stage with a hoover. He was hoovering the cloth on the front of these huge bass cabs. Phil, Brian and myself just looked at each other. We had all thought either the guy was totally nuts, or he was doing this to get a great sound from his gear (well, we were Irish). But we found out from Tim that BBA had played some gig the previous night and had the American and British flags draped as a back-drop behind them as they played. This particular German crowd had taken offence to the flags and started throwing beer bottles at the stage. The cloth which covered the speakers in his bass cabinets was soaked with beer and he was using the warm air from the hoover to dry it out. We had to tell him we thought it was to improve his sound and we all cracked up.

Later that night, after Lizzy had finished playing, I went out and got right to the very front of the stage and stood waiting, right in front of Jeff Beck's amp. Then, suddenly this German policeman walks on stage and asks everyone to move much further to the right to make more room. I had no choice and was swept along with the crowd and, by the time it stopped, I was directly in front of Tim Bogart's amp. The group then walked on and started. Tim Bogart's bass was deafening and he was using a fuzz-box or something like that on the sound he was getting. I didn't hear a single note Jeff played. Right, I thought, I won't miss it tomorrow, but I did.

The next day was an open-air gig, like a biker's festival, with tons and tons of beer and smoke. We went on about 3 o'clock in the afternoon and, again, I made my way to the front of the crowd. But this time, the crowd were sitting on the grass a few yards away from the stage. I sat down between these young German ladies and beer and brandy and hash was passed up and down the front row of people. "Wow, this is great!" I thought. Family were just coming on stage, and after that was BBA. But, just before they were to appear, I started to disappear. "Oh, no," I thought, as everything I looked at was wavering and moving up and down. After five minutes of willing myself to stand up, I staggered over to the stage and somehow found Frank Murray, our driver and personal road manager. He helped me to the car we had parked near the gig, and put me in the back seat where I passed out. The next thing I remembered was Phil gently pushing me and saying, "Hey, Er, come here, Jeff Beck is standing up there on top of that hill. Look!" I managed to half crawl out of the back seat and looked to where Phil was pointing. I did see a figure, but it could have been anyone the way it appeared to me. I just moaned something to Phil and crawled back onto the back seat again, and missed it all.

A couple of days later we were back in London. I wanted to get out of the attic room I was living in and move back to Belsize Avenue, now that Eleanor and Robin had moved to Canada. I knew some people and liked and knew the area. But, the only place I could move into right away was a very small room, which I found out later was a converted bathroom. I had a very drunk Irish friend sitting on the bed waiting for me to get ready to go out and, as he slowly started sliding to the floor, he saved himself by grabbing onto these metal bars at the side of my bed, which I had never really noticed before. "Fuck me, man, this is a converted bathroom, you're living in a bathroom!" he shouted, and we both started laughing about it for quite a while.

A week later, Gary Moore told me that Skid Row were playing in the Marquee, a very famous club where everybody had played one time or another (unfortunately not there any longer). A lot of us went down to see them play that night and it was a great gig. But, after he'd finished playing, Gary seemed very depressed. He later told me he had had some sort of row with Brush, Skid Row's bass player, and was thinking of leaving. I ended up in Gary's room that night, helping him drink this enormous bottle of scotch.

Gary did leave a few weeks later, and Brush got in touch with me to stand in for him on a couple of gigs. I found it very difficult as it was a completely different type of playing from what I was doing with Thin Lizzy. It was funny, though. At one of the gigs, a few hippie types came floating into the changing room. At that moment, Brush was doing a headstand in the middle of the floor. One of the hippies went over to Brush holding a huge joint. "Want a drag, man?" he said. "No tanks," said Brush, in a very broad Dublin accent. "I don't smoke that stuff." But, Brush seemed more stoned than anyone else in the room. Gary Moore went on to form his own band, The Gary Moore Band, and record an album, *Grinding Stone,* I think it was called. He had one of our old friends from Belfast on bass, Sammy Cooke. Sammy played bass in the very first group I was ever in.

The next thing for Thin Lizzy was a UK tour, which lasted around three weeks. We were sharing the bill with Kokomo, Barrabas and a folk singer. We all travelled around on this tour bus, and you can imagine what it was like. Kokomo were an excellent soulful outfit with amazing vocals. There was Paddy and Frank, two really nice gay guys, sharing vocals, Di, the female vocalist, who was amazing as well, and I became infatuated by her. Phil was as well for a while, and he used to sit beside her and give her all the Irish charm he could, but she was a lady of the road and had heard it all before. Then, there was Raffi, a bisexual Indian guitarist, and Tony O'Mally, a very cool piano player. The rest of the band, I can't remember the names, but I remember the people. There were some good times on that tour. I was pissed every night, and every night I would ask Di if she would go out with me after the tour. "Ask me when you're sober," she would always say.

We had a night off and were staying in an old dingy hotel in Glasgow. That night, we all went out to some pub in Glasgow, there must have been around 25 of us, including the roadies, and we all got very drunk. Then, at closing time, we were let out the back door into some cobblestone alley. Myself and Di were lying on top of a car bonnet. Everyone else was shouting and singing and wondering where to go next, then they all slowly drifted off from the alley. We left the alley and walked around very unsteadily and ended up sitting on these stairs leading into a Chinese restaurant. Some waiters eventually came out and told us to move and we ended up back at the hotel we were all staying in. It was very dingy and really old-fashioned with an old cage elevator. We ended up on top of Di's bed and the both of us just passed out. Next morning, everyone had a terrible hangover, including Philip. We all climbed in the bus and drove off for the next gig. After the tour finished, myself and Di started seeing each other for about six months. She lived in this lovely house in Richmond that she shared with Paddy and Frank, the two other singers in the band. I used to love going there with a bottle of Blue Nun and staying the night, it was so quiet and peaceful. Both of us were still playing gigs, and then one afternoon, Di told me that she had met someone else, and didn't want to see me any more. So I was back on my own for a while.

CHAPTER 12

It was around this time, just before playing on the Slade tour, that I started to become worried about the state I was in. Ever since the bad acid trip, I found that sometimes when I smoked some hash, I would become too stoned and lose all sense of reality. This situation was very difficult for me, and I suppose for Phil and Brian as well. Ever since Lizzy had formed, we had been a smoker's band and really enjoyed each other's company. But now, as we would be sitting in our car (we had just said goodbye to the old white transit), travelling to some gig or other, the joints would be passed around as usual, and I would be wishing that I was somewhere else.

One night I found out something else. I found that I couldn't play the guitar 'straight' anymore. We were in the changing room and were going on stage in 45 minutes. As we were getting ready, I asked Phil was he going to roll a joint as I had none and I don't think Brian had any either that night. Phil told me he couldn't spare any as he had only a little bit left and wanted it for when he got home that night. I said OK and took my guitar out of its case and started to play something, but it felt all wrong. My hands felt weak and clammy and the guitar strings felt very cold and tight. The more I tried to get into playing, the worse it all became. I ended up pleading with Phil to roll even a small one, but he wouldn't.

Outside, the club was packed with people waiting for us to come on. I was really starting to dread the gig when there was a knock on the door and this black guy walked in. He seemed to know Philip and they started talking. Then I noticed the guy reach into his inside coat pocket and pull out this enormous joint. I just sat there, willing him to stop talking, light the bloody thing up and pass it around. The time to go on stage was getting closer, and then at last, it was passed to me. All I can say was it was like magic. A few minutes later, I picked up my guitar… no problem. I could now play with the best of them. But, somewhere within me, I realised there was a problem.

It was around this time I started to drink more, as I would need it to cancel the negative moods the weed would cause. But, if I drank too much, I got sloppy on the guitar. I was starting to walk a thin line. One morning, on my

way to the local shop, I got the fright of my life. As I was walking down the street, I just looked up and realised that the pavement and road were sitting at an odd angle. I had to stop and hold on to some railings as I was very frightened. "I must be losing my mind," I thought. "I haven't even taken anything and I'm seeing things." I made an appointment with a local doctor, who helped me on my way to Cuckoo Land by putting me on a long course of valium. Taking the valium felt like having cotton wool balls inside my head, which did help take the edge of things but, along with the smoke and drink, which I couldn't stop taking, took me further from reality... and further still...

Our management pulled a great stroke and got us playing support to Slade, who were as popular as The Beatles at this point in time, around the end of 1972. They had about five No.1 hits behind them and mega selling albums, they were the biggest act in the UK. I thought, why are we on tour with them, a Glam pop group? But, I remember the first show, I think it was Newcastle City Hall. When we arrived in the afternoon at the sound check, we walked in and saw Slade's equipment. We worked out that Noddy Holder, lead singer and rhythm guitarist, was using about 400 watts of amplifier (and that was for rhythm) and Jimmy Lea, bass player, had three acoustic bass amps with reflex cabs. You could demolish buildings with that kind of gear. When I heard them that night, they were deafening, the loudest band I had ever heard, very raw and exciting. The crowd went crazy as soon as they walked on. Slade themselves were great guys, friendly and very down to Earth. We shared their changing room some nights and I couldn't believe the amount of alcohol supplied. There were crates and crates of beer and cardboard boxes full of different kinds of spirits.

Also on the tour, playing support, was Suzi Quatro, an American rocker girl dressed in leather and singing and playing bass. She was really good, as were her band. But both Suzi and Lizzy died a lot of nights on stage in front of Slade's audience. Both bands were booed off stage and cans and other missiles were hurled at us. It must have been a bit like the atmosphere at a Roman arena. Also, it's a real difference to playing in small pubs and clubs to a crowd who are basically there to drink and listen. The stages are smaller and you can come across larger than life much easier. That's what we were used to. Then, when we walked out onto the stage in these huge City Halls that Slade were playing, it felt like a football pitch and Phil seemed about 20 feet away from me. We felt really small up there, especially being a three-piece band. And we didn't put on a show, we just stood there and played like we did in the clubs, and played some slow songs as well. In front of a Slade crowd, hanging off the balconies, waving football scarves, this meant

DEATH! And it was the same for Suzi Quatro's band. We would see her some nights, running past us in tears, holding her bass, having just been booed off stage.

The turning point for Lizzy was when Chas Chandler, Slade's manager, came into our changing room to give us a right bollocking. Chas had been around, first of all playing bass with The Animals, a very successful R&B group in the late 60s, then later on, he managed Jimi Hendrix. He tore into us, especially Philip, and told him to wake up more, wear more colourful clothes, move more, speak to the people. He said he would give us a few more nights to get it together or we were off the rest of the tour. "You're here to wake the crowd up before Slade comes on, not send them to bloody sleep!" and he stormed out. It was one of the few times I ever saw Phil close to tears. One of Phil's biggest heroes was Hendrix, and to be torn apart by his manager was hard to handle.

So, God love Philip, the next night I saw him in front of the mirror and he was putting on black mascara. "It looks great on stage," he said. Also on stage, now and again when I looked over at him, he would, as he used to say, be "throwing a great shape", meaning trying out a pose, a cool movement.

We would watch Slade most nights and try to learn how to project better on stage. But the way I saw it, if everyone in the country knows what you look like from TV, records, magazines and music papers, you do have a better chance of delivering on stage.

We stayed in some great hotels, and I got an idea for a brilliant TV game show. The game is: 12 people are booked into an expensive hotel for one night. They are told to drink as much alcohol as they like and stay up until 4 o'clock in the morning. Then they must get up at 9.00am, walk around this huge breakfast room and try to find all the bits and pieces for their breakfast. The person who gets it together first is the winner. Even today, this is what it feels like to me, especially after a few drinks. I think the breakfast rooms in the good hotels in Sweden are my favourite. In the last one I stayed in, it took me about five minutes to just find a cup, plate, knife, fork and teaspoon before I found something to eat!

At the end of the tour, Slade invited us back to their local pub around 2am, and we all had an old-fashioned sing-song around the piano. But, when the tour finishes and you go back to a very small room all on your own after four weeks of non-stop playing, drinking and all the rest, you realise how far from reality you are. Plus, I was still taking valium and, lately, taking a few extra ones as well. Everything in my life was starting to feel very strange, and now instead of being stoned, I felt totally spaced out.

We were back in the pub where we rehearsed once a week and we were working on new songs. But, on this particular day, nothing much was happening. Phil had a few ideas for songs and we would try them using different approaches, but we just couldn't create anything that grabbed our attention. After a while, we all just sat around smoking and were even thinking of packing up and going home early. Then, Phil put down his bass and picked up the Telecaster (the extra guitar we had in case I broke a string on stage). He started messing about, singing these corny old songs just for a laugh, and at some point started singing *Whiskey In The Jar.* For some reason, I put down the mag I was reading and started playing along with him, then Brian came in with drums.

A few minutes later, Ted Carroll walked in and asked us what we were playing. "Oh, we were only messing around," said Phil. But Ted had obviously heard something we hadn't and asked again what it was. "It was *Whiskey In The Jar*, Ted. It's nothing. We were only messing about. I told you." "Have you any songs suitable for a single? You know, you're lined up to record a single for Decca in about four weeks." We told him that we had a song called *Black Boys On The Corner*. Then he asked if we had a song for the B-side, and when we said we had nothing definite as yet, he suggested we record *Whiskey*. He kept going on about it, and obviously his ears were more in tune with what a commercial hit record should sound like than our own.

A week later, we were playing a gig somewhere in England and, at the end, we walked into the changing room. Phil put away his bass and just sat there, looking at the floor. One of the roadies came in. "Great gig, lads!" then saw Philip looking really pissed off. "What's wrong Phil? Was there something wrong with the sound on stage? Phil looked up and said with a lot of bitterness and frustration, "We've been playing this fucking circuit over and over and over again. Can anybody tell me what you have to do to get out of this fucking circuit of pubs and clubs?" "You need a hit record, mate," said the roadie, and walked out.

Two weeks later we were in the studio recording *Black Boys On The Corner* for what we thought was going to be the A-side of our first single for Decca. When we had finished, we sat around wondering how we were going to approach the recording of *Whiskey In The Jar.* Philip and myself played it on acoustic guitars, with Brian on drums, but I couldn't come up with any ideas for electric guitar. I could have just played a few licks on it, and did in fact try this for a while, but nothing seemed to match the song the way I wanted. So, I was given a cassette of the recording, so I could work on it at home. I don't think I've thought as much about what to play in a song as I did with *Whiskey*. Phil let me borrow the portable cassette recorder that he had just got from his mum, and I played the recording day and night and worked on my guitar, but just couldn't find any ideas I liked. Then, a few nights later, I got the idea for the intro for the song.

We were driving back from some gig and Phil had his cassette player back to play some sounds in the front of the car. He was always playing tapes and it was very varied listening, from Bob Marley and Hendrix to Sly and the Family Stone to The Chieftains. It was the Chieftains tape he was playing when I got the idea. I was in the back of the car with Brian, and was in that dreamy half-awake, half- asleep state, and away in the distance I heard the sound of Irish pipes. "Of course," I thought. "Why don't I play the intro to *Whiskey* more in the mood and style of Irish pipes rather than the guitar?" At last, this gave me the start I had been looking for, now all I needed was the rest of the song.

Back in my room, armed with Phil's cassette player again, another idea came to me. I was starting to think more commercial now for this song, and this made me realise the way The Beatles, The Stones and countless others had used catchy riffs and lines repeating over and over again throughout their songs, especially their singles. So, I worked out a guitar lick, which I repeated throughout *Whiskey.* This just left the guitar solo. Everywhere I went, I kept humming the song, trying to imagine the guitar coming in with the solo, but again couldn't hear anything that caught my attention. It happened when I was in a taxi a few days later. The driver kept talking to me about something or other, when suddenly I heard it. As I don't write musical notation, I had to keep humming the idea in my head so as not to lose it, while still carrying on talking to the driver. He eventually dropped me off at my room and, a minute later, I had the guitar out, working on the notes for the solo. Thank God, as I was starting to be pressured by Phil, the management and Decca record company about when this bloody record was going to be finished.

When it came time to record all my guitar parts, I spotted a Hammond organ in the studio I was working in that day. It had a huge Leslie cabinet, the type that had a huge whirling fan inside that gave a certain sound (this was way before they made effects pedals to create similar sounds). I first played the intro and then the electric backing guitar through the Leslie cab, then double-tracked the intro on sustain guitar, then played the repeated lick and the solo on sustain guitar as well. When we played the finished song back a few times, everyone from the tea boy upwards all agreed that *Whiskey In The Jar* should be released as the A-side. Phil said he still had to put the bass guitar on the song but, the more we listened to it, the more we agreed that it sounded full enough the way it was, which is why there is no bass on the record. Phil, Brian and myself still wanted our original song, *Black Boys On The Corner*, as the A-side as we had planned, so in the end, we all agreed to release the record as a double A-side, and would leave it up to the DJs to play whatever side they wanted.

Young Eric

The Atlantics live in 1965 with Eric, Rodney
Howes, Don Brewster and Sammy Cooke

The Deltones - promo pic

The Deltones Live

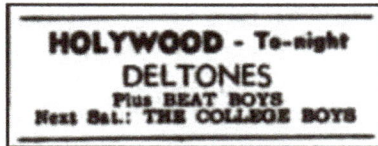

Ticket for the gig where Eric first met Gary Moore, 3 April 1965

Eric with Van in Them

Eric Wrixon, Brian Downey, Philip Lynott, Eric Bell at Castle Avenue

Philip and Eric at Tivoli, Buckley, Wales

1973 Thin Lizzy poster

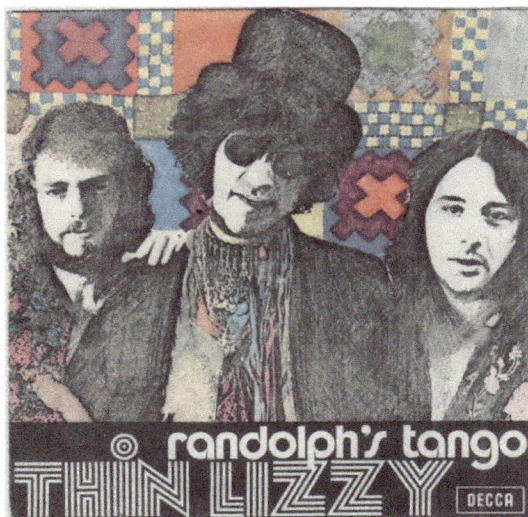

'Randolph's Tango' picture sleeve for Italian single

Brian, Eric and Philip on the road

Philip and Eric on Grafton Street, Dublin

Thin Lizzy in Amsterdam

Eric recovering

Eric and Gary at the unveiling of Philip's statue

Eric from the video of 'Song for Gary'.

Eric and Quique   *Photo by Aidan O'Rourke*

Eric photo shoot in Alderley Edge for 'Exile' album 2016

Photo by Aidan O'Rourke

Mainsqueeze performing live in 1984

Eric and Noel Redding with members of The Noel Redding Band

Eric live at the Sweden Rock Festival, 2016

Eric and Gary Live at the tribute concert for Philip

Eric on tour with Bo Diddley

Eric with Philomena Lynott, 2007

Eric filming the video for 'Gotta Say Bye Bye' from the 'Exile' album

Eric in Cavalier Studios, Stockport for video editing of 'Song for Gary' off 'Exile'   Photo by Aidan O'Rourke

New mural in east Belfast featuring Eric Bell and other local legends

CHAPTER 13

*Whiskey In The Jar was r*eleased by Decca in early December 1972, I think. We, the management, the roadies and Decca kept an eye out and scanned all the music papers and listened to the radio for airplay but, as the weeks went by, nothing much seemed to be happening. "I fucking told you," Philip would say from time to time. "We should have pushed Black Boys On The Corner."

Within a matter of weeks, we were back in Europe for yet another tour. Getting up one morning for a hurried breakfast before getting ready to travel to the next gig, there was a telegram at the hotel reception for Thin Lizzy. We couldn't believe it and thought it was a joke. It read: "Congratulations, boys, *Whiskey In The Jar* has just entered the English charts at number 25. Come home as soon as possible."

We got in touch with our London office to find out if it was true. It was! I think we must have made up some excuse and cancelled the rest of the tour of Europe, and got back to England as quickly as possible. We all called around to the Dean Street office a few days later and it was buzzing with excitement. In the office were lots and lots of cardboard boxes and in the boxes were lots and lots of miniature bottles of whiskey. "I've had this great idea," said Chris the manager. "Imagine that you are a top DJ on the radio and every day someone brings you in another lot of singles for you to choose to play. It must get pretty boring and a lot of the singles won't be to your taste. But now and again, there is a little gift with one of the singles. A free hat or a book or... a small bottle of whiskey to pour in your tea. You would tend to give that single a bit of airplay wouldn't you?"

So, a copy of *Whiskey In The Jar* was sent out to each DJ with a little bottle. It seemed to work, because we were No. 6 in the English charts in a matter of weeks, No. 1 in Ireland, and it became a hit record all over Europe.

We then appeared on a TV programme, which I used to dream about back in my bedroom in those early days in Belfast. Top of the Pops. I think the studios were in Manchester and we stayed in Philip's mother's hotel, The Biz. A few weeks previously, our management had sent us to a real showbiz

hairdressers in London to get groomed and then to Kensington Market for clothes more befitting pop stars. One of the pieces of clothing I was talked or bullied into wearing was a chain mail type of waistcoat, made from plastic discs joined together by little plastic hooks. The discs were very shiny and sort of sparkled in the light. I wore this on Top of the Pops and also on stage at gigs. The whole idea came from the tour we played with Slade when Noddy Holder wore a top hat covered with small round mirrors.

Anyway, when we got to the TOTP studios, it looked like a large warehouse with lots of ceiling lights and little round rostrums and stages covering the floor. The three of us just stood there, trying to take it all in, when this guy walked over to us – believe it or not, he was dressed in a black polo-neck with a large gold chain and medallion around his neck. "And who are you lot?" he said. We told him, then he said, "And who's the drummer?" Brian said, "That's me." "Well, I hope you're not like that group The Who. They were here last week and their drummer kicked his drum kit off the stage. There were drums everywhere!" And with that, he minced off.

Apart from the TV show in Germany where I had mimed to the Dreams single, I hadn't mimed on TV before. Miming to me was a strange experience, you're just standing there, no amps, sometimes no guitar leads (which is a real giveaway) and then you hear your record being played and you start moving to it. This time, no one told me, "You must smile ya?"

A few gigs were lined up for us in England but, now that we had a hit record, we would be playing in much bigger venues. One of the first ones was a Mecca hall. These halls were enormous, holding about 3,000 people, with a huge ballroom and a huge upstairs area, one-arm bandits and bars all over the place. When it was time for us to go on, there were about 800 people standing in front of the stage but, as we started playing our third song, we noticed some of them started walking away, and a little later there were only about 50 people left watching us. A few songs later, I started playing the intro to *Whiskey In The Jar* and, within seconds, there were about 1,000 people cheering and dancing in front of the stage. When we finished playing our hit, most of them disappeared again. About 40 minutes later, I started the intro to you-know-what again and about 1,000 people appeared at the front of the stage. You start to realise quickly what it must be like to have had ten hit records – you just arrive at huge venues, play all of your hits and you have an enormous crowd of people staying in front of the stage all night every night to listen to their favourite hit records.

A few weeks later, it was time to play a tour in Ireland, where *Whiskey* was number one in the Irish charts, and would stay in the charts for 17 weeks. What a change a hit record has to a band. When we arrived in the Emerald Isle, we were met by a huge black car and a few of the people who were running the tour. Then, we were driven to our hotel, quite a bit more up-market, I noticed, and after we had settled down and had a lunch fit for a king, we were told how many shows we had and where we would be playing. There were also lots of press interviews. One thing that really knocked me out was the keyboard player and band leader who I had been in The Dreams Showband with, turned up to take me out for a beautiful dinner in a very expensive restaurant. Shay, the leader, was really happy for me and didn't show any kind of jealousy about my success and was great company.

Philip, Brian and myself still didn't really understand what was happening. It seemed like, after the tour with Slade, we had shot right to No. 1 in Ireland and our record was starting to really take off all over Europe. From the back streets of Belfast, working those crummy 9 to 5 jobs, and staying in every night to practice guitar, with no way of knowing anything was going to happen, wishing I was going to get somewhere, make a name for myself, become famous in a three-piece group. It had come true! The only thing was, I found the whole thing very hard to handle. There I was, having longed for and worked hard for this to happen. Taking the huge risk of leaving the Dreams Showband, meeting Philip and Brian, thinking up the name, and now No.1 in Ireland. And all I wanted was to crawl under a stone when I should have been on top of the world. I was becoming even more spaced out with the unreality of showbiz.

We started playing gigs all round Ireland, and the reception was mixed. On one night, we'd end up playing in a country farming area and the people would just look at us as if we had just arrived by UFO. They didn't know what to make of us. Then, on another night, we'd play somewhere nearer a city or town and we'd tear the place apart. I noticed after every show there would be lots of beer and a large bottle of whiskey waiting for us in the dressing room. It had become a habit, as soon as we finished playing, to dive in to the drink. One night around this time, I thought to myself while playing on stage, "I'm not going to drink any whiskey for the next few nights." But, it was basically impossible. As soon as we walked off stage into the dressing room, it would start all over again.

We had a night off and we were staying in a large house that the management had rented for us to stay in while we were in Dublin. Philip, myself and Brian were invited down to a place in Dublin city centre called Morans Hotel. It was a very popular venue in the early 70s. They let us in early, before the doors were open to the public and, of course, we made a beeline for the bar downstairs. At this point, I could get drunk pretty easy and the whiskey would really go to my head. We must have stood there for a while talking to the guys that ran the gig, when I started noticing people slowly coming in to where we were. Some of them were looking at us as if we were really were big stars, and this guy ended up standing right beside me at the bar. My head was really spinning at this point and everything I looked at was waving up and down. "Is it yourself or 20 other people?"

All of a sudden the guy said, "I don't give a fuck who ye are, I want an apology!" I just looked at him, wondering what he was talking about and he became really nasty. "I told you, I want a fuckin' apology!" I told him to get lost, or words to that effect, but he kept on and on and challenged me to a fight. Me, being so fucking proud and thinking I was John Wayne because of the drink taken, said all right then. Big mistake because I was totally pickled, and also wearing high platform shoes which I found hard to balance on even when sober. We crossed the bar and he walked in front of me and went down a small flight of stairs which led to the gents' toilets. There were these two doors that you had to push quite hard to open. The guy had gone in through these doors ahead of me and then, just as I pushed them, Wham! He had been standing behind the doors and used their strong springs to smash them into me. I went down on the floor and remembered him starting to kick me in the head and body.

"Come on now, he's had enough, leave him alone," I heard Brian Downey's voice. "Do you want some, too?" came the answer. But Brian kept asking him to stop and the guy must have just walked away. Brian helped me to my feet and the pain in my head was unbearable. I thanked him and then told him I was OK and I staggered upstairs again. By this time, the place was packed and the only thing in my mind was to spot the guy who had done this to me and stick a fucking knife in his back. As God is my witness, if I had got hold of one, I would have done it, no problem. When I look back on all of this now, I'm so lucky that I couldn't get a knife. I remember staggering around the crowd of people and asking any girl I passed, did they have a nail file I could borrow? But, I hadn't thought how I must have looked, and anyone I spoke to backed away from me. My head and body, as well as my pride, were hurting so much, I eventually got a taxi back to the house where I was staying and passed out on the bed.

When I awoke the next morning, I just lay there, completely numb. I didn't know where I was, who I was, and the pain in my head was frightening. But, none of this compared to the shock I had when I saw myself in the bathroom mirror. It was like looking at the face of a stranger. My face, hair and shirt were covered in dried blood and I could hardly open one of my eyes. Also, half of one of my front teeth was missing. I just sat on the edge of the bath and started crying.

It took me a long time to get myself together and, early afternoon, I went out to the local shops, called into a cafe, had a snack and a few coffees. But when I called into a pub they wouldn't serve me. After being refused in three pubs, I started thinking that they must have thought I was an alcoholic – probably the way I was shaking and needing a drink badly.

The rest of the Irish tour was a blur. I'd had enough of socialising and talking to people, so I just played the gigs and kept to myself. Then, the Irish tour was finished and back to London. We did another few gigs in England – when you have a hit record, the gigs you play are bigger and more select, so there are fewer places to play. Then, after a while, the advantages of having a recent hit start wearing off and you start having to play smaller gigs again.

As I said earlier, we hadn't been as prepared for the second album as we had been for the first, and it showed. *Shades Of A Blue Orphanage* got a few decent reviews in the music papers, but now it was time to record our second single. We still didn't play the game, meaning when you have a big hit record by jazzing up an old Irish folk song, you're meant to follow it up with another jazzed up Irish folk song. We wouldn't listen and went ahead and recorded one of Philip's songs called Randolph's Tango. It was a good song, but a bad idea. It was released but didn't cause much of a stir, and poor Philip would buy every music paper that was printed, looking to see if we had charted or for some reviews, but it just sailed away without much notice. Decca was very disappointed and we had the idea that they were going to drop us, but they kept us on their books, probably because we owed them a third album and a third single.

We still gigged all over the UK and Europe. One night after the gig, I came back to my hotel room and just sat on the bed. Then I got up, put my damp stage clothes on the radiator, made a cup of tea, had a smoke and took out my guitar as I couldn't sleep. I started to play slow blues, but it felt very forced. I wasn't really that surprised as, apart from playing the set on stage, I never really practised anymore. I started becoming very unhappy with the way I was playing. Yeah, I thought, I might as well have stayed with The Dreams Showband as I'm now playing the same songs with Thin Lizzy every night, no more jamming, everything worked out.

Time passed and we found we were to record our third album in about five weeks. But this time we had been rehearsing acoustic and electric and had a good bunch of songs to record. The sessions for our third album, *Vagabonds Of The Western World,* took place in Tollington Park studios. I had made a pact with myself to really fight to get my guitar to sound the way I wanted. So, the first day when we got to the studios, our gear all set up by our roadies, I went over to my equipment, took out my guitar and started messing about trying to get the tone I had in my head. After about half an hour, I went into the control room and said to the engineer, "I'm just going to play something for a minute or so, could you tape it so I can come in to listen to what it sounds like?" "Alright, mate, go ahead." So I went out again and played a few chords and licks then put the guitar down and went back into the control room. The engineer played the tape and I heard this horrible, fuzzy guitar. "Hey, that's not me!" I said. "That's you, mate, that's what you just played." "No, I don't think so," I said. "The sound I'm getting out in the studio is totally different from that crap. Can you come outside and listen to my guitar?" So, he dragged himself to his feet and walked out into the studio with me. I put on my guitar and played for a minute or so. "Sounds the same to me, mate." "Well, it doesn't sound the same to me." I said. He sat down and I stood behind him. "Can you make it sound a bit cleaner?" He twiddled a few knobs. Anyway, the tone became more what I wanted.

When it came to record *The Rocker,* Philip asked what way did I want to record it? I thought it would be a good idea to play it 'live', as if we were playing on stage. So, we just went for it and I thought it really captured Thin Lizzy as we sounded at gigs. For the track, *Hero and The Madman,* Philip had asked Kid Jensen, our favourite DJ, to read some lines in the middle of the song. So, Kid went out and started reading. All of a sudden, Philip went over to the mike in the control room and said, "Hey, Kid! You sound like you're reading the fuckin' news!" But it all turned out alright.

Weeks later, we were in the studio, it must have been around 10pm and I was to record a guitar solo on *Hero and The Madman.* As usual, we were all smoking The Magic Dragon, and I went out to get ready to try a solo. Around my fifth attempt, things started to get a bit strange. I was in this huge studio on my own and everyone else was in the control room. I could see them all looking through the window. I felt very alone and wearing headphones made that feeling worse. As the track kept playing over and over again, suddenly I started thinking, "Wait a minute, this song's about me." Like I'm a guitar hero or a madman. The guitar solo I ended up playing was totally from the heart, like my life depended on it. It was a mixture of fear, anger, pride and also that insecurity that had followed me as a child when I had found out I was adopted. After this experience, things started to change for me. I started to feel everyone knew what I was going through, but I couldn't just turn around to Philip or Brian or the roadies or the management and say, "Excuse me, chaps, but I think I'm going fucking mad."

Looking back on all of this, I should have asked to be put in some sort of a clinic for a few weeks to get sorted out, like a lot of other showbiz people have, and let them get a guitarist to stand in for me. But, in those days, with the lack of money, I don't know whether that would have been possible. So I just battled on.

Around this time, I had met a young English lady called Linda. She tried her best to clean up my act, and I remember when we had just met, I would have a few nights off and we'd go out for a quiet drink. It was nearing Last Drinks time and I went up to the bar and ordered two pints of Guinness and a double Scotch and a drink for Linda. When I came back with the drinks to our table, she said, "Eric, can you not just sit in a pub and have a quiet drink?" I had never really thought about this. "The only reason I come to a pub is to get drunk," I replied. In those days I wasn't a nice type of drunk.

Thin Lizzy's third single was next on the list, and everyone agreed *The Rocker* would put us back on the map. It was released and Philip would, again, buy all the music papers, scanning them page after page to see if anything was starting to happen. I forget what position it reached, but it certainly wasn't in the Top Twenty. (Today, some 40 years later, *The Rocker* is one of the soundtracks from a huge movie called Rush.)

So now, after *The Rocker* had failed to make us pop stars again, we were starting to think we would be known as One Hit Wonders. It was at this point that Philip started to change. He now realised that getting that second hit record wasn't as easy as we had all thought. He really started to think more like a pop star, worked more and more on his image and was trying dramatic poses on stage. Also, our management started to show up at our gigs now and then to see what we were up to. After a gig one night, one of our managers said to me as we were walking to the changing room, "Eric, your guitar solos are too long, you're boring the audience." I just looked at him and said, "Listen, I don't come into the office and tell you what you should be doing, so just leave the guitar playing to me." But, deep down, I realised that big changes were about to happen... soon the original Thin Lizzy would be no more.

We were about to cross the Irish Sea for another tour, when Brian Downey's finger went poisonous. The varnish on his drum sticks had somehow got into a cut on his hand and started an infection. So, rather than cancel the tour, we asked the drummer from Gary Moore's Band, Pearce Kelly, to stand in for Brian. I can picture some of our Irish gigs on that tour. Myself and Philip and Pearce, doing his best, and Brian Downey just playing a steady beat on some tom-toms. They weren't the greatest gigs we had played.

CHAPTER 14

The end was now looming very close for me. The Lizzymobile made its way to Belfast, my home town, and we stopped off at the hotel Philip and Brian were staying at. I would be staying at my family's house, so one of the roadies drove me there and I said I'd see everybody later at Queen's University for a sound check. I knocked on the front door of my house and waited for a minute. Knocked again, but nobody seemed to be home. Just then, one of our neighbours came out of her house. It was Mrs Corbett. "Oh, it's you, Eric! I think they're all out shopping. Do you want to come in and wait for them?" Not knowing what to do, and a bit let down by no one greeting me home, I went into Mrs Corbett's. Out came the tea and cake and then, the bottle of Mundies, the cheap plonk I used to drink in the early days in Belfast. This was around 1pm in the afternoon and it went straight to my head.

Even though I was drinking quite a lot in those days, I very rarely drank in the afternoon as it made me feel like shit for the rest of the day. Another drink later and I said I would see if anyone was home yet. So, thanking her, I tried my house again and saw my Aunt Ivy walking up the hall and opening the front door. "Eric! How are you, my big son?" And gave me a hug. I walked into the front room and sat down. The rooms felt so small but very homely, and I was offered yet more tea and sandwiches and, yes, more drink. I didn't realise how pissed I was getting as I was telling Ivy about being on the TV and having a hit record and all of that.

A few hours later, I said goodbye and got a taxi to Queen's University for the soundcheck, but when I got there, there was just an empty stage. None of our equipment and no Philip or Brian. One of the guys working there showed me to our dressing room and left me there and I just sat there, wondering what to do. Then, I noticed this table covered with a white sheet. I went over to see what was underneath. "YES!" as Father Jack would have said. There were loads of bottles and cans of beer and bottles of spirits. Here we go again. I really tried to control myself and opened a can of Guinness and sat with it for a while. Then the roadies arrived with the gear and started to set up on stage. I can't remember if there was a sound check or not, but what I do remember was time seemed to pass very quickly and the bar started to fill up with people. "Hi Eric, good to see you, what you drinking?" I ended up at the bar with lots of people from the old days, all of them seeming to buy me a drink. So, by the time we were starting to get ready to play, I was totally blitzed. I'm sure I had a smoke as well, which added the finishing touch.

I don't remember walking out on stage that night. The place was stuffed and we started playing our set but I shouldn't have been there. I was in no state to play the guitar. I felt sick and just seemed to hear a type of feedback in my head. Now, looking back on it all, I see it very much like someone standing at the very edge of a tall building. He has got two choices. He knows if he makes the decision to jump it's just a matter of taking that one more step, and if he does there is no going back. There's no changing your mind as you're zooming towards the ground. It's too late. And, as I was standing there trying to play my guitar, this voice was in my head saying, "You know you have to make a decision, either you get out now or the circus will carry on. You can end it all now." And I made the decision to get out. I threw my guitar up in the air, kicked my speaker cabs over and just staggered off stage, down the stairs and crawled under the stage, where I fell down on top of some gym mats.

Frank Murray, our personal road manager, came over to me. "For fuck's sake! What have you done? Just get back on stage and finish the gig." "No," I said. "I've left. It's finished." But, he talked me into going back on by promising me three bottles of Guinness. As he went off, about four young guys were standing close to me under the stage. "Fucking amazing," they were saying, as they thought what I had done was part of the stage act, part of the show. I saw one of them was holding a bottle of lemonade and my throat was parched. "Hey, could I have a drink of that?" And the guy handed me the bottle. I took a large swallow and then realised that it was straight whiskey. The effect was like an electric shock at either side of my head. By then, the roadies had set up my amp and cabs again, and they helped me out from under the stage and put my guitar on. It must have sounded tragic, as my guitar was totally out of tune – not surprising, as it had hit the stage from about ten foot in the air.

The rest of the show was all a big blur and the last thing I remember was being in the dressing room with a lot of people. I was cursing and falling about the place until someone ordered a taxi, told him where I lived and the next thing I remember was trying to open my front door, which took about five minutes. This must have been around 1.30am and, luckily, everyone was in bed. I say luckily as, if my Uncle Harold had seen the state I was in, I don't know what he would have done. I sat down in the tiny sitting room in front of a coal fire and just stared into the flames for a very long time. "Well, Eric, you've done it. It's over."

The next day, I woke up late, hungover as usual, and made my way downstairs. I had some breakfast and Ivy asked me about the show at Queen's University. I just mumbled something and said I was thinking of leaving Thin Lizzy as I was really burned out. A little later, there was a knock at the front door. It was one of Lizzy's roadies. As we hadn't got a phone, he had driven over to tell me. "Eric, Chris Morrison (one of our managers) is going to phone you at the hotel in about an hour's time. Get ready and I'll drive you over." I got myself together as best as I could and we drove over to the hotel. When I walked into the reception area, they were all sitting there – Philip, Brian and all the roadies. I felt very embarrassed as they all took no notice of me, and I went to a chair and sat down a few yards away. I went up to the bar and ordered a coffee, and then someone from reception came over to me. "Are you Eric Bell? There's a phone call for you from London." She pointed to where there were a few wall phones and I picked one up.

"Hello?" "Eric, is that you? What the fucking hell is going on?" I just listened as Chris raved on for a few minutes and then, when he had stopped, I just said. "Chris, I've had enough, I've left the band." "Right, Eric, and you won't finish the Irish tour?" I said I couldn't and then he said, "Is that your final word?" "Yes'. So, they got in touch with my old friend and fellow gunslinger, Gary Moore, and that, as they say, was that.

A week later, I flew back to London and told my girlfriend, Linda, all that had happened. I think she was relieved in a way I was no longer in the band. I thought about what I was going to do in the future and came up with the idea to first of all get out of London. I thought about moving to Dublin where the pace of life was a lot slower. A few weeks later, Linda and myself caught the boat to Dublin and made our way to an address I had been given by one of Thin Lizzy's roadies. It was a flat in the Rathmines area and this was where they had been staying. When we got there, the roadies were just packing up their gear and getting ready to leave. I couldn't believe it, sitting against one of the walls was all my equipment – my amp, two speaker cabs, a small suitcase with all my guitar leads in it, and my guitar.

The flat itself was alright, the only snag being that it was a basement flat. We settled in as best we could, cleaned the place up a bit, went out and got some shopping, and Linda said she should see about getting a job. We would buy the morning paper and look through the job section and she ended up working in a travel agency. She seemed to like it as the people were very easy going and there wasn't too much pressure from the job. I started thinking about what I was going to do. First of all, I wanted to get myself a bit fitter, so I bought a bicycle and cycled around the area every day for a while. I found it really hard going for a while, but started feeling a bit more solid.

Then, out of the blue, I got a phone call from Brush Sheils, the bass player from Skid Row, the group Gary Moore had played in along with Brush and drummer, Noel Bridgeman. We agreed to meet in a cafe in Dublin city centre and had a long talk, catching up with things, and then we decided to form a three-piece group. We found a drummer, Timmy Creedon, and soon we were rehearsing in the Countdown Club (the place where I had first met Philip and Brian) once a week. The whole thing felt very new and very strange. For a start, Brush didn't smoke dope or cigarettes or drink alcohol. And Timmy only smoked the odd fag. So, when I took my guitar out to play, the sound I and Brush and Tim were making sounded so different from the drug-induced tones I was so used to hearing in the past. It really was like learning to play all over again, and it took a very long time for me to get the confidence to play straight.

A lot of places were interested in booking us because of Brush and myself being ex-members of two famous Irish bands. But I noticed we didn't really go down that well with the audiences. The music we were playing was very strange to say the least. We did a radio session, playing live on an RTE programme. As we were playing nearly all original songs, and at this point in time most radio programmes wanted you to play covers of other people's songs, we would pretend our original stuff was, in fact, songs by other famous bands.

We played a gig one night in Belfast and, as we were travelling there, we were stopped at Newry by an Army checkpoint. The soldiers were decked out in full combat gear and armed with machine guns. They asked us to open the back door of our van and saw the two guitar cases. "Can you open them, please?" said one of the soldiers. I opened mine and he checked the guitar and the rest of the case. Then Brush opened his bass case. The soldier raised his machine gun when he saw the guitar strap in Brush's case. The guitar strap was lined with about 12 large bullets. "Sorry, mate, but you're going nowhere with these." He explained that they could be used again. So, Brush told him there was no problem and they removed the bullets and we were soon on our way again to Belfast. It was a good night there, as we had added a lot of well known songs to our programme, songs by The Beatles, The

Stones, The Faces, etc. Thank God.

One of the hardships with the Bell Brush Band was that, after every gig, we had to drive to The Countdown Club, take our gear out of the van, and carry two large 4x12 cabinets, a bass amp and cab and a drum kit up two flights of stairs, sometimes around three in the morning. This was because we had no van of our own and the guy we hired to drive us about needed an empty van the next day for his job. One time, we drove to Countdown to pick up our equipment and, as Brush and myself started to lift one of my cabinets, we both stopped and put it down. It was really light. I walked around the back of the cab and noticed the four screws that held the back panel on were sticking out a bit. I undid the screws and couldn't believe it! Some bastard had opened the back and stolen the four speakers out of the cabinet. I never found out who had taken them, and luckily I still had another cab so could play the gig that night.

Talking about theft, a few weeks later, the van dropped me off at my flat in Rathmines. I opened the front door and walked down the hall to the door of my flat, put the key in the lock, but it wouldn't turn. Linda was in London for a few months on a secretary course that her father had wanted her to do, so she wasn't around. I tried to open the door but it wasn't happening. I walked back down the hall, opened the main door and walked around the back of the house to where my bedroom window was. I knew there was something not right. The white lace curtains were hanging and being blown outwards from the window. There was a small window that I always left open a little so that my cat, Toby, could get in and out as she wanted. Again, some bastard must have noticed this and opened the larger window below the small one. This was around 3am and it was still dark. I went to the window, opened the large one and, as I was crawling in, I started to feel very nervous. What if someone was still in the flat, in the front room? I shouted out and started to make a noise as I dropped into the bedroom, which was in darkness. I had that strong feeling that at any moment someone would grab me. I made my way to the light switch and turned on the bedroom light. All of the drawers had been pulled out and lay on the floor, which was covered with all types of clothing. I went into the sitting room and noticed a few areas of carpet that looked very clean and new. Oh yeah, that's where my record player and speakers used to be. I had about 50 or so vinyl albums and they had taken most of them and, to add insult to injury, had left all the Thin Lizzy ones. Over near the window was a small kitchen area and the floor there was covered with knives and forks, spoons, pots, pans, etc. I got in touch with the police who took a few details but nothing was ever done about it. Welcome back to Ireland!

The Bell Brush Band was slowly grinding to a halt. On one of our last few gigs, we were playing some hall somewhere in the North and, as we were on stage, this lady was standing behind the curtain trying to get my attention. At one point there was a break between songs and I walked over to her. "Yer fuckin' cat!" she said. In English this means that you are really useless. What could I say? She was running the gig.

The last gig we played was in Arklow, in a huge marquee. We set up our gear, did a small sound check and went to the local cafe for something to eat. When it was time to play that night, we walked out onto the stage and there were about 300 chairs set up and in the front row were six people. That was it .We played for a while, thanked the six people, took down our gear and climbed in the van for Dublin. Brush split the money between us and we had made the princely sum of five euros each. As the driver was just about to move off, Brush said, "Wait a minute, Joe." He then got out and walked over to a small shop that was still open. He came back a few minutes later. "I thought I might spend the money on sweets for the kids." As we drove home, Brush just sat there rubbing his chin. "Right, that's it, that's the last gig I'm playing with this band, lads. I'm fucking fed up trying to play music and not earning anything. I'm fed up with my family having to do without. But it's all going to change. I'm going to play the most commercial music you have ever heard and start earning some real money!" That night, Brush, Timmy and myself said our goodbyes and went our separate ways.

CHAPTER 15

Linda was back now in Dublin, having finished the course in London, and was back working in the travel agency. I was going into Dublin city centre about four times a week, just walking about the shops. From time to time, I would meet musicians, talk about forming bands, but nothing really came of it. One day, Linda told me she thought the girl who lived opposite us was on the game. "Every time the phone rings, she comes out, always in a lace nightgown, and about 20 minutes later, some guy rings the front doorbell and she comes out, opens the front door and they go into her room." I was playing some gig one night and, when I got back, which wasn't too late, Linda told me the girl had been in our flat for a few drinks, and had told Linda she was indeed on the game. "She's a really nice girl," she said.

Another turning point. Sitting in the flat one day, the phone (the old black one with press button A and B) that was in the hall, started ringing. I thought it might be a client for our friend across the hall, but she must have been out as no one was answering. I went out and picked it up. "Hello, could I speak to Eric Bell, please." "This is Eric Bell." I said. "Oh, hello matey, this is Noel Redding." My first thought was that someone was taking the piss. But it turned out that it was indeed Noel Redding, the bass player from The Jimi Hendrix Experience. "I got your number from a guy who said you were with Thin Lizzy." It turned out that Noel was forming a new band and asked if I'd be interested in getting together for a jam. I just stood there, mouth open. Hendrix's bass player, fuck me. Noel then told me that he wasn't living in London, but in West Cork. So I said I would get the train down to Cork and Noel said he'd be there to pick me up.

A few days later, with my guitar and bag, I stepped off the train and, through the crowd of people, spotted Noel. It was just like he had stepped out of a Jimi Hendrix poster. A huge afro hairstyle, pink shirt, brown bell-bottom trousers and pink national health glasses. He walked over and we shook hands. "Hello matey, pleased to meet you, I'm Noel," then "do you play darts?" "Ah, sometimes," I replied. "Right, you're in the fucking band!" He led the way to the bar that was on the train platform. "Right, what you drinking, Eric?" I made it a point in those days never to drink until the evening but, under the circumstances I said, "A pint of Guinness, please." Noel had a pint of beer and we walked over to the corner of the bar where there was a dartboard. He showed me some game he played and we had a few rounds of darts and another drink, which was going straight to my head. "Right, Eric, you ready to head off?" and he led me to this very flash yellow and black Ford sports car.

We drove through Cork City, and past Cork Airport, and soon we were driving down narrow country roads. "Sorry about the traffic," Noel laughed, as I hadn't seen one car passing us in about ten minutes. We drove on through small country towns and eventually to Clonakilty, where we stopped for another drink. Everyone in the town seemed to know Noel and, as we stepped into one of the many pubs, Noel even went behind the bar and poured another two pints himself. He introduced me to loads of the local people and soon we were on our way again.

About 30 minutes later, as we were nearing Noel's place, he said, "What happened that you left Thin Lizzy, Eric?" To cut a long story short I just said, "I sort of freaked out". He said "Yeah, I know what you mean. We've all been there mate, don't worry about it." And, at this point, at the end of a very narrow lane, I saw Noel's house. There was a stone wall and open gates and a drive past a duck pond and through a small forest up to the driveway, where he parked the car. I just got out of the car and stared. The house was huge and painted pink. He led the way in and I noticed the gold albums on the wall and the music room filled with guitars, amps, etc. "Carol, we're home!" he shouted and Carol, his American girlfriend, appeared and we shook hands. "Come and I'll show you around the house and to your bedroom." The house looked very old and some areas of it needed quite a bit of work. Then he showed me his office and I noticed pages and pages everywhere. "Yeah, I'm writing a book about The Experience."

"Ok, you guys, come and get it!" shouted Carol, and I followed Noel to a dining room where there stood a huge old wooden Henry VIII table. We had some homemade soup and real Irish brown bread. "I hope this is alright until I make dinner later on," she said. It was beautiful.

I went to bed that night and, I'm sorry to say, that I was freezing. The room was minus zero. I wasn't that surprised as it would have cost a fortune to heat a house that size. The next morning, when I eventually forced myself to get out of bed, my teeth were chattering. It was so cold and I'm one of those people who love heat. I went downstairs and felt every radiator I could see. They were all cold except the one in the dining room, which I stood as close to as possible. Then Noel appeared. "Good morning mate, have a good sleep?" I muttered something and he noticed me making love to the radiator. "Are you cold? I'm used to it, I don't feel it anymore."

That night, I was to meet the other members of the band. Dave Clarke (nothing to do with The Dave Clark Five), singer, songwriter, keyboards and sometimes guitar, and the drummer, Les Sampson. This was the first shock I had. All along I had been expecting that Noel was forming another three-piece band, and now I had just found out it was a four-piece lineup with keyboards. I met Dave Clarke, a real friendly guy who made me feel like a long lost friend, and the drummer Les. We sat down in front of a huge turf fire, thank God, and then Noel played some tapes of the songs the band was going to learn to play. I listened and thought, "What the hell is this all about?" I just couldn't relate to any of it. They were good enough songs but featured lots of keyboards, and I really couldn't hear much room for my guitar style. Anyway, they gave me a copy of the tape for me to listen to back in Dublin, and we went to Noel's music room to have our first play together.

Music can be very strange sometimes... You can have a group of musicians who are all great players but, for some reason, it doesn't seem to work, and some average players who can make the whole thing sound amazing. I believe it's all to do with the right chemistry. The situation I was in didn't feel right, but I thought I should give it a bit of time. Maybe I'll become more used to it eventually. Next day, I caught the train back to Dublin and, that night, told Linda all about it. She sensed I wasn't too happy about it all, but like myself, thought I should give it all a bit of time.

I remember going out for a drive with a friend of mine, and as we stopped at a view overlooking Dublin, I let him hear the tape of the songs Noel had given me to work on. They sounded just as strange to me on second listening. "I don't know what to do," I said. "What? Fuck that, Eric. This is Noel Redding's new band. It's bound to open lots of doors. Stick with it." So, next day, I started listening to the 11 or so songs on the tape and really got down to some serious work trying to somehow hear what I was going to play. I found it very hard going, being so used to a three-piece lineup.

A week or so later, the phone in the hall rang. It was Noel. "Hi Eric, when can you come down again? I want to start rehearsing those songs. Can you stay for a week or so?" So, we arranged a date, and about ten days later, I was standing in Noel's music room with Noel, Dave and Les. I had worked out quite a lot of guitar parts and wanted to see if they would work. It sounded better than I thought, but I still longed for a trio to play with, where I could play much looser and more natural.

Something happened over the next few days that really threw me. Around this point in time, Noel was drinking quite a bit and smoking grass, and sometimes he would become cynical and moody. We were playing through one of the songs when he just stopped playing and turned around to me. "Fuck me, mate, can you not get a better sound out of that amp?" And he put his bass down and started fiddling with the controls on the amp (which wasn't mine). In all my long years of playing guitar, no one had ever done this to me. I just stood there and, for some reason, didn't tell him to fuck off. I think I was a little star-struck because Noel had, after all, played with Hendrix, so I took a lot of crap from him. Another thing happened a few days later. I was sitting in my bedroom reading a book when Noel, Les and Dave came in. "We're going into Clonakilty for a drink. You coming?" I said I just wanted to relax and have a read of my book. "Fuck me," said Noel, "he's reading a book!" I just looked at him and he stood there for a bit then walked away. "This really doesn't feel right to me," I thought, and started thinking about leaving. But Noel's house was really in the middle of nowhere, so there was no way I could leave at that moment.

We kept rehearsing the same 11 or so songs every day and, at one point, Carol, Noel's girlfriend, came in to have a listen. "Hey, you guys sound good. You should start thinking about playing a few gigs and getting management." "What?" said Noel. "I don't want no fucking manager. I'll manage myself." "Noel," she said, "you're a musician, you can't manage yourself." It seemed a very sore point with him but he must have thought it through. I went back to Dublin and, on the train, was still trying to make up my mind whether to stay or get out.

The dreaded phone in the hall rang. "Eric, it's Noel, can you come down next week? There are some managers flying over from London and would like to hear the band." Something told me to give it all a bit more time, so a week later, I was back at Noel's house. Around that week, there must have been five different blokes who had flown in from London to Cork to check out Noel's new band. One or two of them were right gobshites, and at the end of it all, Noel went for a set-up with two managers who I'll call Bill and Ben, to save later embarrassment.

Bill stayed for a few days and hung out with the band, and Ben flew back to London. These two guys were loaded, having a huge office in Wardour Street in Soho, central London, a Rolls Royce and God knows what else. They seemed to like the overall sound of the band, and we had a meeting in which Bill said he would like to put us out on tour in the UK to see how the band went down with English audiences. We then went our separate ways and met up again in a few weeks at Noel's.

We started rehearsing in a huge ballroom in Clonakilty, and then Bill had this idea. He flew a guy called Rufus Collins over from London to work with us. Rufus was a huge black guy with dreadlocks and had been in charge of the dancers from a musical called *Hair*, which had been very successful doing the rounds in England. He was a very friendly guy and stayed with us in the cottage at the back of Noel's house. There was talk of the band doing an American tour and Bill the manager bought us all tracksuits. "You guys need to get fitter for all these gigs coming up," and he had Rufus getting us to run along the country roads near Noel's. I can see it now, it was like a comedy movie. Noel would make a beeline to the nearest pub and everyone else disappearing in different directions. Rufus was showing us a yoga exercise called Salutation to the Sun, and Dave Clarke had a pint of beer in front of him on the floor doing a Salutation to the Pint!

One of the managers, Bill, flew over from London again to see the band, and Rufus was with us. We were to rehearse again in the ballroom and, as we were playing one song called *There's A Light,* Rufus told us all to turn to the right and sing "Window". That was it for me. I couldn't believe this was the bass player from Jimi Hendrix forming a new band. More like the fucking Wombles. I got into a mood and really didn't want any part of it and was looked on as a sort of traitor.

We decided to play a gig in Clonakilty, I think it was the ballroom in O'Donovan's Hotel. So, a week later, we were playing to a packed hall and seemed to go down really well. After the gig, there were lots of free drinks, and when it was time to leave, we ended up in the hotel's car park. Everyone was pissed as a newt and nobody could drive. I said I would drive back to Noel's and nobody seemed to mind. I got behind the wheel, turned on the ignition and, a few minutes later, found out how to turn the headlights on. After a few jumps I got the car moving. I then drove at a steady 20 miles an hour and made it back to Noel's. To this day, I don't know how I managed it, as I was nearly as drunk as everyone else.

It must have been a month later, when our management got in touch with Noel and told him we had a small tour of the UK coming up. So Noel and myself flew to London and met up with Dave and Les outside the airport car park, where there was a mini-bus and driver waiting. We all said hello and were driven to our manager's office in Wardour Street. The office was very impressive, very big with a bar and music room at the back. We had a bit of a meeting and were given a list of the gigs we were to play. We stayed in some hotel that night and the next day sat off for the Magical Mystery Tour. We went down pretty well in most places, but the odd gig didn't know what to make of us. If they were expecting a Hendrix-type trio, we must have looked like some sort of a joke. I was just playing all my guitar parts, which I'd spent a long time working out, and couldn't have ad-libbed if my life had depended on it. Deep down, I was wishing to be in a band where I could play more naturally, rather than everything worked out and the same show night after night.

At one point, Noel decided he wanted to record a few demos of the songs, so we ended up at Steve Mariott's house, a beautiful country cottage-type place. Steve was the guitarist and singer from The Small Faces, a very popular group from the mid-60s, and later on with his new band, Humble Pie. I found him to be a really nice guy who, on meeting me, gave me a present of a Fender Stratocaster neck. Anyway, we settled down and started recording a few demos at Steve's home recording studio. It was well into the night when we packed up, and Noel arranged to go over to Steve's place in a few days to start to mix the tracks. But the next day at breakfast, Noel turned up, seething with anger. "You won't fucking believe it! That silly cunt Marriott just phoned me and told me he had got up during the night, as he couldn't sleep, and started to mix the songs – and wiped the lot by mistake. Probably coked out of his fucking head." It took Noel a long time to calm down again, and we all just kept our heads down.

Once the tour was finished, Bill, one of our managers, said he was going to try and get us a few gigs in and around London, one being at the famed Marquee Club. There was also maybe a tour of Europe coming up. So, back home to Dublin until the tour was arranged. Linda was still working at the travel agency which was a good thing as, for all the playing and touring we were doing, I didn't seem to ever have much money. I went out to Dublin city centre most days and met some musicians I knew, until the next thing with Noel's band. One night, Linda said that she needed a holiday as she was working so much, so we sat and worked out what date to have the holiday that would suit us both. But it didn't quite work out as we had expected.

CHAPTER 16

I got a phone call from Noel saying that the gigs around London, including two nights at The Marquee Club were in a few weeks' time. So, off I went to London again. I got a phone call from the office asking if it would be ok to do an interview with some music magazine in an hour or so? I said yes, and was told the guy doing it would call up to my hotel room. But, before he arrived, I had another call from the office telling me the dates of some gigs we had in Europe. I looked in my little pocketbook and, yes, it was around the time myself and Linda were going on holiday. I tried my best to remain cool as I explained about the holiday, but the answer I got was something like, "Eric, you're in a professional band, we can't keep chopping and changing gigs just like that. Can you not change the holidays around?" But I knew it was useless. Linda had arranged the holiday with the travel agency she worked for and that was that. I was really pissed off to put it mildly and didn't know what to do.

Before I knew what I was doing, I had opened the little mini-bar that was in my hotel room and took out a miniature bottle of scotch, poured it out and started drinking. I hadn't done anything like this since my Thin Lizzy days, but at that moment, I couldn't have cared less. There was a knock on my door, and it was the guy from the music magazine. "Oh, hi, come on in," I said. He sat down and took out a small tape recorder. "Is it ok if I record the interview?" "Sure," I said. "Would you like a drink?" So I took out another two small bottles of scotch and in about five minutes or so, my head was quite numb. "The music business, it's a load of fucking shit, isn't it?" "Would you mind if I quoted you on that, Eric?" "No, I don't mind, it's the truth, isn't it?" So, the interview went on along those lines.

About a week later, the two gigs at The Marquee came up. I phoned my mate Gary Moore and asked him did he want to come down to the gig? We arranged to meet in The Ship, a popular pub near The Marquee. So, at around 8pm, Gary and myself were standing at the bar having a laugh, when Noel walked in and spotted me. "Hi Noel, this is a friend of mine, Gary Moore." "Hello matey, pleased to meet you." Then Gary said to him, "Did you play the bass on the end of *If 6 was 9?*" "No, mate, that was JH," which was what

Noel called Hendrix sometimes. "Oh," said Gary, and just sniffed and turned away.

Anyway, it was time to get down to the gig and, when we got there, the place was packed. I told Gary I'd see him later and started walking through the bar, which was stuffed with people. I was making my way to the dressing room when I saw this hand holding a magazine waving at me. "Eric, Eric, I want a word with you!" It was Bill, our manager. He came over to me and was foaming at the mouth. "What is the meaning of this? What are you trying to do, fucking break up the band?" We went into the dressing room and he showed me the interview. It started: "The music business is a load of fucking shit." Strong words indeed from guitarist Eric Bell". "Well?" I said. "What's wrong? It's true, isn't it?" Bill said, "Maybe it is and maybe it isn't. The point is you don't tell the whole fucking world about it." Ah, I was rocking the boat again.

We played the two gigs at The Marquee and seemed to go down very well. But I don't think Gary could believe the type of band we were, as it had nothing whatsoever to do with the Jimi Hendrix Experience. A few days later, I phoned Linda to tell her about the gigs and the news about the holiday. She was pretty angry and told me that she was still going to go, with me or without me. "I need this holiday, Eric." And she ended up going with a few girlfriends.

The Noel Redding Band's next stop was a ten-day tour of Europe. One night we played in The Paradiso Club, a very popular gig in Amsterdam. During the day, around 3pm, we were in the club doing a sound check, and there were a few people hanging around. This young lady was walking around with a small basket giving out sweets to people, so I walked over and took two of the sweets. I started eating one and put the other one in my pocket. Soon, we were all walking back to the hotel to relax and freshen up for the gig that night. I opened my hotel room door, switched on the TV and went into the bathroom to have a wash. As I was washing my hands, I became aware of this voice coming from the TV. It was echoing around the bathroom, someone talking in Swedish or whatever. I then looked down at my hands in the sink and the water running down the drain, and I started wondering how long I had been standing there. Then, slowly, I realised that old feeling that I hadn't experienced for a long time. I was stoned out of my head. I hadn't had a smoke of hash or grass for quite a while and here it was after eating one of those sweets. My first feeling was panic, then I started reasoning with myself. "Eric, there's nothing you can do about it, so why don't you just relax, go with it and enjoy it?"

I dried my hands and walked into the bedroom. I turned the TV off, walked over to the window and looked down at the trams and people. I was up on the 5th floor and there were about 12 people down below waiting for a tram. I felt like about eight of those people were looking straight up at me and they all knew I was stoned. I made myself a cup of coffee, lay on the bed and looked at my watch. There was about another four hours to go before leaving for the gig. It should have worn off by then I thought, but eating hash is much stronger in its effect than smoking it. Also, a lot depended on how much had been in that sweet. I got up and went over to my guitar case and took out my guitar. I'll never forget the thing that happened. I wish, somehow, I could have made a tape of it. I sat down and started playing and as I played, this large orchestra followed me. No matter what I played, it followed me perfectly. It was amazing and will always be with me.

Anyway, time passed and I somehow got myself together enough to go down to one of the many cafes around the hotel and bought a burger and chips and a coffee to take away. I went back to the hotel and thought, if I have something to eat I would feel more solid. Then, it was time to walk the short walk back to the gig. Before we went on to play I had a beer... wrong! The stoned feeling was still with me as we walked on and played the first song of our set. The only problem was I didn't know which part of the song I was in – was this the second verse or the first? Had I played the guitar solo yet? The next second, I realised the song had finished and I was still playing, but all on my own. "You must forgive our guitar player, he's had a bit too much to drink," laughed Noel into the mike. After that, the tension broke and it ended up a really good night.

Another thing that happened. A few nights later, we were playing in the Milky Way club, I think it was called. We were into our third song and I saw this huge Indian guy standing with his arms folded and looking directly at Noel. He walked away, but a few minutes later was back holding what looked like a pint of water. He then walked closer to the stage and threw the water all over Noel. It was one of those moments when time seems to stop still. Noel took off his bass, went over to his amp, dried himself with a towel and walked down the few steps that led to the dance floor. He walked up to the huge Indian and grabbed him by his collar. "Right, cunt, I want a public apology!" and walked him up the steps onto the stage. He shoved the guy up to the mike and the band and the audience waited to see what would happen. "I'm so sorry," the guy said and then walked down the steps again. That was it! I couldn't believe it in a way. Noel was a pretty small guy and if the Indian bloke had started something, Noel wouldn't have had a chance. So, I admired him for the nerve he had shown. Afterwards, in the dressing room, we were talking to some people who had come in to meet the band, when I noticed the Indian guy. "Hey, excuse me, what did you do that for, throwing the water over Noel?" He replied, "I probably had taken too much coke. I thought Noel was taking the piss out of the audience." He didn't seem to realise that he could have killed Noel. Water and electricity don't mix.

One of the things I just couldn't understand was I started getting a bad name for playing too loud – what a fucking joke! I was in a four-piece band playing nearly all pop songs. And Noel had been with one of the loudest guitar players that had ever lived. I wonder if anyone told Jimi Hendrix his guitar was too loud?

Our European Tour was now coming to an end. One of our managers wanted a meeting before we left for home. "Right, boys, I think it's time to record your first album, and there's a chance of doing an American tour." But, one thing that was never talked about was money. We seemed to be playing a lot and no one seemed to ever have any money. "I think when we get the record deal, there should be some sort of an advance, and you all should get something." We got a record deal with RCA, and we were each given a cheque for £1,000 and I think Noel got £2,000. Big fucking deal. Where did the rest of it go?

I was back in Dublin and just relaxing until the next chapter with The Noel Redding Band. It started with the phone call from Noel. "Eric, I think we should rehearse a bit and work on some new songs." So, one week later I'm in Noel's house, and we're all there – Noel, Dave, Les and myself.

I seem to remember one night Noel had a few guests over for dinner. Sitting at the huge Henry VIII table, there must have been around 14 people. I'm not sure what happened but I got pretty drunk and there was some sort of misunderstanding between me and Noel. Surprise, surprise. I ended up sitting in one of the rooms in front of a blazing fire drinking whiskey. I think somebody else was sitting with me. "I've had enough of this band, I'm leaving." "Oh, don't be like that, Eric, everything will turn out alright." But, a day or two later, I was looking out of the window of the train bound for Dublin.

I got home and had a talk with Linda about the band. She knew I was really unhappy with the music, and also with Noel. The phone in the hall started ringing and I just wouldn't answer it. The next day I did. "Listen, Noel, I've left the band, it's just not happening for me, see you around." Next day I had a phone call, this time from Bill, one of the managers. "Eric, what's going on between you and Noel? We're putting an American tour together, you can't just walk out. And there's an album to record." I just listened to what he had to say, then said I really couldn't see it working between Noel and myself. "I'll tell you what, Eric, what about if I fly over to Cork, and you, Noel and myself have a nice meal at The Arbutis Lodge Hotel and try to iron out your differences? We do need you to stay in the band." So, we met up at the hotel and the dinner was great, and Bill ordered an old bottle of port, which turned out to be one of the most beautiful things I have ever tasted. (We probably ended up paying for it as well.) So, I just explained to Noel the way I felt. I'd been through the mill with Thin Lizzy and I didn't want any more. Noel grabbed my hand and squeezed it. "Sorry, Eric. I realise how you feel now. Let's try and make this work."

CHAPTER 17

The American Tour came. Noel had got in touch with Tony Henderson. When we had been at Steve Marriot's house we had met Tony. He was a bit of a character, Scottish and built like a wrestler. He was working for Steve and tried his hand at lots of things, minder, cook, driver and, later on, I found out he was a really good artist. So, Noel talked him into touring the States with us. The night before the flight to the USA, we stayed in a hotel somewhere in Essex and, the next day, boarded the plane. It was a good flight with good food, movies and drinks. I remember my first view of America as I looked out of my porthole window. It was at night time and we were preparing to land soon. The lights down below were amazing – pink, green, blue, yellow, red. It really did look magical, something like a Christmas tree. I'd never been to America and I started to feel that excitement.

I think it was Atlanta, Georgia where we landed. After being checked out at customs, we got taxis to the hotel and I'll never forget the feeling as we entered the lobby – the size of the place! I looked up and saw that the ceiling was so high, and there were little balconies on each floor. And lifts with glass floors. Myself and Dave left the rest of our party at the reception and made for the lifts. I haven't got much of a head for heights and when the lift started to move, I couldn't believe how high this hotel really was. It was like something out of *2001: A Space Odyssey.* We checked into our rooms and, every now and again, I would open my hotel room door, take a few steps and peer down at the reception. It was just unbelievable, and I would get that fear of falling feeling each time. Later, we all met in the bar and I noticed all the different colours of the bottles of spirits lined up. Strawberry brandy, peach brandy, apricot brandy. I started thinking... America what a place! Everything seemed to be really flash.

Our management had hired a large Range Rover for us to travel around in, with Tony Hat the wheel. As we were in America for 11 weeks, I can't really recall the names of a lot of the gigs we played. I remember walking on to the stage of our first gig to check out the equipment as we weren't using our own backline. I think it was a Sun amp I was supplied with, and I could never get the tone I liked from it. At one point, I noticed that a few young ladies had appeared and they were talking and laughing, looking like they were checking us out. Noel had told me about the groupies in America and I was looking forward to it all. We had a rough sound check, played a few songs and went back to the hotel for something to eat and relax before our first show. The gig seemed to go pretty well, but I kept thinking that a lot of people couldn't quite believe that this was Jimi Hendrix's bass player with a band like us.

So, the tour was now underway, and I just loved the feeling and the total difference all around me. A few nights later, we were in Dallas, Texas and I think the venue was called Mother Blues. I went in during the afternoon just to check the place out and was standing at the bar when this huge black guy appeared a few stools down from me. "Hi, man, what's happening?" he said to the barman. I looked and then did a double take. It was Freddie King, the amazing blues guitarist and singer. I wanted to say something but just hadn't got the nerve. What I didn't know was that we would be playing on the same show with him in LA later on the tour. We played that night to a full house and all I could think of was longing to be playing in a blues band.

Noel had told me about the groupie scene in America but we'd got to our third gig and not a chick in sight. Oh well, the same old crap, nothing happening. We finished playing and I was walking down the club and making for the dressing room upstairs, when just out of nowhere I heard this voice, "I like your shirt." And standing in front of me was this lovely looking young lady. "Oh, thanks," I answered. "Are you staying in town tonight?" she asked. I said yes and told her the name of the hotel. "Have you got a room on your own?" My heart started to beat faster. "No, I'm sharing it with the keyboard player." "You wanna come back to my place?" Now, after every gig, I always cleaned my guitar strings, but not this time. I told the girl (Barbara was her name) I wouldn't be long, ran up the stairs, threw my guitar in the case and was downstairs in a flash.

Our manager Bill was hovering about, saw me and came over. "Good gig, Eric, everything alright?" "Yeah," I said. "Good gig. Listen, I'll be staying with Barbara tonight." Bill looked a little shocked. "Can a have a word with you, Eric?" So, we walked over to the bar. "Listen, Eric, now I don't think it's a good idea for you to just go off with her. This isn't England. You could get kidnapped." I started laughing. "Who the fuck would want to kidnap me?" So, I told him I would get Barbara's phone number and, if I could have the number of the hotel the band were staying at, I would ring him later to say everything was ok. I could see he wasn't happy, but there wasn't much he could do. So, we said our goodbyes, and myself and Barbara walked out to the car park. She walked over to this huge looking car (I was nuts about old cars) and we got in. As she was starting the engine, she asked me to pull down my sun visor and as I did, two small cigarettes fell onto my lap. "Light one up for me, honey, and have the other one." So, off we went, with me feeling like Jack the Lad. Ten minutes later, Jack the Lad was out of his tree, seeing little green men floating around the outside of the car. "Are you ok, honey?" she asked. "You seem very quiet." I forced myself back to Earth. "Yeah, I'm fine," I said. "America sure is some place," and we cracked up laughing.

We eventually got back to her place, which was a real nice flat, covered in house plants. I sat down and Barbara went to fix some drinks. On the table in front of me was a little box with 'Pet Rock' written on the sides. It had a few small holes in which, when I looked through, I could see a small brown rock. When she came back with the drinks, I asked her about it. "Yeah, that's my pet rock," she said. "But, what does it do?" "Nothing," she said. That was it and I fell on the floor, hardly able to breath with laughing. We had another smoke and drinks and ended up in her bedroom. We made love, which I really don't remember much about, and as I slowly woke up next morning, she was in bed sitting up and talking on the phone. It was a phone conversation to a friend and Barbara was saying that she was going to the doctor to get some more sleeping pills. She said she would give some of these to the friend for some grass, and she would try and score some coke with the rest of the sleeping pills and some of the grass. I just lay there listening to all of this, feeling a bit like a wimp.

Eventually, we got up and she made some breakfast. As we were eating, Barbara went over to a drawer, took out a large book and handed it to me. I opened it and it was a photo album with Barbara posing with lots of very famous rock stars. "They call me The Butter Queen," she smiled. "Do you know Mick Jagger mentions me in one of the Stones' songs. That night in Texas with the Butter Queen." This is true and I think it's a song from *Exile On Main Street*. To this day, I still don't know why she was called that. I phoned the hotel and told Bill I'd be there in an hour or so. Barbara dropped me off before her visit to the doctor and we said our goodbyes. Then the *Noel Redding Band* checked out and we started off for the next gig.

As I said, I can't remember all the shows or places we played as, unlike Noel, I didn't keep a diary. Noel had kept a daily record in his diary ever since his days with Hendrix. One night, we did a gig at some college and there was a few bands playing on the same bill. I remember walking down a huge corridor with Noel. We walked into a large room with the lights on dim, and sitting on his own was the guitarist from The Grateful Dead, Jerry Garcia. "Hello matey, 'ow are you?" was Noel's greeting to nearly everyone he met. "Do you mind if we have a couple of beers?" "Have them all, man," said Jerry. "I don't drink the stuff." And, as Noel introduced me to Jerry, Jerry handed Noel the end of a small joint. The beer was in a huge bucket on wheels and full of ice and lots of bottles. We smoked the joint which was all but dead, or so I thought. As we were wheeling the huge bucket of beer back to our dressing room, we just looked at each other and cracked up laughing for quite a while.

The place I do remember is Los Angeles. Noel had told me about LA in his days with Jimi, but I was thinking it was a bit tamer now having left the 60s far behind. But this wasn't really the case. I found, as the American tour progressed, Noel had become much more mellow and really seemed to be enjoying it all. He was good company and we became quite good friends.

We checked into our hotel in LA and Dave Clarke and I shared the room, or I should say suite. It was enormous – huge sitting room, huge telly, huge fridge. America, just like I pictured it. After a while, we all met at reception and then out for a stroll around the town. We ended up in a burger bar and noticed lots of long-haired musician types hanging out with lots of tasty young ladies. As we sat down and ordered, I noticed this really pretty girl looking over in my direction now and again. I thought LA was amazing and sometimes I'd go out walking on my own dressed in my stage gear, a real flash, loose-sleeved shirt, real tight black jeans and boots. Nobody gave me a second look, as everyone around was dressed to kill and strutting their stuff. I tried to imagine walking through Dublin or Belfast dressed like this… no way!

We had a meeting with our manager Bill in his hotel room and found out that we would be playing in one of the clubs right in the heart of town, seven nights in a row, supporting Freddie King.

We had a night off and we all went down to a club (I think it was called The Roxy). It was full of lots of weird and colourful people and we ended up splitting up and going our separate ways. Sometimes, on tour, you are with each other so much during the day and at night, that it's a good idea to avoid each other from time to time. I was sitting on my own in the corner of the club, having a quiet drink, when someone said, "Excuse me, can I have a light?" I looked up. It was the girl I saw at the burger bar. Up close, she looked like a real honey. I handed her my lighter and asked her if she wanted a drink. "Thanks, but I'm with someone at the moment. But I'd love to have a drink with you sometime soon." I introduced myself and she told me her name was Amy, and then she left.

A few nights later, we played our first gig at The Roxy. As soon as we finished our set, I cleaned my strings, put my guitar away and made my way downstairs and stood at the front of the stage, waiting on Freddie King. His band appeared and started playing a really funky number, then taking the volume down low as the keyboard player walked out to the front of the stage. "Ok, ladies and gentlemen, we've got a real natural blues high for you tonight. Freddie is ready, are you ready for Freddie? I said, Freddie is ready, are you ready for Freddie?" And Freddie King walked on the stage, plugged his guitar into a Fender amp and hit the first note. That note. I'll never forget the tone, the attack, the vibrato. It was perfect. I just stood and watched him all night. His singing was so soulful and powerful. I noticed the other guitarist in the band was the only white guy on stage. I started daydreaming that Freddie would somehow hear me playing and ask me to join his band. But, it wasn't to be.

After the fourth night playing in the same club, I'd made a few friends, one of them being a young, black bass player called Nick. We would hang out together and one day, after borrowing a car from his mum, we went for a drive to the outskirts of LA. I noticed the sign I think everyone on planet Earth has seen at one time or another – the huge sign that spells 'HOLLYWOOD'. "Oh man, I gotta go up there!" So we parked the car and walked up the hilly ground until we were standing right beside it. I walked around the back and noticed it was all scaffolding holding the sign up. Myself and Nick started to climb up and we eventually reached the giant H, and the both of us sat on the middle bar. It was one of those moments when you think you're dreaming. I just wanted everyone I knew to see me now. I was as high as a kite and hadn't even taken anything.

We played the gig that night and after Freddie had finished his set, I went upstairs again to our dressing room. It was packed with people, everybody talking at once, when this guy came in and shouted, "Let's party!" In less than a minute, the whole crowd of us were outside the club, climbing into various cars and driving off. This young girl ended up sitting on my lap in the back seat as the car was overflowing with people. She opened her handbag and took out a little bottle, snapped the cap off and started sniffing it. Amyl nitrate. I couldn't believe it. I don't think I met one person in America who wasn't into taking something. Everyone seemed to be stoned.

We arrived at Silver's house (that was the guy whose house the party was in). He opened the back door and right in front was a very large swimming pool with little clouds of steam floating on top. He led us into the house and over to the biggest fridge I had ever seen and said, "Just help yourselves." It was stuffed with food of all descriptions and six packs of beer and bottles of wine.

Then, we all followed him into a large sitting room where he emptied his pockets at a large round table and again shouted, "Let's party!" On the table were pills, powders, tablets, coke, grass, hash and God knows what. A half hour later, there were people on the floor, in the pool, upstairs, music blaring, people dancing. I was thinking, what a place America is. If I lived here, I'd probably be dead in a week.

I had gotten very friendly with a lovely young lady that night, and we ended up back at her place. I had no idea how we got there, and after a great night, I woke up next morning with no idea where I was. I went into the sitting room and found a note on the table: "Hi, Eric, sorry to leave you on your own but had to go out. Thanks for last night. Help yourself to breakfast and please lock up. Might see you at Roxy. Helen xx." I couldn't believe how trusting some people are. I could have just helped myself to anything in her house, never to see her again. Instead, I had some cereal and coffee and wrote her a Thank You note. Then I opened the front door, locked it and posted the keys through the letter box. Where the fuck am I? What with a hangover and not knowing what part of LA I was in, I started getting a bit worried. But, I had to do something so I just started walking. It seemed like I was in a sort of housing estate, and eventually, I came out on a main road. I managed to get a taxi to take me back to the Sunset Marquee, our hotel. Dave was in the hotel room and we swapped stories about our night out.

We got a phone call from Bill suggesting that the band should have a practice session later on that afternoon in the function room in the hotel. The hotel manager was a big fan of Jimi Hendrix so he was cool about us having a blow there, as long as we kept the volume down. We had a rehearsal but it was really a waste of time, as no one was into it at all. Tonight was our last show in the Roxy and I thought I would have a night on my own, come back to the hotel after our set and have a long, hot bath and just relax. Later on, about an hour before we were to play, I saw Nick, my black bass player friend. "Hi, Eric, what's happening?" I told him I was planning to have an early night. "Call yourself a guitar player, you're going to miss the jam tonight. Eric Clapton's coming down to play a few songs with Freddie King." "Yeah, right," I said. But then I started thinking it's possible this might happen… and it did.

After we finished our set, we were upstairs in our dressing room and there was definitely a buzz in the air. As I walked down the stairs that led onto the stage, I saw some guy setting up a Marshall amp and placing a chair in front of it. I saw Nick down in the audience and went over. I couldn't believe it – Amy was standing beside him. I said hello and she smiled. "Nick," I whispered. "Are you two together?" "No, Eric, we're just good friends." So, I edged in beside her and asked if she would be around and could I see her later? "That's why I came down tonight, Eric." Amazing.

I went backstage and went upstairs to the dressing room again. There were a lot of people and then Buddy Miles walked in. Buddy played drums on Hendrix's album, *Band Of Gypsies.* He was dressed in a black suit, white gloves and a bowler hat, with a lovely white lady hanging on his arm. Freddie King and his band were already onstage and, about 40 minutes later, everyone started to go downstairs to the club. I sat down on the bottom of the stairs and had a view of the stage. Then, this guy walked out and placed a black Fender Stratocaster on the chair beside the Marshall amp. And out walked Eric Clapton. He really looked out of it and picked up his guitar and sat on the chair. At this point, Buddy Miles came on and sat behind the drum kit. Noel came on with his bass, some sax player joined in and then Freddie King. They started an up tempo funky blues, and Freddie started taking a solo. He walked over to where Clapton was sitting and tried to get him to trade some licks. But Eric just smiled, played a few notes which could hardly be heard and really just sat there till the end of the song. Then, Freddie King started a slow blues, sang a few verses and walked over to Clapton again to try and get him to start playing. Eric again played a few notes but it just wasn't happening. He shook his head, got up and left his guitar on the chair.

Then, he started walking to where I was sitting on the stairs. 'Excuse me, mate, can I get past?" I couldn't believe it. Eric Clapton was standing right beside me. "Yeah, sure," I stammered. As he was walking up the stairs, I said, "Hey, Eric, can I borrow your guitar?" He looked down and smiled. "No fucking way, man, no fucking way." I was dying to go on and play some blues with Freddie, but it wasn't meant to be. Anyway, any time someone asks me did I ever meet Eric Clapton, I always say he told me to fuck off.

But, to end on a good note, Amy and myself went back to the hotel – and the rest is censored! When we woke up and had some coffee, I got a phone call from Bill. "Eric, I've just found out six of our gigs have been pulled. Now, that means that the next gig is in San Diego. What do you want to do, stay in LA for another five days or make our way to San Diego?" "Stay in LA?" I begged. Amazing! Another five days and five nights off.

Later on, the phone rang in my suite. "Hello, are you a member of the Noel Redding Band?" "Yes," I replied. "Hi, I'm one of the roadies with Back Street Crawler (this was the band that the guitarist Paul Kosoff from Free was now fronting). "I wonder if you would do me a favour? We've just checked into the hotel. If Paul asks you or anyone else from your band if you have any dope, can you tell him no? Paul had an accident and broke his arm, which is in plaster, so he can't play at the moment. We have another guitarist playing his licks and Paul walks on the stage just to show people he is on the tour." I said of course and he said thanks and that was that. Paul Kossoff was into taking heroin and his roadie had told me he had been clean for a few weeks, but was probably looking for something else to ease the pain.

That evening, Amy and I went out for dinner and then to a bar for a few drinks, before walking back to the hotel. We opened the door and, to our amazement, there were about 20 people standing and sitting about. A few of the guys were even playing a sort of cricket game with a squashed tin of beer for a ball and an empty bottle of wine for a bat. I soon found out these were the members of Back Street Crawler and their road crew. Dave, our keyboard player, came over. "Hey, Eric, come on over and meet Paul Kossof." .So, Amy smiled and sat down with some girls, who were probably groupies, and I went over. Paul was sitting at the end of the sofa with his arm in plaster inside a sling. I sat down and we started talking guitars – he was a really nice guy.

I really don't remember how it happened, but a bit later, myself and Paul ended up lying beside each other on top of my double bed, smoking a huge joint. I started telling him that hundreds of guitar players in and around Belfast were crazy about his guitar playing. He seemed very pleased with this and then I started giving him a lecture. "Jesus, Paul, look at you now, your arm in a sling. Listen, man, you've got a talent and you're not even playing on your own tour. "I suddenly realised I didn't even know the bloke and was waiting for him to tell me to fuck off. But he didn't, and maybe he was starting to think about the talent he had. It was about 2am when everyone started to leave the suite and Amy and myself fell into bed. We drifted off but, some time later, I woke to some movement in the room. Dave Clarke, who I was sharing the suite with, had came in from wherever he had been, thrown himself on his bed, bounced back off and had hit his head on something.

I turned the bedside lamp on and Dave was sitting on the edge of his bed, his head and shirt covered with blood. "God, Dave, that looks bad." I phoned Noel's room as he was well used to dealing with things in America, and he walked in. "Fuck me, Dave, what have you done? You better get to a hospital, that looks like it needs stitching." We got him down to reception, found out the nearest hospital and phoned a cab. Then we went back to our rooms and Amy and myself went back to sleep. A while later, I thought I heard voices in the bedroom. I really got a fright! It was two cops. The lights were off and they were shining torches around the room. I didn't move and pretended I was asleep. "Hey, will I wake these two up?" one of the cops said. "Nah, just leave them, doesn't seem like they had anything to do with it." answered the other. I found out later that anything like this is reported to the police and they always turn up to check everything out.

The next day, after some life-saving coffee, Amy told me she had to go and visit her mother and would see me later. I went down to this health cafe called The Source and got some beautiful veg soup with brown bread, then bread with honey and coffee. As I was sitting there looking around, I spotted piano player, singer and songwriter, Tom Waits, in deep conversation with someone, and also spotted a dwarf actor out of one of the James Bond movies. He was sitting with a beautiful lady about three times his size. Some guys have all the luck. Well, it was LA.

Later that evening, Amy showed up back at my hotel room. She told me she saw her mother. "It's a bit of bad news, Eric. My mom has a sort of boyfriend that she sees now and again. He's a waiter in this hotel that's in Buffalo Springs, right in the desert, and she wants me to go along. We leave tomorrow." We spent a few hours together, but before she left, she said she was going to ask her mom if I could go along. Dave and myself had a bit of a talk about the tour and how we were going down, but mostly about the money, or the lack of it. His wife had phoned him and there was a bit of a heated discussion about money. Poor Dave. I heard him tell his wife to sell one of his guitars, a Gibson, to help her out. So, at this point, we would start to ask the manager where the money from the shows was going. And we were told the same old shit. "I don't know whether you know it, lads, but the expenses of doing your first tour in America is fucking frightening, most bands do their first tour at a loss. It's when you play your second tour, you'll see more money coming in." What can you do?

Next morning, Amy was on the phone. "Eric, I asked my mom and I don't believe it, she said yes." "We'll call round for you in the next hour or so." I phoned Bill's room and told him where I was going. This time he didn't seem to mind. "How long will you be gone? You know we're leaving LA in two days." "We're just going for one day, staying overnight and driving back the next night." I then started packing a few things, and a short time later, there was a knock on the door and Amy walked in, followed by her mom. We said hello and she asked me if I was ready, and we made our way downstairs to the car. The cars in America were just amazing, really wide and low, with fabulous leather seats and fins and pastel colours. Why no one makes cars like that anymore is a mystery to me. Amy and her mom got in the front and I had this enormous leather couch type seat in the back. The roof was down and the sun was shining. We stopped at a garage and filled up with gas. Amy bought an ice cold six pack of beer and away we went. It was another 'I wish my friends could see me now' moment. I sat there thinking that, sometimes, being in the music business had its good times. I really felt good.

Eventually, we arrived at the hotel in Buffalo Springs, unloaded our luggage and Amy's mom had a talk with the people at reception. Then, she called Amy over and after a few minutes, Amy walked back to me. "I think we better stay out of my mom's way for a while. She's just found out that her boyfriend isn't here this season, so he's not working here at the moment." One of the hotel staff showed us to our rooms, or should I say room. Oh my God, I thought, the three of us are sharing the same room. Where else would it happen but America. I've known Amy for a week, and I'm sleeping with her in the same bedroom as her mother who I've only just met. The thought did occur to me we might end up as a threesome, but later on this guy knocked on the door, wheeled in a sort of camp bed and put it up in the middle of the room. Phew!

As it was such a beautiful day, myself and Amy hired two bikes and cycled off and soon we were in the desert area. I was buzzing out of my head, singing at the top of my voice, and then she spotted a bird rushing along the ground. "Look, it's a roadrunner." It didn't look anything like the cartoon, its colour mostly a darkish brown. Later on, we had dinner and quite a few drinks, as I wanted to be numb sleeping in a bed with Amy and her mom only a few feet away. I had a pretty sleepless night, and next morning over breakfast, it was decided that we would check out of the hotel and head back to LA. I was dropped off at the Sunset Marquee and shared a few last moments with Amy and told her we must meet again on the band's next American tour. Noel and the rest of the band and Tony and Bill kept asking me about any sordid details from my trip, but I just told them the high point of it all was cycling in the desert.

I had a few hours to pack my belongings before we sat off for the next gig, which was in San Diego. San Diego was as different to LA as day is to night. It looked like a seaside town with lots of open space. We checked into the hotel, which was more like a motel, and this time I was sharing a room with Les, the drummer. There didn't seem to be very much to do here, but I went out for a walk and found a few shops, one which sold beautiful turquoise jewellery. I bought myself a silver ring set with the blue stones. Later, as we were having something to eat in the hotel, a few young ladies joined us. They seemed to know Les and Noel and just talked over old times. We weren't playing until the next night and, for once, I went to bed early. The next morning I woke up, drenched in sweat and feeling pretty lousy. Noel called in to see myself and Les and thought I looked a bit rough.

"Yeah," I said. "I thought having an early night would make me feel rested, but I had hardly any sleep." "You're having withdrawals, mate!" Noel told me. I hadn't thought about that fact, but he was probably right. I was taking anything I could get in LA, where everybody was taking something, and being in a popular band, you were offered lots of free samples. I remember dope of any kind was like gold dust in San Diego. It seemed to be a drinking town, which I found out after the gig that night.

Before the gig, we had a beautiful dinner, which really made me feel a lot better, and we played a good show to a pretty large crowd. Afterwards, the owner of the club seemed to be in the partying mood, and he invited us up to the bar for a few drinks. I seemed to hit it off with him and, at one point, he asked the guy behind the bar for a special bottle of Tequila. After what seemed like a ceremony to the bottle, he eventually opened it. I'd never drank Tequila before, and it sort of creeps up on you. I was in a deep conversation with the owner and halfway through I forgot what I was talking about. We both cracked up laughing, then he said he liked the shirt I was wearing and would I swap it for the t-shirt he had on? So, we both stripped off our shirts and swapped them. He was about twice my size and his t-shirt was like an overcoat on me, while my shirt barely fitted him.

The next morning, I awoke with a dreadful hangover and picked up the phone and ordered breakfast for both myself and Les. The waiter wheeled in the trolley and I lifted off the covers from the plates. Fried eggs, hash browns, toast, coffee and melon. After that, I felt reasonably human and went out for a walk and some fresh air. When I got back, Les must have gone out. I noticed this long black line on the floor, going up one of the legs of the trolley. I looked closer. Ants! They were after the remains of the melon. Soon, they were spreading everywhere. I picked up the phone and told reception, and a few minutes later, this guy knocked on the door and came in. He was so cool about it all and must have dealt with this hundreds of times before. He took out a can of something, sprayed the ants, then lit a lighter and set fire to it. It was all over in a few moments, then he cleaned up the mess, wheeled the trolley out and closed the door. I felt really bad about the ants, but I suppose there was nothing much else to do about it. They would have taken over the room.

It was early afternoon and we all met in reception, then went outside where the Range Rover was waiting for us with Tony Henderson at the wheel. Off to the next show. At one point, we stopped for gas and this young guy came out to fill us up. It reminded me of earlier times, those days when you stopped at a filling station for petrol and an attendant would come out and fill the tank for you and clean the windscreen, the good old days. As he was cleaning one of the side windows on my side of the Rover, I heard him say, "Man, I don't believe it... is that Noel Redding?" Then he knocked on my window and I opened it. "Hey, man, fucking far out. Wait till I tell the guys about this!" and he handed me a large ball of silver paper. Just as I was thanking him, we drove off. "Hey, Eric, did that guy give you something? Give it here." I reached over and passed it to Noel. "Hey, Eric, you have to be careful over here. This stuff could be laced with anything." It turned out to be quite a lot of very strong weed.

We eventually reached our destination, St Louis. The gig looked like a large college, and Noel and myself were walking around the building and ended up in a very large kitchen. As we were standing there having a cup of coffee, this guy walked in. "Hey, you guys, pleased to meet you. My name is Buddy. I work here. Did you hear the news? Paul Kossoff's dead." Noel got really angry. "What do you fucking mean? No he isn't, we were at a party with him only last week." "Well, sorry, man, but it was on the news on the radio. I heard it. I didn't mean to upset you." Noel calmed down, said he was sorry and explained that he was shocked by the news. We found out later that Paul had a sort of heart attack on a plane.

An hour later, the sound crew for the gig showed up and we did a sound check. On the whole of the American tour, I could never find an amp that I could get a tone I wanted from. I would have given anything to plug into a Vox or Marshall, but they were not available. Noel had bought a magazine called the *Gourmet Guide to American Restaurants,* and when possible, would look them up and we would end up in one of them. This night, we ended up in a place called *The Abbey*. It really had been a church at one time and someone had made it into a top class restaurant. They even had the waiters wearing monk's robes and sandals on their feet. And the menus were rolled up scrolls. The stained glass windows and the pews were still being used. The waiter was taking our orders, and when it came to Dave's turn, he ordered venison. "Dave, you're not going to eat venison before a gig, are you?" said our minder/driver, Tony Henderson, in his strong Scottish accent. "You'll never digest it before the gig. It's too heavy." I have to mention at this point that Dave and Tony didn't really hit it off as people. Nothing serious, but just didn't really get on. "Listen, Tony, just leave it out. I'll eat what I want, ok?" answered Dave. Tony just threw up his hands. "Well, don't tell me I didn't warn you."

I remember another two moments when Tony would wind Dave up. At one of our points on the tour, Tony had gone to check out the local shops He came back to the hotel and knocked on our door. (Dave and myself shared most of the hotel rooms.) He walked in to show us what he had bought, and one of the items was a huge bull whip. "Look at this, lads." As soon as I saw it, I knew what would happen and I quickly ran into the bathroom, leaving the door a few inches open. Tony started cracking the whip and the room being so small, just missed whipping Dave at the side of his face. "For fuck's sake, Tony, be fucking careful, will you?" "Ah, come on Dave, what's wrong with you? I know how to handle a bull whip," said Tony, and cracked it a few more times. Then, rolling it up, told Dave not to worry so much. But I could see Dave was not a happy man.

The other time was in some hotel room and Dave and myself were sitting down with these two pretty young ladies. A knock on our door and it was Tony. He came in to tell us something about the gig or whatever, saw the two girls and probably wanted to show off a bit. Tony wasn't that tall, but he was very strong, and at one point I think he had done a bit of wrestling. "Come here, Dave, and I'll throw you over my back." and he started walking towards Dave. "No, Tony, don't! You'll rip my jacket," said Dave. But Tony, smiling at the two girls, made a grab for Dave who was sitting on one of the beds, and picked him up. "Come on, Dave, it won't hurt, you'll land on the bed," and quick as a flash, grabbed Dave and threw him over his shoulder onto the bed. There was this loud ripping sound as Dave's leather jacket separated in two pieces right up the back. "I told you that would happen, you fuckin' idiot!" Dave said, getting up from the bed and taking off the remains of his jacket. "I'm really sorry, Dave, let's look at your jacket. Look, it's only ripped at the seam, that can be easily mended." "Listen, Tony, just leave me alone. I've had enough. Please just stay out of my way, alright?" Tony just looked at everyone, shrugged his shoulders and left the room.

At one point on the tour, when we were in Houston, Texas, our manager booked a few sessions at Sugar Hill Studios for us to record some tracks for our second album, *Blowin'*. We met the engineers and set up for recording, and they told us *The Big Bopper* had recorded *Chantilly Lace* here, which was a big hit in the 60s. I, for one, was never happy with my playing on the songs in Noel's band. I felt I was sort of waiting all the time for the band to change direction and start to really play. It always felt like a cabaret rock band to me. But, looking back, apart from the music, I had some great times and saw a lot of the States, which I had missed out on with Thin Lizzy.

Our tour of America was now coming to an end and, after a day or two of hanging around, we drove to the airport and had our last drink together in the airport bar, and boarded the plane. I'll never forget landing at Dublin Airport. It was a grey sky and grey buildings that greeted me as I looked out of my window. I was wearing this real flashy shirt and cowboy boots as I left the plane, and it now felt completely out of place. And as the bus drove through Dublin city centre towards Rathmines, I just got more and more depressed. How am I going to live here? I thought, as I hadn't fully realised the effect America had had on me.

CHAPTER 18

I opened the front door of the basement flat, put my case down and made myself a cup of tea. The flat was empty and I felt really exhausted. I just lay down on the bed and had a bit of a sleep. I must have slept for a few hours and slowly woke up to the flat door opening and Linda walking in. It felt like we were strangers for a while, as I had been away for nearly 11 weeks. We had a long cuddle and went out for a meal, and while we were eating, Linda told me she was really pissed off working at the travel agency. She really wanted to do her own thing and be self-employed. She had met this girl called Betty and they got on really well and wanted to open a clothes shop in the Dandelion Green Market, which faced St Stephen's Green Park. I said she should definitely give it a go and, next day, we went to look at the shop premises, which were pretty small but in a great location, being in a long narrow alleyway with shops on either side. Betty had some money to start them off and soon the shop was filled with colourful clothes, hats, shawls, etc, and Linda was much happier being her own boss.

Since I had come back from America, I hadn't played any gigs. I'd been back about six weeks and was getting a bit worried about what to do and the lack of money. But one of the things about being in the music business is you never know what's going to happen from day to day. I got a real surprise when I got a phone call from the Noel Redding Band management. "Eric, this is Bill, how are you? Listen, do you know the bass player Tim Bogart?" (Tim Bogart was the bass player from the rock trio Beck, Bogart and Appice, the guy who was hoovering his bass cabinets earlier on in the book.) I told him of course I did. "Well, he's in London at the moment, the thing he was trying didn't work out and he's here for another few days. If I send you a ticket and book you into a hotel, do you fancy coming over to have a jam with him?" In my head, I was already on the plane.

I was picked up at Heathrow Airport and taken to a small rehearsal room somewhere in central London. When I arrived, I walked in and saw this guy setting up a kit of drums. He saw me and walked over. "Oh, hello mate, I'm Mickey Waller." My God, I thought, this is getting better and better. Mickey Waller was the drummer who had played on the classic Jeff Beck Group album, *Truth*. "I'm really pleased to meet you, Mickey. I'm Eric Bell." As he went back to setting up his kit, I told him that so many drummers in Dublin really loved his playing on the Truth album, trying to work out his parts. "Oh, thanks mate, that's really nice." Then Tim Bogart walked in. Dressed in denim and wearing the trademark glasses. He said "Hi" in a very strong American accent. There were various amps about the room and we plugged in and fiddled about for a while, tuning up and trying to get a sound. Mickey's drum kit was set up and we started jamming around some riff Tim had started playing. I couldn't believe the volume he played. It was really loud and he was using a type of fuzz box on the bass, which was giving it a sort of growling sound. We played various shuffles and slow blues and a few soul tunes and that was that. As we were packing up, Mickey came over and said that myself and Tim should definitely get something together, but at the moment he couldn't be a part of it as he was with a band. He had just come down to help out with the jam.

Tim and myself walked to Wardour Street, where the Noel Redding Band office was, and we had a bit of a meeting with Bill. Then, Tim asked me was I free to go back with him to his hotel to listen to some songs he had written? At one point, he asked me about living in America. But, in his hotel room, when he played the tape of his songs, I thought it was the wrong tape he was playing to me. Here we go again, I thought. The songs were more like ballads, quiet, soft music. It was the same with Noel. Both Noel and Tim had worked with two of the best guitar players on the planet. Yet, when forming their own bands, they steered clear of that type of music. Maybe they just felt burnt out with so much guitar playing and wanted something different? I think Tim sort of picked up that I didn't really understand his new direction in music, because the next day I found out he was on his way back to the States. I phoned Bill's office but no reply, so I checked out of my hotel and got the tube to Heathrow. Arriving at the airport, I went up to the ticket desk and got the shock of my life. "I'm sorry, sir, but this is just a single ticket, they won't let you on the plane with this. Do you want to purchase a new ticket?" I just took the ticket I had handed her and kept looking at it.

Oh for fuck's sake. I had a bit of money with me, but not enough to buy another single ticket back to Dublin. I went to the nearest phone and called Bill at the office again. A lady's voice. "Yes, how can I help you?" I explained who I was and that Bill had only sent me a single ticket, and could he please organise it so I could get home? She really didn't want to know and told me Bill was out of the office and she didn't know where he was or when he would be back (this was before we had all mobile phones). I slammed the phone down and went for a coffee to think what to do. I had a little phone book with me and looked through it. As I looked through the names, I got a feeling to call John Brady, a really good bass player that I knew a little. I went to the phone and got through to John and explained what had happened. He asked me would I like him to wire me the money for my ticket? Man, what a gentleman! I eventually got back to Dublin and home to my flat. Sometimes, you can't help hating the music business, the amount of shit that goes on and the many disappointments that you have to survive.

Linda and I went out for a drink and a serious talk about what I was going to do with myself. I knew I had to do something soon that would bring in some money. "Why don't you go and see Brush Shiels?" Linda said. "He seems to be working all the time. I see posters and ads in the paper showing where he's playing." I said that Brush already had a guitarist, but she started me thinking about calling up to see Brush. I had his phone number and gave him a call and, an hour or so later, I was talking to him. He was still in bed, having played the night before, and after he shouted down to his wife Mar for two cups of tea, asked me what was going on. I told him all about the Tim Bogart thing and did he know any band that needed a guitar player? He said he would put the word out and let me know as soon as he heard anything. At this point I just said, "Listen, Brush, can you give me a job? I'll even be a roadie. I don't know what to do. I really need to make some money." I then found out the way he ran his band, which was basically helping out of work musicians. He kept a steady bass player, Gentleman John Brady, who had wired me the money to Heathrow to help me get home, and sometimes he would change the drummer and lead guitarist. He would get in touch with players who were good but not working a lot, and offer them a gig for six months. They could then save up their weekly wage and, after the six months was up, leave the band with a bit of money to live on for a while.

The guitarist he had at the moment had only been in the band a few months, but Brush said he would still pay him his wages and take me on as guitarist. Within a few days, I was travelling in the van with Brush and his band, Skid Row. The guitarist stayed for a few days while I picked up the songs they were playing. I couldn't believe the change in Brush and his new approach to playing music. I remembered the last gig the Bell Brush Band had played, and Brush saying he was going to go commercial, just to earn some money for a change. He was an excellent bass player, but had stopped playing the bass and was out the front now as lead singer, dressed up in very colourful clothes and putting on a great show. The music was very popular songs that everybody knew – Stones, Beatles, Rod Stewart, Creedence Clearwater and some soul music like *Land Of A 1000 Dances* and *River Deep Mountain High*. His was one of the first groups in Ireland to play in the famed Irish Ballrooms, where only Irish showbands were allowed to play a few years previous. In fact, it felt very much like The Dreams Showband all over again, as we were playing four or five nights a week. In the van, off to the gig, get something to eat, play the gig, pack up, drive home, into bed, up again, back in the van and so on. I was earning good money for a change, and this really helped my relationship with Linda, though we really didn't see much of each other now.

Skid Row had a resident gig every Thursday in The Baggott Inn in Baggot Street in Dublin, and it was always stuffed to the rafters. Playing gigs in the country could be a bit hairy sometimes, as there was no alcohol sold in the dancehall, so the men would get tanked up before paying in and be in a right state entering the hall. One night, as we were on stage at one of these gigs, playing to a packed hall, I felt a stab of pain at the top of my head. It felt like being stung by a wasp. I put my hand up and rubbed my head. I looked at my fingers and they were covered in blood. Then, something hit my guitar. I saw a few coins laying on the stage Some guys had been flicking coins up at the band. I started to get real nervous and took my guitar off to go into the dressing room behind the stage. You could easily lose an eye with this going on. Brush came over to me but the rest of the band were still playing. "Don't leave the stage, Eric. I'll get it sorted out." There would always be a few bouncers in the hall at these gigs in case a fight broke out between the guys that were drunk. So, Brush somehow signalled to one of them and, a few moments later, they spotted the guys who were flicking the coins and they were grabbed and roughly taken out of the hall – and probably got the shit kicked out of them.

The strangest thing that happened while I was with Skid Row was one night, when we were playing somewhere in Donegal. Towards the end of the night, this small crowd of people came into the hall. They came up to the front of the stage and started this weird dancing, wearing hippie type clothes. After we'd finished playing, and as I was packing up my equipment, I saw Brush talking to the hippies. Brush told us that they were called The Screamers and they lived on Innisfree, a sort of island off the coast of Donegal. They asked him if the band would like to stay overnight, as they had a huge house with plenty of room. I can't remember how we got there, but soon we were on this small island and looming in front of us was the house. The lady who seemed to be the leader of The Screamers told us it was called Atlantis. She showed us around and the place looked really old, with a huge kitchen that had a massive black cooking range. She led us through the house and we came to a door with a small glass window. She told us this was where the screaming was done. Then, she opened the door and we saw the floor was completely covered in mattresses, blankets and pillows. She explained that what they did was based on Primal Scream Therapy. To me, it sounded like a good idea. If you were stressed or uptight, it would be a great way to let it all out without worrying about what other people thought. We then went back to the kitchen for tea and homemade bread and, after a while, we were shown to our bedrooms. I was to sleep in a single room, and the way it looked I will never forget. Someone had painted the four walls from floor to ceiling so that it looked just like a forest. It did look very real. And the ceiling was painted with overhanging branches and treetops. It took me a while to get to sleep, and luckily, I never heard any screaming.

On the Thursday night, where we had our resident gig at the Baggott Inn, Brush asked me if I fancy a coffee in one of the many shops in and around Baggott Street? We sat down with our coffee and I had a feeling this was going to be a serious talk. "Well, Eric, you've been with the band now for about seven months or so. I think it would be a good idea to start thinking about forming your own band. I should be able to help you out with finding musicians. All you need is a bass player and drummer." "But, Brush," I said. "I haven't a clue about running a band and finding transport and getting gigs." But all he said was, not to worry, as he wanted to help out some other guitarist who needed money. "You stay in the band for another month, Eric, then I'll have to let you go. But we'll keep in touch and you can let me know how you're getting on."

After the month was up, I was dropped home to my flat after my last gig with Skid Row. The driver opened the back door of the van and took out my amplifier and guitar. It was all so final. Everyone then shouted their goodbyes to me and the van drove off into the night.

CHAPTER 19

I had saved quite a bit of money from all the playing, so at least that would keep the wolf away for a while, but now I needed to do some serious thinking about how to form my own band. So, I started going into Dublin city centre and hanging around Grafton Street. Dublin was small enough to see the same people every day, and soon I started to meet lots of musos and, eventually, found a drummer, bass player and keyboard player. I wanted to try out keyboards for a while as I was writing a few songs that might not have suited a three-piece lineup. So, we started rehearsing and, after a few weeks, I managed to get a few gigs, one being in Moran's Hotel. There was always a really good crowd that turned up at Moran's and we seemed to go down really well. The guys in the band were ok players, but to me they were more posers than real musicians. We did a few more gigs in and around Dublin, then Linda said she was going to London for a week or so for a break and to see her parents. I thought I fancied a while in London myself.

When we got there, I went into town and called into Thin Lizzy's office on Dean Street. I saw Chris Morrison, one of the managers, and we sat and talked about this and that. I told him I had this great band back in Dublin, and did he think I could get a few gigs in London? He asked me if I was free, and if so, he would introduce me to a great agency called Asgard, who had their offices in Oxford Street. So, a ten minute walk took us to Asgard, and Chris introduced me to Paul Charles, one of the guys that ran the agency. Paul was from Belfast (small world) and asked me would I and my band be up for playing a few gigs in London, say in one month's time? And that was that.

A week or so later, Linda and myself were back in Dublin and I couldn't wait to tell the news to the band, but I held off until I got some definite word from Asgard. The definite word arrived about ten days later in the form of a large envelope, which held contracts for five gigs in London. Amazing! The next day, we were rehearsing and I waited until the end of the rehearsal and then took out the contracts and told them we had five definite gigs in London in two weeks' time. They thought I was joking, and then the truth sank in. "Fuckin' hell, Eric, we better start rehearsing a bit more!" said Paul, the keyboard player.

Linda really helped me organise everything, from the tickets for the ferry over to England and back, to a house we could rent for a week, which would be so much cheaper than staying in a hotel. Time passed, and soon we were on the ferry heading to England. It was after a very long drive around the streets of London, that we found the house we would be staying at. It was a nice clean place with lots of room and we started making ourselves at home.

It felt strange doing a sound check at our first gig, which might have been at The Hope and Anchor. I felt it was so much more professional at that time in England, and people took the running of gigs much more seriously than back in Ireland. We played that night to a crowd who didn't know what to expect and we went down alright, but the band was very nervous. Another gig we played was at Dingwall's, and this gig would turn the tables on me. There was a good crowd that night, but the band were still very nervous. The rest of the gigs I can't remember, and around five days later, we were making our way to the ferry and back to Dublin. On the way, we stopped at one of the services for a break and something to eat. A few of the guys went to the area that sold papers and mags and bought a few of the music papers. I think it was *Melody Maker* that had a review of the gig we had played at Dingwall's. The band crowded around as Dave the drummer read the review, and then they handed me the paper. I could tell by their faces that something was wrong. "Fuck that!" they said, one after the other. It basically said that 'The Eric Bell Band was pretty average and couldn't keep with Bell's musical imagination'.

The attitude of the band towards me had changed. I got the impression they thought I had written the review myself. Lots of funny things have happened to me as a guitarist, but I think this is one of the funniest. Back in Dublin, I made my way to the rehearsal that we had arranged for the following week and arrived at the drummer's house, rang the bell and walked in the front room. The rest of the band were sitting around and I nodded to them, but nobody looked me in the eye. "Ok, what songs do you want to run over?" I said. Then they started to tell me that they had found themselves another guitarist and were changing the direction of the band. This was a new one on me. I was fired from my own band. There was an embarrassed silence as I picked up my guitar, mumbled something and left. Walking down the street to the bus stop, I couldn't help laughing to myself. It was obviously the review from Dingwall's that they couldn't face, and this was how they reacted. Wait till I tell Linda and my friends this one. I was fired from my OWN band!

I got a bit of a surprise a few weeks later, when I received another large envelope in the post. It was from Asgard with contracts for another seven gigs. Bollocks! Another seven gigs in England and no band. I got in touch and told them the news and they didn't seem in the least bit worried. "Just come over yourself. I know some bass players and drummers. All you need is a three-piece band, and we can get you some work." A few weeks later, and this time I was flying over. I had arranged to stay in Linda's parents' house. As soon as I settled there, I got the tube to Oxford Street and went to talk to Paul at Asgard. He told me he had found a bass player and drummer for me and they were both Irish. A few days later, the three of us met up at a rehearsal room in central London. We ran over a few things, and they were good enough to play basic blues and rock, but I couldn't stand their attitudes. Every time I would make a suggestion about some part of a song, they would just look at me in a pissed off way, and then try the suggestion with a very half-hearted attitude. Looking back now, I should have gotten rid of them, but the gigs were close and there was no time to work anyone else in.

We played the gigs, which were mainly universities, and went down alright, but there was no togetherness between us and my playing sounded tense. I couldn't wait to try other players, but found out a lot of them were real bread heads and wanted fucking retainers, and one guy even wanted me to pay his insurance stamps. But at least I had a good agent working for me, and gigwise everything looked great. Putting the word around, I met some more bass players and drummers, and it was easier than I thought to meet the right guys, as I could offer them steady work. I got rid of the two Irish guys and started rehearsing with another bass and drums, and soon we were out gigging again.

It had now come to the point that I felt I wanted to move out of Linda's parents house, as I didn't really get on with her father. I got a room in Willesden, though why I moved there, I'll never know. The room was very cheap and the land lady showed me I could get free electricity by putting a coin in the meter and then getting the same coin back again, as the lock was broken. What she didn't tell me was the electric shock you could receive if you touched a certain part at the back of the meter. I found this out myself one night when I was feeling for the coin. This incredible sensation shook straight up my arm and threw me right across the room. I didn't touch the meter for quite a while after that.

Because I now had some steady work coming in, Linda told me she was thinking of coming over to London for a while, as Betty, her partner in the clothes shop, could keep the shop going by herself. They had made some sort of a deal that she could send Linda some of the profits every few weeks. At this point, we hadn't that many possessions, and what we had, Linda had packed in her car and got the ferry over to England. She had also rented our flat in Rathmines to a friend that worked in the travel agency she had worked for, so if we ever needed to come back to Dublin, we could get the flat back. Linda stayed at her parents' place, as the room I had was crummy to say the least. She ended up working for her father, who had his own business, and things went on reasonably smoothly for a while.

We decided – or rather Linda did – to get our own place to live, and ended up in a comfortable flat in Acton. But, lately, I had noticed that the amount of gigs I was playing was dropping from four or five a week down to two. I called into Asgard one day to pay them their commission, and asked what was happening about the gigs situation. I was told that to keep the gigs coming in, I would have to get myself a deal with a record company. I took round a tape of some songs to the various companies, but nobody was interested, as they all wanted me to form another Thin Lizzy.

So, as the gigs went down to one a week, and then stopped coming in all together, I decided to put an ad in *Melody Maker* about giving guitar lessons. As soon as the guys heard it was someone that had been with Thin Lizzy, I got about 40 phone calls asking for lessons. Most of them only wanted to learn a few things, and I ended up giving seven lessons a week to regulars. Giving lessons can really do your head in as you have to get the student to repeat the same thing over and over until it starts sinking in and then staying. And then the change started again as, one by one, they said they had learned more than enough, and needed to digest it for a while, and ended their lessons. So, here I was, with no money coming in, and Linda was starting to hate her job working for her dad as there were lots of arguments starting to happen.

Linda's brother Sam worked down at Camden Town Market. He had an open air stall and, with his girlfriend Ann, sold second hand clothes at the weekends. They also had a small clothes shop, which they sold from during the rest of the week. One night after dinner, Linda said she wanted to have a talk. She brought out a writing pad and then showed me what she'd written. "Eric, I've been working out how much money I have earned in the past two years, and how much you have earned. You're going to have to do something about this. I seem to be paying most of the bills and it's starting to worry me." I got very depressed about it all, and she said would I try and work at selling clothes at Camden Market to help out for a while? At this point I didn't really care anymore and said I might as well give it a go. Linda knew some contacts that sold second hand clothes and we ended up in Brighton, where two gay guys had a warehouse full of clothes, handbags, scarves, etc. We spent an hour or two looking at the stuff and left with about six large black plastic bags.

The market was open on Saturday and Sunday, and that Saturday, I was dropped off there around 9am. Being a musician, my body clock was different from a lot of other people. I was used to going to bed around 2 or 3am after a gig, and getting up around 10:30am or so. Now, I was standing at this stall with brush poles hanging from a tin roof and clothes on coat hangers hanging from the poles. There were stalls everywhere, selling clothes, belts, overcoats, records, pipes, cigarette papers, ornaments and all types of food. The place would be crowded and, I must say, had a great atmosphere. But, when the weather changed, it was pretty unbearable. I remember standing there on a winter's day with two pullovers under a huge overcoat, scarf, hat, gloves, moon boots and a pair of thick track bottoms. Anything I sold, I jotted it down in a little notebook, but sometimes, I couldn't feel the pen and kept dropping it as my fingers were so cold. The market closed around 6pm, and by that time, I just wanted to crawl somewhere and die. I thought I was a fuckin' guitar player?

Weeks passed and I got to know some of the stall holders and they were all really nice people. Linda knew this married couple and, one weekend, they invited us over to their place. Over dinner, the guy, Brian, kept talking to me about the importance of getting quality clothes to sell and making sure they were washed and ironed and all that stuff. Then, after the dinner, he showed me upstairs to a small room where he had his second hand clothes all hanging up. "See, Eric, this is what you want. All the shirts are washed and ironed, with little tags to show the sizes and really good wooden coat hangers. You should start to take it more seriously." I just looked at him. God Almighty, let me out of here, I thought.

As luck would have it, one bitterly cold Sunday afternoon around 6pm, Linda called for me at the market to take me home. She asked me how much I had made – it was not a lot of money – and she started moaning about it. "Listen, Linda, our clothes are so crap, I can hardly give it away." And it was true. All around us were stalls that were selling decent stuff, the people selling it were serious at what they did, whereas we just wanted to make quick money. It wasn't working, and we drove home in silence. I ran a hot bath, as my whole body was numb with coldness, and just lay there thawing out, wondering what to do. Maybe guitar lessons again?

A few days later, the phone rang. I picked it up. "Could I speak to Eric Bell?" "Speaking," I replied. "Do these names mean anything to you, Eric? Dick Heckstall-Smith, Victor Brox, Keef Hartley, Keith Tillman..?" Of course they did. Most of the names had played with the English 'Godfather of the Blues', John Mayall. They were my heroes. "Well, Eric," the voice continued, "the guitar player we have isn't working out and we'll be going on tour in Europe in a few weeks. Do you fancy coming down for a jam?" I was there already! He gave me the address and asked if I could show up around 2pm the next day. So, next day, I arrived at what looked like a builder's yard. It turned out to be a sort of carpenter's workshop, with planks of all sizes, machines and a strong smell of sawdust. It turned out to be Keef Hartley's place, who had been one of John Mayall's drummers. I went out to the car, got my guitar and amp and set up in the middle of the workshop.

After we all said hello, we started a loose jam around a slow blues. I couldn't believe the sound. Up to now, I had been playing with three-piece bands, apart from in the Irish showband scene. These guys were players – there were drums, bass guitar, a girl singer who played sax, another sax player, a guy who sang and played trumpet, a harmonica player and a guy on keyboards. We played for another hour or so (I could have played with this lot all day). They all seemed happy with my playing and singing, and we went out to a local cafe for a talk. As we were walking to the cafe, Keith the bass player told me to watch Dick Heckstall-Smith, the famous saxophone player. "He might walk out without paying, so watch it, Eric," he laughed. Sure enough, as I was the last to pay my bill, the girl on the till told me how much I owed. It was about three times what I had expected. I told her she must be making a mistake. "No, one of your lot left without paying. You'll have to pay for him, you can sort it out later." This was my first experience with the band, Mainsqueeze.

Around this time in England, punk music was very popular, which was why a blues band like Mainsqueeze would play and tour in Europe. I told Linda I was now playing music again and would be going off to Europe in a couple of weeks. She seemed happy for me, as my heart wasn't into selling clothes at a market. The day we left for Europe, this enormous Mercedes van stopped outside my flat. Saying my goodbyes to Linda, I packed my amp, guitar and suitcase in the back of the van, and we set off towards the ferry to Sweden. The Mercedes was very old and as cold as a fridge, which I thought in a funny way would help us to play the Blues with a feeling.

Playing in Europe was really enjoyable as the audiences are very into their music, especially blues and jazz. I noticed this when I took a stroll around one of the cities we played. In the front window of a record shop, there would be the current pop bands' albums on show alongside Howlin' Wolf, Muddy Waters and Buddy Guy. A lot of the gigs we played were in really long halls, one or two in bars, and some of them stayed open until three in the morning.

On one of the tours in Sweden, we got a phone call from the agent who had arranged a ten-day tour for us. She said she would meet us the next day at a cafe in a town near her office. So, we met up and she told us a few gigs had been cancelled, but she would try and fill the gaps. Outside, she asked us if we would follow her to our hotel? I got in her car and we drove off with the Mercedes following behind. We seemed to be driving away from the town and into the country. Then, she turned right and we were driving through the start of a forest. "Is this a shortcut to the hotel?" I asked, starting to feel what was about to happen. "No," the agent replied. "This is where you are staying," She stopped the car and in front of us was a large wooden hut. "Oh, my God," I thought. "Wait till the band sees this." She saw my face drop and asked if there was anything wrong. By this time, the band had pulled up behind us. One by one they got out. "Is this a fucking joke?" someone said. I think by now the agent had got the message and wanted to leave as quickly as possible. "Don't worry, I'll be in touch," and drove off. Welcome to the big time!

We went into the hut and it was really primitive. I spotted a small room with a bed. Great, at least I'll have a room to myself. Then I thought how difficult it would be for Diana Wood, one of the singers and sax players, in a room with six guys. "Hey, Diana, why don't you have this room?" She looked very pleased and I was glad that I had acted like a gentleman. That night, there was no gig to play, so we drove to the nearest town to get something to eat, then back to the hut. We sat around talking, wondering what we had got ourselves into. Then Keef, the drummer, brought out this huge bottle of duty free whiskey. At this point in time, only about three of us were into having a drink. We all sat around the table in the middle of the room and Keef poured out a few glasses of the whiskey.

John, the harmonica player, and Victor, the singer who also played trumpet, had the whiskey. I can't remember how it happened, but Keef started saying how he could drink anyone under the table. So, John took up the challenge and Keef poured out a large measure for each of them. I noticed that Keef had filled up his own glass half full of water, which he had slyly done under the table while he was talking. About 20 minutes later, after another large glass of the whiskey, John started slurring his words and staggering around the room... and then passed out on one of the beds.

Next day, the agent arrived and told us we had a gig that night, followed by another four in a row. We all looked a lot happier as, apart from playing, we would be staying in proper hotels instead of the effing hut. Making our way to gig number four, we had to stop at a border where lots of huge lorries were standing idle, and their drivers standing smoking, talking to each other. It seemed there was some sort of a strike problem and the border checkpoint wasn't letting anyone through. We just sat in the van, and it got colder and colder, and I started getting very restless. I noticed a large wooden building and found out it was a restaurant of some sort for truck drivers. One thing about being in a band the size of Mainsqueeze was the lack of money. Eight people in the band and a driver and a huge fuckin' Mercedes that guzzled most of our wages. I asked John, who handled the money, for some cash to get something to eat. But, as I guessed, he told me we needed the money for petrol and couldn't give me anything at the moment. That was it. I stood up, climbed out of the van and slammed the sliding door. It was freezing outside, just a little bit colder than in the van. I checked all my pockets and, to my surprise, found a crumpled ten pound note right at the bottom of my jeans pocket. Brilliant, I thought, let's hope they take Sterling.

I walked up to the restaurant and pushed open the door. Inside, it was steamy,and warm and looked just like a film set. There were two huge wooden tables and about 40 drivers sitting on either side, smoking, drinking coffee and eating. I made my way to a woman standing by a till and asked her would she take an English ten pound note? She looked at me and smiled, took my money and pointed to one of the huge tables. Maybe you just help yourself, I thought, and walked to the table and sat down. There were enormous pots filled with what looked like stew and large pieces of bread. So, I watched what the drivers did and copied them. It was one of the most welcoming meals I ever had and, after two bowls and the bread, I started to thaw out. What was also great was the drivers didn't take a blind bit of notice of me, and I felt really at ease. I noticed some of the band were standing up at the till and saw me sitting at the table and came over. "Good idea, Eric," said Dick, and soon he was sitting at the table with me, digging into the stew and bread. A few of the others joined us and I noticed most of the drivers and truckers getting up and talking as they made their way outside. Then, John and Keith came in and told us that it looked as if the trouble was over and they were now letting the lorries through. After everyone had some coffee, we made our way back to the van and started our journey to the gig.

Some of the things that happened on the road with Mainsqueeze... we were playing somewhere in Yugoslavia and we were booked into a really nice hotel for a change. Myself and Dick Heckstall-Smith (also known as Thick Oxtail Soup) were sharing a room. It was a lovely room with deep white carpets on the floor and a beautiful bathroom. I was really looking forward to a long hot shower and, about 40 minutes later, came out of the bathroom and couldn't see anything. The bedroom was filled with thick, grey smoke. I thought it might be the steam from the bathroom and groped my way slowly around the room, found a window and opened it. As the smoke started to clear, I saw Dick sitting on the floor with a small Primus stove, on top of which sat a small saucepan with six eggs boiling away. If the flames of the stove had touched the white carpet, I don't know what would have happened. Or how much it would have cost us. "For fuck's sake, Dick, what are you doing?" I said. "Oh, hello, Eric, have you seen the prices on the menu here? There's no way I'm paying that money. I went out for a walk and spotted a supermarket and bought six eggs, a loaf of bread and some cheese. I'm going to make some sandwiches!"

Another time, we were playing in Germany, and we stopped at a small garage for petrol, coffee and the toilet. We were all in the small shop looking around, and then I went outside to use the toilet. The men's and women's toilets each had a black silhouette of a man and woman on the doors and I saw Dick peeling the little black figure of the woman off the door. I walked back to the van, followed by Dick, who then stuck the little figure on the side of the white van, and we sat and waited for the rest of the band. With everyone on board, we were getting ready to set off when this little old lady came walking towards us, waving her arms and shouting something in German. We opened the door and she peered in. "You must pay me three marks for the figure off the ladies' toilet!" Everyone looked around at Dick, who was hiding behind a huge newspaper. He pretended as if nothing was happening, but the old lady kept on and on about wanting three marks. "Ah, come on, Dick, pay her for the figure." And, knowing the game was up, Dick came out from behind his paper and, looking very embarrassed, paid up, and off we went.

Another one from Germany, although not so funny this time. We were booked to play a blues club in Munich and had a day off before the gig. Keith, the bass player, Dick and myself were all interested in the history of World War II, so we decided to drive to Dachau concentration camp. I'll never forget that day. We arrived there after a short drive from Munich and it was quite a sunny day, but as we parked the van and got out to walk across the courtyard, there was a definite chill in the air. It really felt cold. The huge courtyard had just the remains of where the prisoners' huts once stood, with just the outline of them on the ground. But they had left one hut standing for people to see what the conditions used to be like. We went in and the hut had four bunk beds. The wood looked very thin and soft, like wood from orange crates, and each bed was covered with straw. On one of the walls was a notice that read: 'If one piece of straw is found on the floor, there will be severe punishment carried out.'

We walked across the rest of the courtyard and came to a small bridge that looked very pretty, with small shrubs and flowers around it. We crossed the bridge and noticed a few large grey buildings standing nearby. One of them was the gas chamber. It looked just like a huge shower room – in fact, it reminded me of the shower room they had in the old public swimming pool I used to go to as a kid in Belfast. As I stood there, I thought how strange time and place really is. I'm standing in the very spot, free to go or stay as I pleased, where years ago, people were ordered about and punished and gassed. We walked over to the other building, and this turned out to be where the ovens were to burn the bodies. It just looked like an old Italian restaurant where they make pizzas – old brickwork surrounding small iron doors, which opened into the ovens. That day will stick in my mind forever.

None of us knew it, but Mainsqueeze was slowly grinding to a halt. The last gig we played in Germany, we had gone down a storm with the audience. We waited in the dressing room to walk out again for an encore but, as we were getting ready to make our appearance, we heard a voice say, "Forget about it, I'm not going on." It was our drummer, Keef Hartley. We looked at him in amazement. "What do you mean? The audience are going apeshit!" "Don't care, I'm not interested. I'm leaving the band. I've had enough. There's no fucking money!"

CHAPTER 20

About three days later, we were back in London and, a week later, I was back at Camden Market, freezing my bollocks off, trying to sell crummy second hand clothes again. Things just carried on like this for a month or so until, one Saturday morning, I heard someone call my name. I looked around and it was Dave 'Munch' Moore, the keyboard player from Mainsqueeze. "Listen, Eric, Mainsqueeze is getting back together and there's a few gigs lined up. Are you interested?" I was interested – interested in getting the fuck out of this market.

So, we started rehearsals again, and the first gig was in Battersea Town Hall. There was a drummer turning up that we had to try out before the gig. He was a huge black guy called Stretch, with a huge beard, glasses and a build like Arnie. We said our hellos and myself and Keith Tillman, the bass player, walked out on stage to run over a few things with Stretch. We started a slow blues to jam around, but half way through, we stopped. "Ah, Stretch, I think there's something a bit off, mate," said Keith. It was like he was playing a 13 bar blues instead of the usual 12 bar version, so when it came to the end of the 12 bar measure, Stretch would play an extra bar. This happened on a blues shuffle as well. But, as the rest of the band came out, we eventually ironed things out and he turned out to be a great drummer. This was around 4pm, and we were due to play around 9pm that evening. So, we all split up and went our various ways to get something to eat, etc.

Back in the dressing room, about an hour before showtime, these two guys knocked on the door and walked in. They went over to where Keith and Dick were standing. "Hello, guys, I'm just wondering if this young man could get up for a few songs with you tonight?" one of them said. We all looked over at the young man, curly hair nearly down to his shoulders. "Hi," he said. "I'm Jeremy Spencer." We all looked at one another and talked among ourselves. "Do you think he's the real Jeremy Spencer? We didn't know whether this guy was the real thing or some nutter. He did get up to play that night, but it was nothing special. To this day, I don't know if it was him or not. If I remember correctly, I think there was some mention of it all in a local newspaper, and I think the guy turned out to be an imposter.

Our management had at last woken up and told us the amazing news that we were to play six nights in a row at Ronnie Scott's Jazz club, a very famous venue right in the middle of Soho in central London. Wow! None of us could believe it .And, we were told that the last gig was going to be recorded live. The five nights we played before the recording were all great gigs and a good crowd turned up for each night. On the day of the recording, John O'Leary, the harp player, told us he was going out for a while to buy some new harmonicas in the nearby music shops. As the rest of the band were setting up for a sound check, bass player, Keith Tillman, asked us all if he could have a word with us. "Listen, John is out buying a few new harps for tonight's recording. Let's have a laugh!" And he said, when John comes back and we try a few songs out, let's play everything a semitone down from what it's supposed to be." About a half hour later, John turned up with five new harmonicas. So, we started the first song, and after a minute or so, John stopped playing. "Hey, is something out of tune?" We all looked at each other. "John, let's try another song in a different key," said Keith, trying his best not to laugh. So, John got out another harp and we started into another song. Yeah, the harp sounded awful. "I don't fucking understand this, I just bought these. They're brand new!" We tried one more song, and each time everyone in the band was still playing a semi-tone flat. "Fuck it!" said John and walked off the stage and into the dressing room. As far as I thought, the joke was over, and we had finished the sound check anyway. I made my way to the dressing room and walked in to see John pacing nervously up and down. "Eric, I don't know why all of the harps sounded out of tune, they are all new." I felt sorry for him, as we all were feeling a bit wired up about being recorded live. So I told him we were all playing a half-tone down, just for a laugh. "I bet it's Keith behind all this, isn't it? Fuck it, as if I'm not nervous enough." But later that night, I thought the band played a great set,

The album, *Mainsqueeze Live at Ronnie Scott's,* was out in SOME shops. But, the management and record company couldn't give it away, as punk music was the whole scene in London at this moment in time.

Another memorable night... Mainsqueeze were booked to play at The Embassy Club, another gig near central London. It looked very plush, with one-arm bandits and a few celebrities swaying about the place. We went on and played and seemed to go down very well. When I made my way to the dressing room, there was only Keith and Dick there. "Is all the money there, Dick?" Keith asked. "No," Dick answered. "It's £45 short. Would you mind asking the guy who paid you to come into the dressing room, please?"

answered Keith. A few minutes later, Dick walked in followed by the guy who had paid us our fee. "Oh, hello," said Keith, "I think you've paid us £45 short, mate." "No," said the guy, "that's my commission." "You what? £45 pounds for a fucking phone call? How much is a phone call these days,

Dick?" Keith asked. "I'd say about 75 pence or something like that." On hearing this, Keith searched in his pocket and handed the guy a pound coin ."Right, mate, there's the money for your phone call, now give me the £45." The guy started to look very worried to say the least. "No, it doesn't work like that…" and he started to explain, but Keith was having none of it. "Ok, show me your watch." The guy asked what he meant. "Show me your fucking watch!" Keith said, looming over the poor bloke. I couldn't believe it as the guy took his watch off and handed it to Keith, who took it, looked at it and said, "Cheap rubbish", and then asked the guy to give him the ring he was wearing. He handed Keith the ring. I should say at this point that Keith Tillman was a big guy and reminded me of Oliver Reed a bit. It all got too much for me and I left the changing room. Half an hour later, as I was getting a lift home, the last thing I saw was Dick and Keith standing beside the poor guy's car outside the club, as the guy was searching through his glove compartment.

Our manager called us to meet him in a cafe near his office. "Well, I've got some good news for you. Bo Diddley is in town and is looking for a backing band. He'll be in Dingwall's club tomorrow, and I've spoken to his manager, Marty. So, if you guys can be down there around 2pm, you can try a few songs with Bo and see how you all get on." This piece of news cheered the band up a bit and, the next day, as our roadie started setting up our gear on stage, we all went over to where Bo and Marty were standing. Bo was putting new strings on his famous square guitar. "Wow," I said, "the old Gretsch square guitar!" Bo looked at me through his red tinted glasses. "This ain't no fuckin' Gretsch," he said. "We don't do business anymore. I got this one made for me by another guitar maker." What a good start to meeting Bo Diddley.

Anyway, 20 minutes later, we were ready to try a few of Bo's songs that all had the famous Bo Diddley beat. When Bo started playing the catchy rhythm and doing his dancing, I thought what it must have been like the first time this type of music had been heard around the end of the 50s. We played for quite a while, and Bo seemed very happy with the way Mainsqueeze was backing him. Marty, Bo's manager, called over to us. "Hey, you guys, there's some hamburgers and coffee over here." We all made a beeline for the table and Marty said he would like to have a small meeting with us. "Well, it's like this, guys. Bo seems very happy with the way you play. Now, we're going to be playing Europe, possibly on a three-week tour. Me and Bo work in a certain way." And he explained a few things, which we all agreed on. "And we leave each hotel around 9:30am for the next show." "But, what if the next gig is not too far to travel?" I said, as I really wasn't a morning person.

"Could we not leave later then, and have a few more hours in bed?" Marty looked over at me, chewing on a toothpick that seemed to be permanently in his mouth. "I knew I was going to have trouble with you," he said, then started laughing. "We'll see, Eric, we'll see."

Within a week or so, we all met up and this beautiful 1950s coach was waiting with a driver to take us over to Europe again – but this time with Bo Diddley. Bo was a real gentleman, very young in his outlook, and a great sense of humour. I would sit in the back of the coach with him sometimes, and he would be talking about the early days of rock 'n' roll and Elvis and all the blues guys. (Next time I come back, I'd love to be living around that time in America.) Everything seemed so tasteful. The beautiful cars with their pastel colours, fins, leather seats and enormous front grills, and the Art Deco furniture and the clothes. Where did we go wrong?

The first few gigs we played were packed and, on the first night, as we were waiting to go on, I noticed Bo holding on to this great big wallet. "Hey, Eric," he said, pointing to the wallet. "This sucker (he called a lot of things 'sucker') goes everywhere with me and sits right on top of my amp where I can keep an eye on it. Back in the past, I left it in the dressing room, until one night, coming off the stage and walking into the dressing room, I saw it lying on the floor empty. One of the many lessons you learn on the road." It was great being on stage with Bo, as you didn't know what to expect. He broke a guitar string and would take it off his guitar and walk out to the very edge of the stage and start chanting voodoo spells, while wrapping the string up in knots. Then, he would hold it out for a pretty girl in the audience.

On one of the drives to the next town, we would all be talking away and, somehow, I got on the subject of the Daleks, from the Dr Who programme. There I was, sitting with Bo Diddley, trying my best to explain what a Dalek was. "Where can I buy one of those suckers?" I said if I spotted one – a toy one that is – that I would get one for him. I couldn't believe it! A few nights later, we were playing to about 800 people. Bo walked over to me and said, "Leader, the people are waiting for you to talk to them." From the talk in the coach about the Daleks, Bo had started calling me the Leader. Having played on stages for so long, sometimes you get over stage fright or nerves and can do things spontaneously. Bo just stood there looking at me through his tinted glasses. I walked up to the mike. "Do not move! Do not move! If you move you will be exterminated!" The audience didn't know what was going on, and neither did the band. Bo then walked over to Dick and put his hand down the bell of Dick's saxophone, pretended to pull something out and threw it on the stage. Then, he started grinding his heel on the thing and, at the same time, he scraped the bass string of his guitar with the plectrum, making a rasping sound. You just didn't know what was going to happen next, but it was all clean fun and very entertaining.

One of the gigs we played was somewhere in Yugoslavia, right out in the country. After the gig, we came out to the coach to drive back to our hotel. It was pitch black, as there were no street lights. We all got in and Dave, the keyboard player, was going to drive. He switched on the engine and the headlights and we started off. A few moments later, the coach seemed to go out of control. There was a really loud judder, and the coach came to a stop. "You're not going to believe this, guys, but we're in the middle of a fuckin' river!" Before the headlights went out, we all looked out the front window and saw the grey, black water. We were very lucky that our coach had four steel steps at the door and, as we opened the door, the river was lapping around the third step. The other piece of luck was the agent who had booked us for the gig was with us in the coach. He only spoke a few words of English and he eventually explained that he was going to get help. I'll never forget him taking off his shoes and socks, rolling his trousers up to his knees and walking down the four steps into the river. There was a torch in the coach, and we shone it at the agent, who was now up to his knees in the water. It looked really freezing. He climbed out of the river onto the other bank and disappeared. It must have been about 40 minutes later when we heard the sound of an engine and a small truck with a crane and winch on the back came into view.

The driver got out and attached ropes and a hook to the coach and had us out onto the bank in 20 minutes. We thanked him and paid him some money and away he went. We all got back in the coach, laughing now at the idea of driving into a river. Then, Dave got behind the wheel and we started again on our way to the hotel. But, the brakes in the coach were soaking wet, and we hadn't noticed that we were parked at the top of a steep hill. Dave let the handbrake off and we started rolling backwards down the hill. There was a loud bang and the coach stopped. By now, we were all freaked out, especially Dave. We all stood up and got out with the torch and had a look. Our coach, rolling down the hill, had crashed into a large tree, which was stopping it from rolling down the rest of the hill. "Right," said Dave, "I've had it. No more driving for me tonight." So, another one of the guys got in the driving seat and, very slowly and very carefully, we drove back to our hotel.

There were only a couple more shows to play in England before Bo and Marty flew back to the States. We picked them up at their hotel and made our way to the first gig. Bo had just bought himself a digital keyboard and it was still in its cardboard box. I went down to the back of the coach where Bo always sat, as he examined the keyboard. There was a book of instructions and a few cables and plugs and some stickers. "Hey, Eric, you want a few stickers to put on your guitar?" He gave me the two stickers, which I stuck on my guitar, and to this day they are still there. We finished the last of the gigs, drove back to London and said our goodbyes.

That seemed to be the end now for Mainsqueeze. It was such a good band, but with so many people in it, we never seemed to earn decent money. I still listen to the live album we recorded at Ronnie Scott's. There's such good playing on it, it's a real shame the band had to fold.

CHAPTER 21

I was back in London, wondering what I was going to do. Linda, who was now my wife, was thinking this as well! A few weeks passed, and I got a phone call from Noel Redding. "'Ello, matey, 'ow are ya?" He asked me what I was up to, and said he had a two-week tour in Italy, and would I be interested? Great! The drummer was John Coglan from Status Quo. I think being on the road was becoming a little difficult for Noel around this time. Every morning, when we got in the car, Noel would ask the driver how far it was to the next gig. "About two hours' drive, Noel," the driver would say. In reality, it was probably four hours, but the driver was trying to keep Noel sweet. The hotels were good, we had a room each, and the food and drink were enjoyable as well. But the downside was very hard to handle sometimes. As I said, Noel was finding touring a bit of trouble. He had got to the point that he wouldn't travel on planes with his bass guitar any more. "It's too fucking heavy, carrying it about airports, off and on planes," he would say. So, it had been arranged that he could borrow the support band's bass guitar every night. We mostly had a different band before us at the gigs and Noel seemed so tired that he wouldn't even bother to see if the bass he was using was in tune with my guitar. I found this out at the first gig – it sounded really shit. So, from then on, I would tune the bass Noel was going to play that night. The other thing was, we had to play through different amplifiers each night. And the biggest hurdle I forgot to mention was Noel wouldn't do sound checks any more. So, we would hang about our hotel rooms, get picked up, driven to the gig and straight to the dressing room. I would tune Noel's bass and then I would go backstage with a little torch and see, first of all what side of the stage my amp was set up, then look at the settings on the amp and try to become familiar with them. It was really starting to do my head in, as some of the amps were really shit. We went down OK with most of the audience, but it could have been so much better if we had done sound checks.

air gig. There were about four bands on and we were the last band to play. I plugged into the amp that belonged to the guitarist out of the last band, looked at it and had to call the guitarist over to help me. All the controls were in Italian, and there was a small digital screen at the front and push button controls. If my life had depended on it, I couldn't have worked out how to use it. The guitarist came over, looked at me like I was some sort of cretin, and asked me what I wanted. "Can you get me a clean tone, you know, not too much distortion?" He fiddled about and it was OK but not great. Then he left me to it and jumped down from the stage into the crowd. We were halfway through our third song when, all of a sudden, the power went off and all that was heard was John playing the drums. Five minutes later, the power came back on, but the amp I was using was a modern digital thing and all the settings were now changed. The echo effect of the amp was now in full swing and it was impossible to play, as echo joined more echo and I didn't know where I was in the song. I had to announce through the mike if the guitarist could come up on stage. A very pissed off guitarist loomed over to me. I thought he was going to punch me at one point as I stood there helpless to stop the fucking echo from happening. Then, we somehow soldiered on to the end of the gig. I was starting to wish this tour was over. We struggled on and finished the last few gigs and then we all flew home and went our separate ways.

A few weeks later, I moved out of the flat my wife and myself had in Acton, and moved into a small flat in Shepherd's Bush. I had exactly £1,000 to my name. My wife and I stayed good friends, but eventually, she met someone else and we drifted further apart. As usual, being a musician, one of my main concerns was money, or should I say, the lack of it. About a month later, I was giving a few guitar lessons a week, but needed to earn more money so, for the first time in about 40 years, I went out one day to look for some sort of a job. I called into various places, like Manpower, but they didn't want to know a musician who had none of the usual documents that the average working person has, like P45s, insurance cards, insurance stamps, etc. I tried a place called Gentle Ghost that some musician friends had mentioned. It was a removal firm but they couldn't, or wouldn't, give me a job either. I tried a few more places that were mentioned in the local papers but no luck. I really was getting desperate and all my streetwise knowhow didn't seem to be working.

Sometimes, I really believe that there is some sort of outside force, or if you want something badly enough and you've tried and tried and you've sent out all of this energy, then out of the blue, your luck starts to change. I couldn't believe this... I was in my flat, drinking tea, looking out of the window, when my phone rang. "Hello, is that Eric?" It turned out to be a Dublin bass player friend of mine who I hadn't seen for about 12 years or so. "Jesus, Dave," I said. "How are you?" Anyway, we talked a while and then he asked me was I still playing, and was I free to play a few gigs at the weekend? I still find the timing of it all very strange. I ended up playing with Dave and his drummer, Derek, full-time, playing four or five nights a week and sometimes Sunday afternoons, and making a lot of money.

Remembering - Eric Bell

I still had a few guys who were coming to me for guitar lessons. This one night, I had given a lesson to this guy called Steve and, as we were packing up, he asked me what I was doing that evening. He mentioned this blues band that were playing and said the guitar player was just as good as Peter Green, the fabulous blues guitarist from John Mayall's Bluesbreakers and early Fleetwood Mac. So, we got in Steve's car and drove for an hour or so and came to what looked like a youth club type of building with lots of young people standing outside. We went in and a five-piece blues band were playing. The guitar player just sounded like Peter Green. We stood and listened for a while, then the bass player went up to the mike and said the guitarist from Thin Lizzy was here tonight, and would I like to get up and play a few tunes? Next thing, I was standing on stage and the rhythm guitarist handed me his guitar. We played about three songs and it sounded really good. They were called The Sunsets.

Next night I was back playing with Dave and Derek in the three-piece Irish group, Treat. I'd been with Treat now for a few months, and even though some of the music was shit, it was a good little band and the two guys were a good rhythm section. One of the best gigs we played was a Saturday night residency in a huge pub called The Archway Tavern near Holloway Road. There must have been 800 to a 1,000 people who would show up every Saturday night ,about 80% being Irish. On one of these nights, I met a girl. Let's call her Sandra. After a few weeks, we were going strong and Sandra would turn up at most of our gigs. I have always thought that girlfriends and wives and gigs don't work. They can either get jealous seeing you talking to other girls or make you jealous by dancing close to other men or getting too drunk and shouting out of their heads. It takes a special type of relationship to let the night go slowly by. Sandra thought I was screwing every female that was at any of our gigs and this started to cause a lot of trouble.

After one of Treat's gigs, we were invited to this couple's house for a drink. At this moment in time, I'd given up drink, drugs and cigarettes for roughly seven years. There were about 20 people in the house, a lot of them I knew to see as they would come to a lot of Treat's gigs. I was talking to some girl about music or something, when I heard someone shouting in the next room. Here we go, I thought, and sure enough, it was Sandra. "For fuck's sake, Eric, you're over 40 years old and still trying to pull young birds," and I thought, right, she's out to lunch, I better apologise to the people that invited us and order a taxi. Someone phoned a local taxi service and, five minutes later, we were heading to my flat in Shepherd's Bush. In the back seat of the taxi, Sandra was screaming at me and, at one point, punched me hard in the face. The taxi driver had had enough. "Right, sir, I'm dropping you off here."

It was only a few minutes walk to the flat, but it took more like 20, with Sandra screaming, then lying on the pavement. I was thinking, what the fuck have I let myself into this time? The next few days were very tense between us but, thank God, she had a job to go to.

Things settled down a bit, and the weeks went by until, one night, Dave, the bass player from Treat, had had one drink too many at one of our gigs. He started arguing with me about something and started to get a bit physical. I tried my best to control my temper but, as we made our way home, he kept on at me. "Derek," I said to the drummer, who was driving the van. "I'll be taking my amp home tonight." When we reached my flat, Derek opened the van's back door and I started to carry my amp into the flat. I heard Dave shouting, "Eric, you better turn up at the gig tomorrow night or I'll fucking come down and sort you out." "Any time, mate," I answered, looking at Derek, who didn't know what to do. And the van drove off. I didn't turn up at the next night's gig – and that was me finished with Treat.

As luck would have it, I got a phone call from Tony, bass player with The Sunsets, the blues band I had jammed with at the youth club. "Hello, mate," he said, "are you doing much at the moment?" I told him I had just finished up with Treat a few weeks ago and wasn't playing. "Do you fancy doing a few gigs with The Sunsets? My first gig, without any rehearsing, was in a few days' time. It took a bit of getting used to playing with another lead guitarist, as I was nearly always in three-piece bands, where I did the lead and rhythm guitar parts. Anyway, I adapted my style and started playing more rhythm parts and fill-ins, and learned quite a lot of new ideas, which kept me happy.

Sandra now started showing up at some of The Sunsets' gigs, much to my dismay. Everything was OK, but I noticed she would be drinking and talking to Marty, the Peter Green clone, nearly every chance she could get. This led to us having a blazing row a few weeks later after a gig. We got dropped off back at the flat in Shepherd's Bush, and the row started up again. Exhausted, we went to bed, the both of us lying like two ironing boards, not touching or breathing properly. I must have drifted into to a light sleep when, suddenly, I heard the phone ring in the front room. Sandra was up like a shot and I heard her speak on the phone. "Hold fucking on and I'll fucking get him!" She came back into the bedroom shouting, "Who the fuck is Clair? What's going on?" I got up, my head pounding, and lifted up the phone, thinking there would just be a dialling tone. "Oh, hello, Eric…" I could sense the blood draining from the top of my head to the soles of my feet. All I could think of was, "Clair, do you know what time it is ? (It was 5:15am.) "Oh," she said.

"Maybe it's a bad time to call." I muttered something and put the phone down. I went back into the bedroom, wondering what to say, but by now Sandra was hysterical. I went down to the tiny kitchen, made two cups of tea and brought them back. "Listen, Sandra, I know you won't believe me, but I haven't seen or spoken to Clair for over a year since we split up." But it was pointless. I went back into the front room and tried to figure out what had just happened. The whole thing felt weird, like it was planned. Things didn't get any better between us and I thought the best thing to do would be for me to go to Belfast for a week, just to give us a bit of space and, hopefully, when I came back, things would be better. But, as I was getting ready to leave the next day, Sandra had asked me what girl I was going to see in Belfast. At this point, I just couldn't be bothered with it and said goodbye and made my way to the tube station to get to the airport. I stayed with my Auntie Irene for a week, saw my cousins and a few old friends, and then it was time to go back to London.

I got home to Shepherd's Bush, opened the door to the flat, put down my case and went to the kitchen to make a cup of tea. As the kettle would take a few minutes, I went up to the sitting room and had a look around. Sandra was at work and would be home in an hour or so. I wondered how she would be feeling. Then, I noticed something. On the shelf above the fireplace was a coloured photo of The Sunsets – but there were only three people instead of four. I picked it up and looked at it more closely. Marty had been cut out of the photo! I felt something was going on, but at the moment I couldn't be sure. I started unpacking and then heard the front door open, and in walked Sandra. "Oh, hello," she said, and walked down to the kitchen. A warm welcome home, I thought, and saw Sandra's handbag sitting on the floor with the piece of the photo with Marty's smiling face looking up at me. Sandra came back from the kitchen, lit a cigarette and sat down. "Eric, I've got something to tell you. Since you've been in Belfast, I've been seeing Marty." I'm not into hitting women, but at this moment, it took all my willpower to stop jumping from my chair and grabbing her around the throat. "Oh, fucking great. Right, I want you out of this flat tonight!" and I got up, left the room and made for the front door. "But, I've nowhere to stay, Eric!" shouted Sandra. "Ask fucking lover boy to sort it out!" I shouted back, and slammed the door.

Out in the street, I didn't know what to do. I ended up in some cafe, looking into my cup of coffee and seeing nothing. What's going to happen now? I thought. I got back to the flat later, and Sandra was on the phone to Marty, as I paced up and down. "Right, what's happening?" I said, after she put the phone down. "Marty lives with his mother, he can't put me up." "Sandra, I don't give a shit! Get in touch with one of your girlfriends, but I want you out of here tonight." I couldn't bear staying in the same room, and made for the front door again. I passed an hour or so walking fast around Holland Park, trying to get rid of the tension that was eating me up. When I got back, the flat was empty.

A few days passed and then I got a phone call from Tony, bass player with The Sunsets. "Hi, Eric, I just got a phone call from Marty. He's told me what happened. Are you alright?" I told him I was just getting on with things. "OK, Eric. We've got a gig at lunchtime tomorrow. I'll pick you up around 1pm. Will you be OK to play?" Next day, being Sunday, Tony called at the flat and we had a bit of a talk and then headed for the gig. We were on stage, setting up our gear, and I was feeling nervous, wondering what was going to happen if Marty turned up. He did. We all made our way to the bar, and Tony was talking to Marty. Then Marty saw me and walked over. "Hey, Eric, I wonder if we could have a talk?" "Is it about Sandra?" I said. "Yeah," he said. "Don't worry about it," I said, but I didn't feel it. "Go ahead, and the best of luck. You're going to need it." "What do you mean by that?" "You'll find out," I answered, and walked back to the stage to finish setting up.

When it was time to play, we just went through the motions and there was a lot of tension on the stage. Marty packed up his amp and guitar and left. Next day, I got a phone call from Tony, telling me Marty had left The Sunsets. That more than suited me. Back to being a good old three-piece again. I also got a phone call later from Sandra, saying she and Marty would be over later to collect some of her things. So, I got ready and went out to get something to eat and then walked around High Street Kensington, killing time. A few hours later, I made my way back to the flat and got the shock of my life when I walked into the sitting room! Most of the furniture was gone – the three-piece suite, a couple of wooden chairs, and the double bed was gone from the bedroom. "Fucking great!" I hadn't thought that most of the furniture had been Sandra's when she had first started living with me. At that time, I had got rid of my bits of furniture to make room for her stuff, which had been better than mine.

Now, as I sat on the floor with my back against the wall, I started thinking about having a drink for the first time in about seven years. My head started having a fight with itself. One part saying, "Stick with it, it'll all pass in a few weeks," the other part saying, "Fuck it, you've had enough, just enjoy yourself and have a few drinks." Not really knowing what I was doing, I made my way to the front door and headed down the street to the Off Licence. I felt like it was someone else picking up a six pack of Guinness, a small bottle of whiskey and a packet of cigarettes. I came out of the store, holding my goodies in a brown paper bag. I might as well let it all hang out, I thought, and called at a friend's house to score some hash. That done, I slowly walked back to my flat, shaking my head, wondering what I was about to do.

I had a pint of Guinness, a small glass of whiskey, and rolled a small joint. About 20 minutes later, I was laughing and dancing around my front room to the sounds of some of my favourite records. I was determined not to get depressed or weighed down by self-pity. As there was no bed, I had to sleep on the floor, but at least it was carpeted.

The Sunsets were now a three-piece and we started playing around London and beyond, changing the name to The Eric Bell Band. Tony, the bass player, somehow got in touch with an agent in Sweden and we had a two-week tour lined up, but had to find a replacement drummer as Brian, our drummer, had a day job. After finding a drummer and a few days rehearsing with him, we were on the plane to Gothenburg. I hadn't played in Sweden for a few years and wondered what the audiences were like... were they expecting a Thin Lizzy type of band or would they give me a chance to play some of my own music and some old blues and rock done my way? We soon found out. It seemed about half the audience wanted Thin Lizzy and the other half let us play what we wanted.

The agent we worked for in Sweden was called Dave. He was English and introduced us to a musician friend of his who had access to a recording studio. We went to look at the studio and we all started talking about recording an album. This led to us thinking that maybe recording a live album might be a better idea, as it was cheaper and more atmospheric. So, we recorded a few of the gigs on a mobile studio set-up, and picked the songs that showed the band at its best. We called the album *Live Tonite: The Eric Bell Band. I'm pretty happy the way the album sounded – a bit raw and loose and the guitar up front.*

We played in Sweden a lot after this. In fact, I think we overplayed Sweden. We seemed to be doing a small tour there every few months. One of the highlights for me was meeting Bo Winberg, the guitarist with a group from Gothenburg called The Spotniks. They were a very famous group in the 1960s and dressed up in space suits and helmets. They had a few hits in Britain and I bought their first three albums. They were Sweden's answer to The Shadows, but had their own sound and Bo Winberg's very quirky guitar.

Remembering - Eric Bell

Now back in England, we parted company with the drummer we had, as I think he was on the verge of getting married, and after a few weeks, found another drummer. We were still going out as The Eric Bell Band and lined up a few shows around Britain. One of these shows found us playing a pub called The George Roby. It was on a Sunday in the afternoon and lots of Irish bands were playing. I think we were the only electric group playing that day. Anyway, it was time for us to do a sound check and, as we were setting up our gear, I saw this young lady appear on the stage and start to place mics around the drum kit, then shift the vocal monitors. "Oh no," I thought, with my male chauvinist pig attitude, "not a fecking chick!"

A lot of sound engineers turn out to be posers, wearing black jeans and a key ring attached to their waist with about 50 keys on it. I'm not saying all sound engineers are chancers, but I have worked with a few who were definitely in the wrong job. The ones who ask the drummer to hit the snare drum and, ten minutes later, he's still hitting it but it still sounds exactly the same. There's other ones who ask you to play the guitar at the loudest volume you are going to play that night, then tell you the guitar is too loud. As we all know (and some sound guys as well) the difference between playing in an empty room and one filled with a large audience is a bit like chalk and cheese. One of the most memorable sound engineers brought his two sons with him, who were trying to learn the trade, and one of them walked onto the stage at the sound check. He walked past me and somehow managed to stand on my guitar lead, pulling it out of the guitar. Then to finish off, I kicked a can of beer over, which spilled onto the stage, right in front of where I was standing. Next!

Anyway, back to the George Roby. The young lady sound engineer was called Rhona and she got one of the best sounds I ever heard. When we were playing that night, it just sounded like a record. After the gig, I went up to her and thanked her and gave her a big hug – and it was like an electric shock for both of us. I was very attracted to her, and the next time we played the Roby, I asked her to come back with me to my flat in Shepherd's Bush. Rhona told me she would love to but couldn't, as she had a large dog to look after. Well, it's original at least, I thought. But, to my delight, it turned out to be true. The next time we played in the George Roby, Rhona asked me back to her flat. She lived in one of the tower blocks of flats in Ponders End, on the 15th floor. And she lived with a beautiful big dog called Tequila. We ended up seeing each other about three times a week, staying in each other's flats.

I got offered a few gigs in Dublin, playing at the Vibe for Philo, which was run every year on the date Philip passed away, the 4th of January. It was all put together by Smiley Bolger, a real Dublin character, who had been a friend of Philip's. It was all happening in Dublin (or so I thought) as I was playing good gigs, doing interviews on the radio and for the press, and and a few brief appearances on TV. The whole music scene seemed to be alive and buzzing, and I started thinking that it might be a very good idea to move to Dublin.

When I got back to London, Rhona was still pretty busy doing sound about three or four nights a week. My own band was still up and running, but in the back of my mind, I was thinking more and more about Dublin. Then it happened. Rhona told me she was pregnant. We had a serious talk about the new situation, but I still wanted to live in Dublin. Time passed in London and Rhona gave birth to our baby son, who we named Erik. Your life completely changes when you become parents. You go to the hospital as two people and then leave as three. And, then you just have to get on with it. The first three months left Rhona and myself feeling and walking about like zombies. The baby doesn't care if it starts crying at 4am – it either wants to be fed, cleaned or just wants to be cuddled. So, you can lose lots and lots of sleep, and a lot of the time I fell into a deep sleep on a bus or a tube train, waking up miles away from my destination.

By now, I had made my mind up – I wanted to move to Dublin, and one night asked Rhona would she go with me? Eventually, she agreed, and the plan was for me to go over first and try to find a place to live. A few weeks later, I found myself in Dublin with my guitar and a small suitcase. I booked into a cheap bed and breakfast and called into various estate agents, looking for a flat or house for Rhona and Erik. The money they wanted was unreal, a bit like two months' rent in advance plus other bits and pieces added on. I just couldn't afford it. This went on for a few days and I was starting to feel very insecure. As I came out of another estate agent's office, just facing St Stephen's Green, I heard someone calling my name. It was a young guy sitting in a car a few yards away. I went over and he asked me if I was Eric Bell? After a few minutes of conversation, I told him I was looking for somewhere to live and wasn't having much luck. His name was Joe and he told me he had a large house in Phibsbourgh, which he ran for his uncle, and would I like to see some of the rooms? I couldn't believe my luck! It was a strange building, and the rooms were made out a bit like Art Deco. I told Joe I was very interested in having a room and, the next day, I left the B&B and moved into a large room feeling so very much better. A week or so later, Rhona and Erik arrived.

CHAPTER 22

I started going into Dublin city centre where I knew, at some point, I would run into some old musician friends. A few days later, I somehow ended up in a small recording studio at the top end of O'Connell Street. I hung around the studio for a while, but there didn't seem to be much happening. Money was now becoming the top priority and I asked Joe, my landlord, where the dole office was. Next day, he drove me to the unemployment office and I joined the end of a long queue. When I finally reached the desk, a guy asked me my name, and when I told him, he looked at me for a few moments and said, "Eric Bell? Not *the* Eric Bell?" He then turned round and told everyone in the office, "Hey, it's Eric Bell out of Thin Lizzy!" I just wanted to disappear.

I started to get a bit of money from them every week until, one day, I was asked to appear at Room 101 or such. I knocked on the door and was asked to come in. "Right, Eric," said this young man. "It's like this. Are you looking for a job? Because we're going to have to stop your money soon." I told him I was looking for musicians to form a band, and when that happened I would be able to support myself. "And how long do you think it will take to form your band?" "I honestly don't know," I replied. "Right, wait here while I talk to someone." He came back five minutes later. "OK, I've spoken to my boss, who told me you're allowed another four weeks of money."

I went up to the recording studio again and there was a band there recording a few songs, and I got talking to one of the studio engineers. I told him my girlfriend, Rhona, was a gifted sound engineer and the guy asked me was she looking for work? He gave me his card and a few phone numbers, and when I got back to our room, I told Rhona. About four days later, Rhona was working doing sound three nights a week at the clubs, Charlie's and Barnstormers. And I was left holding the baby. Things weren't going the way I had planned, but at least Rhona was earning some very welcome money.

One day in the city, I met a guy called Jim O'Neil, who was a friend of Noel Redding's. We went for a drink and I asked him was he still playing keyboards? He said he fooled around with them still, but was very busy as a very popular DJ on Dublin radio. I told him I was trying to form a new band and when I found a bass player and drummer, maybe he would like to come down for a blow? Also, some of the songs I was writing might sound better with keyboards. We swapped phone numbers and I ended up walking to the recording studios to see if anything was happening. Yes, my luck had started changing. There were quite a few musicians hanging about that day, and I met a bass player and a drummer. They were already in bands but weren't doing that much work. So, I asked them if they'd be up for a jam and they were both interested. I phoned up Jim O'Neil and organised for us to get together in a few days time, and we could rehearse in one of the rooms at the studio.

The first blow together was a bit shy and over careful, but after a few more rehearsals, the band started to shape up. We rehearsed for about three weeks and got a set together – some covers and some of my own songs. Our first gig was in a weeks' time in Charlie's, one of the clubs Rhona worked in. The band went down pretty well and we got more confident. I started going around Dublin, calling into the various clubs and gigs, telling them I had a new band and could they give me some work. But, I soon found out there was a new attitude with the owners of these clubs. "Ah, Jaysus, Eric, it's all changed now. We're booked up for months in advance and we've got our own PA system and all." "Wow," I thought, "things have changed." Ireland was always behind England by about 500 years, and now they were catching up. Look out!

I got a phone call from Jim O'Neil asking me if I could meet him in Neary's bar as he had something important to tell me. "Listen, Eric, I'm really sorry but I won't be able to play with the band anymore. We just had a meeting at the radio station I work for and they've changed the hours that I work. They now want me to be on the air between 10pm and 3am so I won't be able to do any gigs." So that was that. Maybe I'm destined to play in three-piece bands? I told the bass player and drummer, but they didn't seem to care one way or the other. But it meant having to throw out the songs that featured keyboards and replace them with more blues and rock standards.

I still went around Dublin looking for gigs, meeting musicians and finding out where the good gigs were. I was walking in the city centre one day and ended up in Slattery's, a pub near Cable Street, and went in and asked the barman could I speak to the guy that ran gigs? I was shown to an office up the stairs and spoke to the man who booked the bands. "Right, Eric, what about next Sunday night? Can you play that night?" I told him I'd be there and, next Sunday, we arrived at Slattery's and were told that we were playing upstairs at 9pm. I was sitting in the changing room around 8 o'clock and got the feeling that the room we were playing in was completely empty. It's just a feeling that you develop over the years. I got up and walked down the corridor that led into the gig. Not a fucking sinner. I went downstairs to look out into the street to see if there was anybody about. Then, I got the shock of my life. Downstairs in Slattery's, there was a free gig on! A band was about to start playing and I looked in and saw about 120 people shouting and drinking. I overheard someone say, "Hey, Eric Bell's playing upstairs, do you fancy going up?" "Na, fuck that," came the answer. "You have to pay in. I'm staying here and buying another few pints. It was one of those moments when you think God is looking down at you to see how you are going to react.

My band waited an extra 30 minutes to see if anyone was going to turn up, and we ended up playing to 12 people. When the gig had finished, there was a knock on the changing room door and a young barmaid came over and handed me an envelope. "That's your money for tonight," she said. The drummer and bass player were outside in the bar and, when they came in, they hung about waiting, I suppose, to get paid. I handed each of them six punts. "What the fuck's that?" they said in unison. "You're fucking lucky!" I replied. "I only got five." We had a gig the next Sunday night in Slattery's and I suppose the idea was that we try and build up a bit of a crowd, but I couldn't see it with a free gig going on downstairs at the same time. The nightmare begins.

That Sunday afternoon, I was having my dinner when the old-fashioned press button A and B phone started ringing downstairs. "Phone call for you, Eric!" someone shouted from downstairs. I went down and picked up the phone. It was the bass player (let's call him Jack). "Hey, Eric, I'm really sorry, I won't be able to do the gig tonight. I'm at my girlfriend's house and there's no way I can get to Dublin." I looked at the phone in disbelief. "For fuck's sake, Jack, could you not have let me know sooner?" He started to get angry and I just put the phone down, went upstairs and told Rhona. She ended up driving me to Slattery's with baby Erik in his chair, and waited for me in the car as I went upstairs to where I was playing that night.

There was a band playing, and when they took a break, I walked over to the bass player. I knew him to see, and told him I was playing here tonight but my bass player couldn't make it and could he help me out? "How much do we get each?" he asked, as I was standing there, hoping he wouldn't. "About six punts each," I said. "You are joking?" he

said, looking at me. I started to explain that this was just my second gig in the place and

I was trying to build it up. "OK, I'll play tonight for old times' sake and because I like early Thin Lizzy." I went back downstairs to where Rhona and Erik were waiting, and we drove back to our room. Later on, we played that night to 18 people, while over 100 people were going mad at the free downstairs gig. I am not making this up.

Next Sunday afternoon, I got a phone call from the drummer (let's call him Pat). "Hello, Eric, it's Pat. Listen, I'm really sorry, but something's come up and I won't be able to do the gig tonight." I just muttered something and put the phone down. My head started spinning and all I wanted was to get the fuck out of Dublin. After thinking about what to do now, I remembered an old phone book I had with lots of musicians phone numbers in. I started looking through it, wondering were some of these guys still alive or still playing? I found a drummer who I had known years ago but hadn't spoken to for a very long time. I phoned him and it sounded like his mother who answered. "Oh hello, could I speak to Sam, please?" I said. "Who will I say is calling?" she asked. "Tell him it's Eric Bell." He came on the phone. "Ah, Jaysus, Eric, how's it going?" We had some small talk and I asked him was he still playing? "Not that much, Eric, I'm driving the oul taxi now. Anyway, what's happening?" I told him I needed a drummer that night and could he help me? I held my breath as he eventually asked, "What's the money?" I told him. "Are you joking me? Sure, that wouldn't even pay for my petrol there and back." Then he said, "Alright, Eric, for old times' sake. Can you help me lift the drums upstairs when I get there?" I told him no problem and thanked him for helping me out. The only thing I knew for certain was to tell Slattery's what to do with their gig – in a nice way! We played that night again to about 18 people and I told the guy who ran the gig that it just wasn't working, and that was that.

It was getting to the point now, that I was falling behind with the rent. But Joe was very understanding about it all. Rhona was still working two and sometimes three nights a week, so we had some money coming in. Then Joe, our young landlord, asked me for some guitar lessons, which he said would help with the rent. I didn't know how he knew and I didn't ask. Joe turned out to be a pretty good guitarist and he kept up the lessons for quite a long time. As far as gigs and bands went, I had just had enough of it all and I thought the attitude of some of the Dublin musicians a bit strange, to say the least. I think I must have been spoiled working with Philip and Brian.

As far as I was concerned, I'd given Dublin a fair go and it just wasn't happening. The first thing I did was phone Tony (the bass player out of The Sunsets and my last band in England) and told him I was moving back to London, and would he be interested in getting the band back together? He told me he had a band but they didn't seem to be doing much, and to get in touch again when I was back in London. I then told Joe that I would be leaving in a few weeks and he told me I owed him about six guitar lessons, and we started laughing. I did in fact give him about four lessons before we left. Rhona told the clubs she was working at that she would be leaving and, a week later, we were on our way back to London.

Rhona had let her flat in Ponder's End out to someone she knew, and told him we would need the flat back, which was the arrangement she had made when he took the flat over.

He said that was no problem and, as Rhona had got in touch with him before we had left Dublin, it had given him time to find another place to live. We were now back living in London and it felt like Dublin had never happened.

I got in touch with Tony, who found another drummer, and we started a few rehearsals and, later on, started playing around England. Rhona got her old job back in the George Roby. At one point, Tony got in touch with an agent in Spain, or the agent got in touch with Tony, I'm not sure which, but a few gigs were lined up for a small Spanish tour. We flew over to Madrid and met the agent, Michael. He was a real nice guy, with a bit of the Godfather about him, with his black hair slicked back, a pencil slim moustache and a camel hair coat draped over his shoulders. He also had three guys working for him, organising things for him and looking after us. We played a few gigs and seemed to go down quite well, but I got the impression the audience wanted more dance music or more of a disco type band.

On one of the days, Michael called us into his office and wanted to have a meeting with the band. He mentioned that he would like us to record an album. I had just finished writing some songs and thought it would be a perfect time to record. So, we made a date to go over to Spain in a month or so, stay in a hotel in Madrid and have about eight days in the studio. When we got back to England, I gave Tony and our new drummer, Andy Golden, a cassette of each of the songs I wanted to record. Then, we would rehearse them and learn all our parts. The month passed quickly and we were back in Madrid. We were driven to the studio to have a look around and meet the studio engineer. It was a great studio, and the amplifiers and drum kit were of the best quality. The only snag was that the studio engineer only knew about ten words in English. So, some days, Michael's helpers would call in and act as interpreters, and somehow we finished recording and mixing the album, which was called Irish Boy. I had brought over a very old black and white photograph of myself as a boy of about three years of age, sitting on a tricycle, and I wanted this to be on the cover of the album.

Back to England. One morning, along with the bills and letters, came a small package. I opened it and it was a CD of *Irish Boy* – but no black and white photo of myself on the cover. The more I looked at the cover, the less I believed what I was looking at. Up to this moment in time, it must be one of the worst album covers I have ever seen. It was a horrible photo of myself, Tony and Andy, something like the *Three Stooges*. I listened to the album and, given the time we had to record and mix it, it didn't sound too bad, but I just couldn't get the photo on the cover out of my head. (Thankfully, further on down the line, a company called Angel Air re-released the album with the black and white photo on the cover.)

I got a request to play a few gigs in Sweden. The agent told me it was going to be a Thin Lizzy tribute night and he said he had been in touch with Brian Downey and Brian was up for it. So, when the time came, I flew out to Sweden, was picked up at the airport and taken to my hotel. The Thin Lizzy tribute gig was only a few minutes' walk from my hotel, so I walked over to check it out. It was in a big club, and the stage was filled with amplifiers and drum gigs and lots of musicians hanging about. I stayed for a while, talking to various guitarists, found out a few details about what time I was

on stage, and walked back to the hotel. Back in my room, I unpacked my bag, made a cup of coffee and started to roll a few small joints from a small piece of hash that I had brought with me. (I always made sure I brought a little bit when playing in Sweden.) Nobody I met there ever had any, as they all seemed to be beer drinkers. I then realised I had no cigarettes, so went out to buy some, and then went for another coffee in one of the many coffee bars in the street.

Back at the hotel, I opened the door of my room and my blood ran cold. One of the cleaning ladies had been in my room, leaving fresh towels and tea bags and had cleaned up the piece of hash that had been in silver paper, along with the cigarette papers and a few strands of tobacco. I didn't know what to do for a while, and paced around my room, looked out the window, and then opened my door and looked down the corridor. Yes! The cleaning lady's trolley was a few doors down from mine. She was in another room cleaning up. I walked down to where her trolley was standing and peered into the room. She must be in the bathroom. I looked up and down the corridor, held my breath and lifted off the large plastic bag that was hooked on the trolley, then sprinted back to my room. Locking my door, I went into the bathroom and emptied the contents of the plastic bag onto the floor. There was all types of shit in front of me, and I searched through it all looking for a ball of silver paper. I kept looking, but just could not find it. It wasn't there. I wondered if the cleaning lady took it? But, obviously, I couldn't ask her. I just lay on the bed and eventually faced it. Oh well, a few beers and a couple of hot-shots should do the trick.

Later on, in the dressing room, I met Brian Downey and talked about old times and what songs we were going to play that night. The Swedish bass player, who was playing with us, came over and introduced himself. From the way he was talking, he seemed to know every Thin Lizzy song that was ever recorded. The dressing room started to fill up with dozens of musicians, and there must have been five Thin Lizzy cover bands before us. They all sounded great. Then, myself, Brian and the bass player went on and opened with *Whiskey In The Jar,* and everybody went mad. It was a great night.

CHAPTER 23

Back in London now for a few weeks, and I got a phone call from the agent who set up tours for Noel Redding. "Eric, can you please phone Noel and ask him what the fuck is going on. He asked me to book a small tour of the UK and now he says he doesn't want to do it. It seems he fell out of his bedroom window or something!" So, that night, I phoned Noel and told him the agent wanted to know if he was going to do the tour. "What tour? I didn't ask him for a fucking tour." "He mentioned that you fell out of a window," I said. Then, Noel told me what had happened. He said an old friend had called at his house, and they had shared a bottle of wine and a few joints, and later,when the guy had left, Noel went up to his bedroom. He then told me he saw some ghosts standing in the corner of the room and his bedroom window was open. It was the first time it was open since he had moved into the house, as the frame had been held tight by paint. He then found himself lying outside on a piece of grassy ground underneath his window, and he was naked. He eventually got himself up and rang the doorbell. It was lucky his mother, Margaret, was staying in the house, and she opened the door. Noel said Margaret just looked at him and shook her head. What a story. I asked him had he been taking acid or something? He told me he had just half a bottle of wine and shared a few joints. Noel obviously could handle that, and a lot more, having been in The Jimi Hendrix Experience for three or four years.

He said he really should do the UK tour as he needed some money, but first he was going to the doctor to see if anything was wrong after his fall. He phoned me later and said the doctor told him he had twisted his pelvis and didn't think doing a tour would be a good idea. We talked about it and he said he would do the tour, but would be taking it very easy. He would borrow a bass guitar from whatever band was on with us, and wouldn't be carrying anything.

The first day of the tour arrived, and myself and the driver/road manager drove to Heathrow Airport to wait for Noel's flight from Cork. I saw him coming through the Arrivals gate, and he looked about ten years older since I saw him last. I could also tell he had been drinking, and it was only 11.30am. We shook hands and he said let's go to the bar for a swift half. I had a coffee and Noel had two bottles of beer, then we picked up our drummer, John Cochlan from Status Quo.

We had about seven gigs in a row and played the first three, which went down quite well, and it certainly helped to have been three name musicians out of famous bands. On the fourth day of the tour, I got a phone call in my hotel room from the agent. "Eric, for fuck's sake, what's going on? Noel just phoned me and said he isn't playing tonight's gig. It's sold out! Would you mind speaking to him?" Here we go again, I thought. Then my phone rang again. "Eric, it's Noel. Listen, matey, I don't feel up to doing the gig tonight, I'm sorry, but I'm feeling a bit rough." The agent must have realised how Noel was feeling, and he told us he had spoken to the guy running the gig and everything was sorted out. We finished the remaining gigs, and all went our separate ways.

One day, out of the blue, I got a call from a friend of Noel's who worked for Fender Soundhouse. It was from a guy called Dave, who had played second guitar with me in Noel's band on a few of our gigs. "Hey, Eric, I was wondering would you be up for judging a guitar competition in Amsterdam? We'll fly you there and back ,put you up in a good hotel and fix you up with some sort of a payment." "Yeah, just what I need," I told him, and a week later, myself and Dave were in Amsterdam. We were met at the airport, driven to our hotel and, after we checked into our rooms, were driven to a large complex with supermarkets and warehouses all over the place.

The competition was in a large warehouse, all laid out with stalls with guitars, amplifiers, effects pedal boards, strings, and so on. Dave led the way towards the stage and I was shown where to sit, joining another four people who would also be judging the guitar players. On the stage was what looked like an old iron staircase, which curved from about 20 feet up and led to the stage. Some guy came on stage and spoke for a few minutes, and then introduced the first guitarist, who walked down the staircase as searchlights shone to light his descent. He handed what must have been a cassette to another guy onstage and then this very fast backing track kicked in and the guitarist played up and down the neck like someone possessed. Each judge had a paper on which was written how many points each guitarist would score for technique, chords, scales, picking, etc. Then, the next guitarist would walk down the staircase onto the stage, hand his cassette over and play twice as fast as the last player. And this was how it carried on.

I don't really understand why nearly every guitarist is obsessed with playing as fast as possible. I must admit, it's very impressive for the first few minutes, but after that I just want to leave. Anyway, I tried to give marks as best I could, and we all handed in our results. As this was being sorted out, I walked around the huge warehouse and saw a group walk out on another stage. They all wore suits, and I couldn't believe it as they started to play

Apache by The Shadows. This is more like it, I thought. After watching them for a while, I made my way back to the area where the competition had been held, and the young winner walked on stage and was given his prize to a round of applause. Then, Dave and I met up and got driven back to our hotel. We relaxed for a while, had something to eat and I made my way to the numerous cafés that were dotted around Amsterdam. I had a smoke and went back to the hotel for a reasonably early night.

We flew back to London the next day and, as we parted, Dave said he would phone me about calling into Fender Soundhouse. He phoned me back and said I could call in that Wednesday. Then, he had another piece of news, which I just couldn't believe. On that Wednesday, Jet Harris, the brilliant bass guitarist from The Shadows, would be calling into Fender to be awarded a Lifetime Achievement Award for music, and afterwards, we would be going out to lunch with Jet and his wife! Rhona drove me to the Fender warehouse and dropped me off. I met Dave and we walked around looking at the guitars hanging on the wall. I made a beeline to a salmon pink Fender Stratocaster. "Don't even think about it," Dave laughed. as I examined the guitar. It was a Marvin model and really beautiful, with gold fittings and a real ruby embedded in the machine head. When he told me the price, we walked quickly. Maybe I should really be looking at amplifiers, as my old Marshall combo had caught on fire a few months ago. I had it fixed up, but an extra amp is always a good idea. I saw a Fender De-Ville amp with four ten-inch speakers and I fell in love. I still have it and use it on most gigs and I really love the tone it has.

As we were walking back to the entrance, I spotted Jet Harris. He had obviously changed since the days of The Shadows, when he really did look super cool, but just to meet him was an honour. He turned out to be a really nice guy and told me some stories from when he had been a Shadow. He was then presented with the Lifetime Achievement Award and, after that, at the end of the lunch, Jet gave me an autograph. It said 'To Eric, wishing you everything that you would wish for yourself, your mate, Jet Harris'. I still have it.

Two amusing stories from the Eric Bell Band days. We were at a gig somewhere in Wales. It was a Saturday afternoon, and we were playing that night in this huge pub. We were setting up our equipment and there were a lot of people out drinking in the beer garden as it was a beautiful sunny day. As every musician knows, or will find out, the Ladies toilet is very much cleaner than the Gents. They have got soap, towels, a mirror, toilet paper, etc, and this afternoon, Tony the bass player went to the Ladies loo to have a wash and freshen up. As this part of the pub wasn't really open to the public yet, there wasn't – or shouldn't have been – anybody in the loo. But, a few minutes later, I heard this shouting. A girl had been using the toilet as Tony was getting washed, and she came running out screaming that someone was watching her. She ran out to the beer garden and told her boyfriend, who was drinking with some of his mates. He was a bit pissed, as well as very pissed off with Tony, and a fight started to take shape. Now, Tony was a black belt in Karate and taught it in his own club. As the guy started to walk towards him, Tony started to walk backwards, and they carried on like this down the whole length of the club until they reached the stage, and now both had nowhere to go. As far as I could see, Tony seemed to push the guy gently backwards, and it was all over. The guy turned around and, still cursing, walked out of the club and back to his mates.

An hour or so later, the governor of the pub arrived, and I went over to talk to him. I told him what happened and said I was worried in case the guy and his mate, who had been drinking all afternoon, would turn up tonight and start something. The governor told me everything would be OK as he had a few good bouncers who would keep an eye on things. And, true to his word, nothing happened.

The other funny thing that happened was, we were playing at a Thin Lizzy tribute gig in Manchester and were booked into a grand hotel for two nights. We played the gig and, next day, just hung about the hotel as we weren't playing that night. Around 8pm, I was washing up in the bathroom when, all of a sudden, this ear-splitting noise started. I walked into the bedroom and it was the fire alarm on the ceiling going off. My hearing is very sensitive and I just couldn't take the noise. It was really painful and, without thinking, I picked up a Yellow Pages and threw it at the fire alarm. It hit the alarm, knocking its cover off, and it hit the ground. The noise stopped. Just to find out what was happening, I opened the door and looked down the corridor. A few people were standing about, looking as confused as me. We muttered something to each other and I just went back to my room. After 20 minutes or so had passed, I went over to the window to look down the street and got a real shock. There were about 200 people standing just outside the entrance to the hotel. Oh my God, I thought, maybe there really is a fire! I opened the door and ran down the corridor to the nearest lift. None of the lifts were in operation. As I was making my way down the stairs, a fireman in full firefighting gear passed me, talking to one of the guys that worked at the hotel. "Yeah, it's probably some young guys having a laugh and setting off the alarm. It happens quite a lot."

Eventually, I got to the ground floor. I could see the crowd of people through the glass doors still standing about, and as I walked over, I heard this very loud voice. "Excuse me, what's the meaning of this? You should have been down here 20 minutes ago, did you not hear the alarm.?" It was the hotel manager. I have always found it very difficult to take notice of figures of authority (probably from my 9 to 5 experiences) and I just looked at him and said, "I thought it was just to see if the alarms were working. I've stayed in hundreds of hotels being a musician, and this happens quite a lot. There never has been a fire." He got really annoyed with me and kept shouting that I should have come down with the other people. I'd had enough and just walked out into the street and spotted the other guys from the band. They asked me what had happened and then we went out for something to eat and a few drinks and got a reasonably early night.

Next morning after breakfast, I went up to the hotel reception desk to give my room key and pay for a few coffees I had signed for. The girl behind the desk said, "That will be £110, Mr Bell." I really thought she was having a laugh, then realised she was being serious. "What do you mean?" I said. At this point, my friend, the hotel manager, appeared. "Don't worry about this Shirley, I'll deal with it." "Your bill is because of the inconvenience you have caused the hotel. It was you who set off the alarm system." "What are you talking about? How did I set off the alarm?" "One of the hotel staff went into your room when you finally came down last night and said your radiator was really hot and it set off the alarm." This was starting to become like a sketch from Monty Python. I couldn't believe it. He must have thought I was just off the boat.

I said, "So, what you're saying is, when it's Winter, people can't turn up their radiators to keep warm in case they set off the fire alarm?" I could see by his expression that he thought he was losing the game, so he tried a different angle. "The hotel staff said you had somehow knocked the cover off your fire alarm and they found it on the floor. You'll have to pay for it, so please settle your bill." I was really starting to get annoyed by this man's attitude. "Listen, mate, I know how much a fire alarm costs and it's certainly not £110. It's more like six quid." The manager then said he was going to call the police if I didn't pay the bill and I told him to go ahead. Within ten minutes, these two policemen appeared and walked up to reception. "Right, what's going on? The manager said, "This gentleman won't pay his bill." "Right, let's hear your side of the story," said one of the cops, and they led me to an area away from the reception desk. I explained what happened, but really thought, being a rock guitarist, that they would have sided with the hotel manager. But, I got the impression they were bored already by the whole thing and they told me I could leave when I wanted. I went back to reception and paid for my two coffees. The manager was speechless and as I walked past him to the front door, he came up to me. "Don't think you're getting away with this, Mr Bell. You'll be getting an invoice from me in the post." No invoice ever arrived.

A guy called Ray got in touch. I had met him in one of the London music clubs where he used to be the entertainment manager, and he had moved to another country. He was calling from Dubai. We spoke for a while, catching up on things, and then he asked me what I thought about coming out to Dubai to play a few shows. I'd never been there, and when he told me he was now the entertainment manager of one of the biggest hotels out there, I jumped at the chance. So, a few weeks later, myself, Tony and Andy were flying first class (the only way to travel) to Dubai. Mac met us at the airport and we were driven to our hotel. I couldn't believe the luxury of the place. Beautiful marble tiles, Persian carpets and very ornate furniture, and lots of very rich people walking around. We were shown up to our suites. I had a suite on my own that was vast – a huge sitting room and kitchen and an enormous bathroom. I unpacked my case, put on some fresh clothes and decided to go out for a walk to see what type of place we were in. But, ten minutes later, I was back in my room, shivering and sweating and all my clothes clinging to me with sweat. The heat outside was unbearable. Now I knew why there was so much air-conditioning everywhere.

I had a shower and met the other guys and Ray downstairs, and we made our way to the restaurant for some dinner. The menu was amazing, and Ray told us that part of the deal was we could order anything we wanted while we stayed at the hotel. After the dinner, we all went for a small walk to an enormous shopping mall and stopped outside a very English looking pub with a red telephone box outside the entrance. We travel halfway around the world to end up playing in an English pub! But, when we got inside, I saw that the place was huge, with what seemed like hundreds of tables and chairs and a huge stage. We went back to the hotel and got our guitars, then back to the pub to do a sound check. There was a guitar amplifier for me, one of the brand new Marshalls with 500 knobs, which I hate. I always prefer the old Marshall amps with only five controls. Anyway, I plugged in and tried to get some sort of a tone, when this young English guy appeared on stage. He came over to me and asked me was I ready to do a sound check? "Yeah," I said, "once I try to get a decent sound out of this heap of shit." Then he said something which made me realise he was the wrong guy in the wrong job, a fucking chancer. "It's not the amp, your guitar's too old." I bought my guitar brand new around 1970, and have played it since then, and it is now a beautiful, mature Fender Stratocaster. I just looked at him and kept out of his way as much as possible.

We played a few nights there and must have been doing something right as, a few months later, Ray asked us would we like to play Dubai again? We flew first class again and stayed at the same beautiful hotel, but this time we were told we would be playing in a marquee. But, this marquee was like nothing I had ever seen. It was enormous, a bit like a circus tent, and it even had huge chandeliers hanging from the ceiling. I don't remember too much about the gig, except it looked like half the population of Dubai had turned up, and we went down really well with the crowd.

Next day, we were free to just hang out until the evening when we had another gig to play, this time in a small club. I decided to go out for a walk and see if I could get a present for my son, Erik, who was around eight years of age. Tony, the bass player, went with me and, as I was looking around the shops, I saw a great robot toy in one of the shop windows. I thought Erik would love it and went in to ask about it. The owner of the shop showed me what it could do – it talked a few words in a real robot voice and swivelled around and fired space guns. "Yes, I'll have that," and I took out this huge wad of money. "I'm sorry, sir," said the owner, "but we don't take English currency. You'll have to get it changed." He shouted someone's name and a boy of about 12 appeared. "Please take these gentlemen to the shop where they can get their money changed." The boy smiled at us and took off and we started to follow him. We ended up in very iffy side streets, which led into a marketplace, where huge Arabs were chopping up various pieces of meat. The boy was way ahead of us now, and Tony and myself were getting strange looks from the market people and I had this wad of money in the top pocket of my shirt. Maybe there was nothing to worry about, but I started to get this uneasy feeling. "I've had enough of this, mate," I said to Tony, and he agreed and we walked quickly back to the hotel.

I went up to my room to rest and, later, met Tony and Andy in the restaurant, where we ordered some amazing dishes. A few hours later we were on stage playing to a very appreciative audience, and a good night was had by all. Next morning, I was woken up by the sound of newspapers hitting the floor and realised it was part of the deal of staying in a five star hotel. I got up, made my way to the kitchen, where there was a kettle and coffee, and waited for the water to boil. I don't usually read newspapers, as I've enough shit floating through my head without adding more to it. Most of the newspapers were coloured a light pink and in Arabic, but there was one in English so I quickly scanned through it. Then, something hit my eye. "Man beheaded for hashish". I sat down and read the article, which informed me that eight people had been beheaded for possessing hashish in the last ten months. I found this incredibly hard to believe. Different laws for different countries. In another part of the world, like Amsterdam, you can buy hashish in cafés and smoke it in the streets. I cut the article out and when I got back to London, I would send it to Noel Redding.

CHAPTER 24

We got back to London and, about six weeks later, we were playing a ten-day tour in Sweden. I noticed at the end of each show, when fans would come in to the dressing room to get albums signed and photos taken, someone would always ask, "Eric, have you heard Metallica's version of *Whiskey In The Jar?*" I had never heard of Metallica at this point and was curious to hear what they had done with Whiskey. So, when the tour had finished and we were back in the UK, I went to a few of the record shops in Oxford Street. I looked under 'M' and couldn't believe the number of albums Metallica had released. But, I couldn't find any album with Whiskey In The Jar on. Strange things happen sometimes and, a few weeks later, as I was sitting about the flat, the phone rang. "Hello," said this American accent. "Can I speak to Eric Bell?" "Yeah, speaking," I said. "Hi, I work for the band Metallica and we're doing a world tour at the moment. We'll be playing The Point in Dublin soon and we'd be honoured if you could appear with us and play Whiskey In The Jar." Then he asked me if I had heard their version. I told him I hadn't yet. "Hey, man, what planet are you living on?" I told him Jupiter at the moment. He asked me for my address and said a courier would drop off a few CDs so I could hear their version.

Next day, a guy on a motorbike handed me a package and inside were various versions of *Whiskey*, live and in the studio. They didn't play the intro but played the riff that I had made up. Then, I noticed on the booklet that it said '(trad. arr.) Metallica'. I phoned the Thin Lizzy office and eventually got through to Chris. I was just about to tell him about it… "Yeah, don't worry about it, Eric. Our lawyers are in touch with their lawyers at the moment." I think what had happened was when Metallica had heard the Thin Lizzy version, they must have thought it was the original song, the first version. They didn't realise the original song was probably a guy singing on his own to a banjo.

A few days later, I got another phone call from the Metallica crew saying they would be staying at a hotel in Marble Arch, and a car would pick me up and drop me off. I was now standing in the foyer of this grand hotel when, one by one, what looked like a rock band appeared and came over to me. We all shook hands and there were four guys out of the band and about six road crew. "OK, guys, let's go," and everyone walked out into the street where four very modern minivans were waiting. We all got in and away we went, cutting through side streets to miss as much of the traffic as possible. I didn't know what was happening, but it felt like I was in the SAS, as the roadies were talking to each other from each van, giving out different directions.

We eventually got out of London and drove about roughly 30 miles until we came to what looked like some sort of an army camp. And sitting on a runway was this beautiful little silver and red plane, probably their own private plane I thought. We all climbed in and found our seats. It was a bit strange, as the seat I was in faced backwards and the rest was facing forwards, so all of Metallica and their road crew were looking in my direction. The plane took off and eventually, I think it was their bass player, who must have taken pity on me, came over and we started talking. I think at one point in the conversation, he told me he was thinking of leaving the band, but as it was quite a while ago, I could be mistaken. Soon, we landed at Dublin airport where we were met by another four minivans and were driven through the back streets of Dublin to The Point, where they were playing that night.

There were about five or so dressing rooms behind the stage and they were now being set up. One with stage clothes, etc, one for catering and booze, one with a Marshall amp and cab for me to try out, and one that had been set up with computers – this one was used to sell Metallica's merchandising worldwide. Later, as I was trying out the Marshall amp, the four guys in Metallica sort of jogged in, very much like an American army unit, and immediately started playing *Whiskey In The Jar*. Something didn't seem to sound quite right. We stopped playing and I was told that they were tuned down a whole tone from concert pitch. I know some people tune down a half-ton, like Jimi Hendrix, but a whole tone? I thought it would make the strings feel too loose with not enough tension in them. So I stuck to regular tuning, which meant I would be playing Whiskey in the key of F.

Show time arrived and they went on to a packed house and played for about two hours. Meanwhile, I was sitting in the dressing room with all the booze, using all my willpower to drink very slowly, and the only thing I kept reminding myself about was, "It's in F… it's in the key of F". I have been playing *Whiskey In The Jar* in the key of G since 1973. Enough said! They called me on to the stage and I played my party piece and it went down a bomb. After the show, we were in one of the rooms backstage with about 100 fans and, as I was talking to a few people, one of Metallica's crew came over to me. "Can I see you for a moment, Eric?" We went over to a quiet corner of the room and he produced a sheet of paper. "We just need your signature on this." I hadn't got my glasses and, looking back, should never have signed it, but for some reason, I did sign. Then, one of the Sergeant Major roadies appeared and shouted, "OK, everybody, we'll be leaving in 20 minutes!"

A little while later, we were at Dublin airport and got on the little plane and flew back to the army camp. As usual, the transport was all lined up, and there was a car to take me home. One of the road crew came over to me and handed me a big ball of (I found out later) Metallica merchandising – caps, t-shirts, scarves, etc. They all waved goodbye and took off. As I was getting into the car, I suddenly realised the bastards hadn't paid me. I was quietly expecting about two grand, which wouldn't have meant a thing to them, but up to this day I got paid fuck all. It's only Rock 'n' Roll…

Being in the music business can sometimes have a bad effect on relationships. One day, something went wrong, and my girlfriend, Rhona, and I had a blazing row over something. At that moment in time, I was very impulsive and just packed my guitar and a small bag and walked out of our flat, slamming the door. I walked till I reached a cafe, got a coffee and sat down to think things through. "What the fuck am I going to do now?" Then, as I tried to think of old friends and acquaintances who might put me up for a few days, I thought of my old friend Liam, who once helped me out, acting as sound engineer and driver in one of my many bands. I phoned him up and he told me I could stay for a few days. I got the tube to Kilburn, where Liam had his flat, and an hour later, was sitting in his front room, sharing a joint. I usually didn't smoke until the evening, but under the circumstances…

As we sat there, I suddenly realised. I was giving guitar lessons to a few guys and one of them had bought tickets for him and myself to go and see the amazing blues guitarist Albert King at The Mean Fiddler – and it was tonight. I went and got cleaned up in Liam's bathroom and told him I would see him later on tonight after the gig and went out to get something to eat in the many cafes around Kilburn. I walked around the shops slowly, as I'd a few hours to kill before the gig, then made my way on the tube to The Mean Fiddler. By the time I got there, there was a queue forming outside and, after a minute or so, I spotted Pete, the guy who had kindly bought the tickets. Inside the gig, after a few beers, Albert King's band came on and started with a real funky beat, and half way through the number, Albert walked on. Like a lot of the black blues players, he started tuning up his guitar on stage. When I worked with Bo Diddley, he would walk on stage, turn his guitar up really loud and start tuning up. I've never seen white guitarists do this, they are so polite and shy when tuning up. But, after two songs with his guitar still not in tune, Albert King walked up to the mike. "You know, sometimes, up here some nights, you gotta be prepared to lose the first few rounds." Then, he took a few more minutes to get in tune, and the Albert King we all know started playing blistering blues guitar.

As I was standing there, this guy came up to me. "Are you Eric Bell?" I told him I was. "How you doing, man? I took some photos of you once." We talked for a few minutes and he asked me had I seen Gary Moore? I asked him was Gary here? "Yeah, that's him over there, mate," and he pointed to some guy's back. I went over. "Gary, how are you doing?" "Eric!" he said, and we had a hug. "Come on over to the bar and we'll have a few drinks." I then introduced Pete to Gary and Pete shook hands with him and stood there, his jaw touching the floor. Gary told me he had been in the dressing room to see Albert King. "Yeah, I brought him a present. I got him a really small Gibson Flying V, and it works like a regular guitar. He was really knocked out with it." In his day, Gary had played with a lot of the great blues guitarists – BB King, Albert Collins, Albert King, Buddy Guy.

After a while, Pete said he had to get the last tube home, leaving me and Gary at the bar. "What are you up to, Eric?" he said. "Well, actually, I walked out on my girlfriend this morning," I said. "Yeah? And where are you staying?" "A guy called Liam is letting me stay at his place, hopefully for a few days." Gary knew who Liam was. "What, are you sleeping on his floor?" "Yes," I answered. "No fucking way! You can come back to my place, I've loads of room," said Gary.

The gig had just about finished, when these two blokes in suits came up to Gary. "Excuse me, Gary, will I bring the car round?" one of them asked. "Yeah," said Gary, "bring it round the front in about 20 minutes." We walked out of the gig into the street and, standing there, was this huge limo. The driver got out, wearing a peaked hat, and Gary introduced me to him, then we climbed in the back. We got to Liam's place in Kilburn, and it was his girlfriend who opened the door as Liam wasn't home yet. I explained that I'd met Gary and he was going to let me stay at his place, and she said she would tell Liam when he came home. So, I collected my guitar and bag and went downstairs and out into the limo again.

About a half hour later, we were well outside London and into the start of the countryside. Gary and myself were having a laugh and some brandy from the little drinks tray in the back. "Hey, Eric, do you see that wall?" On my side of the car was an old stone wall that had been alongside us for the last ten minutes. "That's where George Harrison lives. He's my neighbour." The car eventually slowed down and stopped outside two large iron gates. Gary pushed some type of signal on a keyring and the gates slowly swung open. We got out of the car, said goodbye to the driver and walked over the large gravel path to the front doors. Once inside, my eyes started to take in the luxury of the surroundings. We passed a little room with nothing in it apart from a baby grand piano. There was a winding staircase that led upstairs. Fuck me, I thought, I'm on the set from Dallas!

We went into the kitchen, had another drink, then Gary showed me up to my bedroom. "I'm knackered, Eric, I'll see you in the morning, have a good sleep." As it happened, I hardly slept at all. I kept thinking, right we're from the same background, we both play guitar, we both played with Thin Lizzy. He's got all of this and I'm looking for places to sleep with a guitar and a fucking bag. The next morning I was woken up by some sort of droning sound. At first, I didn't know where I was, then I started thinking about meeting Gary and it all came back. I got up and pulled the thick velvet curtains aside and saw what was making the droning sound. It was a guy on a small tractor-type vehicle going round in circles on a huge lawn. I got up and dressed and, eventually, found the bathroom.

Downstairs, I saw Gary in a bathrobe, sitting in a beautiful little kitchen. "Hi, Eric, want some breakfast?" I said that would be great, and then the next big thing happened. This young lady appeared. I just looked and looked, she was beautiful. "Can you fix some breakfast for Eric as well? She smiled and wiggled off. "Who the fuck is that?" I asked. "Oh, she's the nanny and looks after my son, Jack." I just asked him out straight. "Are you having a scene with her?" "Oh, no, nothing like that." The young lady came back with mugs of coffee and scrambled eggs, bacon and toast, and left again.

After breakfast, myself and Gary went outside and walked around the garden that looked more like a small park, and we came to a hedge running across the garden. And as we got to the other side of the hedge, wait for it... there was a swimming pool. I sat down on one of the benches and probably looked like I was about to cry. Gary looked over at me and he must have known what I was going through. "Eric, all of this... there's no way I would have anything like this if it wasn't for the people that manage me. It's them that has made all of this possible." I felt better when Gary explained this to me.

I'm not sure when it was, but sometime later, someone showed me a copy of The Sun newspaper. On one of the pages, the headline said: 'Rock guitarist runs away with Nanny'. And there was a photo of Gary. I just had to laugh. But, I know it didn't amount to anything, as they split up after a few weeks.

CHAPTER 25

A few days later, I was back living with Rhona and my son Erik. I got a phone call from Ray, the guy who had brought me and the band over to Dubai a few times. Ray was an entertainment manager, and his job shifted him around a lot. He told me he was now working in Ukraine. "Eric, would you be interested in doing a few gigs in Ukraine? It's going to be a bit special." He didn't tell me what, but I knew we would be well looked after and the money would be good. By now, the drummer with me was a Mr Romek Parol, and the bass player, Mr Brian Bethall. In a few weeks time, we flew to Ukraine and were met by Ray, who took us to the hotel. As far as I can remember, the hotel was on a sort of barge down at a pretty seedy looking area, like a harbour. We booked into the hotel, went to our various rooms and arranged to meet Ray at the bar in 15 minutes.

"Right, Eric," said Ray, "Steven Segal is in town shooting a movie and we're having dinner with him tonight. Ray looked really excited, but then started visibly deflating as I said, "Who is Steven Segal?" Romek and Brian seemed to know right away who he was. I still had a pretty old-fashioned TV at home and could only get four channels. It was a while later, when I caught up with the rest of the world, and had a TV half the size of the room it was in. Then I saw the amount of martial art movies Steven was in, so now I know who he is. Anyway, later that evening, Ray took us in a taxi to this beautiful restaurant and there was Steven and about nine other people with him. As Ray had mentioned, Steven was in Ukraine shooting a new movie and had all these people with him, working on the movie.

Ray introduced us to them all and, about a half hour later, Steven got a chair and came over and sat beside me. He had real charisma, and was a good-looking, friendly guy. He started talking about blues music, and seemed very up on it all. "You know, Muddy Waters and Howlin' Wolf are my cousins." I looked at him, but it was just his way of saying how much he was into their music… I think? The Eric Bell Band was playing in a club not too far from the dockland where the hotel was, and Ray arranged for Steven to come down to the sound check the next day.

So, around 3pm the next day, Romek, Brian and myself were at the club, checking things out and trying to get a sound. Next thing, Steven Segal and the nine people walked into the club, and sat down as we played through a few songs. Then, two guys appeared, one pushing a Marshall amp and speaker cab on wheels and the other carrying a guitar case. They sat the amp up on the floor beside the stage and got out the guitar. Steven started playing a few blues licks and sounded pretty good. After 20 minutes or so, we asked him would he like to get up with us tonight and play a few songs with us? He seemed really up for it, but later on, Ray told us he might not show as he was pretty tired with working on the movie.

Anyway, we played our gig and most people seemed to like what we were doing. After we'd finished, I went to the changing room, got changed and went up to the bar for a drink and to relax as the club was open for another few hours. I left the bar and walked down to this area which was quiet and had a few big armchairs, and sat down on one. A few minutes later, this lovely blonde lady came over and sat down on the arm of my chair. We started talking and I asked her if she enjoyed the music? She said yes and then asked me if I would like her to come to my hotel room. I was up, and halfway through the club, holding her hand – and then she said it would cost me 200 dollars. I looked at her, my ego floating away, and said, "So, you're on the game?" "Yes," she said. "Oh well," I replied. "Would you like a drink?" She said yes, and we went up to the bar and had a few drinks and just talked for a while. She was a really nice lady, but up to this moment, I have never paid for it… though, sometimes, I've been very close.

A few days later, we were checking out of the hotel when Ray came to my room. He handed me an envelope that was full of money and said he also gave me a small bonus. It was quite a lot of money and I wondered where to stash it. I put it in a small area of my toilet bag that had a zip at the side, and put the toilet bag in my case – wrong! There was an airport bus outside and we said our thanks and goodbyes to Ray, agreeing to stay in touch. We got on the bus and started off, but the bus started stopping at other hotels, picking other people up to take to the airport. When we eventually got to the airport, which was crowded with people, we checked in and found a few vacant seats. "Right, lads, I'll buy the coffees and some things to eat," and opened my case and took out my toilet bag. I opened the zip, where all my money was… empty. That shock that you get when the unexpected happens, hit home. "Oh fuck," I said, as the two guys looked at me. "I think someone has stolen all my money." I was shaking, and put my case on the table and took out shirts, socks, underpants, everything, and went through each item. Nothing. I then looked in my toilet bag again, willing the money to somehow be there. No. Some smart fucker had somehow searched my case, probably when the coach was stopping at the various hotels, picking up people for the airport. The two guys agreed to give me some of their wages, which was a lovely gesture. From now on, I keep my money on my person and put it all down to experience!

Now, back in London with my wife, Rhona, and my son Erik, I settled down to home life again. A few weeks later, I got a phone call from Noel Redding. "Ello, matey, 'ow are you?" We had a bit of a talk, then Noel asked me if I would be up to playing a gig in Moscow? It was to be one of the strangest gigs I've ever played.

There was a guy in Moscow who was opening up a sort of R&B club, and he got in touch with Noel to come over and play on opening night. This guy, who was called Stas, I found out later had been in a very successful rock-type band and was one of the biggest names in music in Russia. Noel organised our visas and permits and he and his girlfriend (I think her name was Candy, and if not, I am sorry).

After a long but comfortable flight, we landed in Moscow and I could feel the different vibe very strongly. Stas and a few people who worked for him met us at the airport and, after being checked out, we all got into various cars and were taken to our hotel. The hotel was incredible. It looked like one of the old-fashioned 1950s skyscrapers from the movie *Ghostbusters. I was told there was five or six of them. As we walked up to the entrance, I noticed about five guys in suits all wearing mics, with wires dangling from their ears. They looked at myself and Noel, then looked at each other, but didn't say or do anything. Everything in the hotel looked enormous, huge corridors, huge lifts, huge old-fashioned paintings on the wall and huge bedrooms. After we unpacked our cases, had coffee and rested a while, Stas said he would like to take us to his recording studio and office in Gorky Park.*

The drive took about half an hour, and we drove through a sort of woods and came to a clearing. We got out and in front of us was a sort of outdoor stage, with railings and barriers. We walked past this, down a small alleyway and into a building that led into a studio with amps, guitars, drum kit and lots of leads and speakers everywhere. Then, behind this was a mixing desk and chairs and everything set up to record. Noel and myself went back into the room with the amps and guitars. At this point, two guys walked in and Stas introduced us. We just said hi and shook hands, as these guys didn't speak English, and we didn't speak Russian. One of them got behind the kit of drums and the other, who reminded me of a young professor, brought out a sort of digital guitar. I picked a guitar up to try it out. Noel tried a bass and Stas was playing on a beautiful jazz-type guitar. We started jamming around for a while, but I found it hard to get into it.

After it was finished, Stas asked myself and Noel if we could record about six rock and blues-type songs. There was just the three of us, Noel, myself and the drummer who, as I said, couldn't speak a word of English, so there were lots of hand signals and body language going on. When it was finished, we went in to listen to what we had played. It sounded pretty good, and after a while, we were driven back to our hotel.

Later, all freshened up, myself and Noel and Candy got something to eat and Stas had asked Noel if we would come down to the R&B club. I think this was opening night so we went down with Stas to look the place over. When we arrived, there were quite a few people standing around. We went in and it looked like a really nice place. Stas asked myself and Noel to follow him upstairs, where there was a door which led onto nearly the roof of the building. There was some scaffolding, which we were told to climb up, the idea being that we would sign our autographs and messages on the wall of the club. Down below, people were taking photos. We stayed in the club for a while, meeting and talking to lots of people, and then went back to the hotel.

I wanted to look around the hotel, which was huge, and started walking around the place. I was always watched and followed at a distance by these guys in suits. I found out each floor of the hotel had a sitting area, a bar, and a cafe. Then, I noticed something else. Sitting beside these pillars near the cafe were young girls, all dressed in black, reading books. This was on each floor of the hotel. I sat down with my coffee and watched as men of all ages approached the young ladies. Some would get up and leave with the men. Very discreet, I thought.

Later on, Stas told us that two young American ladies would be joining us later. I found out that one of the ladies had had a relationship with Stas in the past. They were both pretty and very nice and were staying at our hotel. Down at the R&B club later on, there were guitar players everywhere and we all had a few drinks, and it turned out to be a big jam session with anybody who could play. I lost count of the musicians on stage that night. But, one of the strangest gigs I ever played was to take place the next night…

The next day, I went out for a walk. The suits were still standing at the entrance of the hotel. Everything looked grey and concrete looking, and I only walked around for about ten minutes or so. Maybe it was my imagination, but I felt like at any minute, a car would pull up beside me and whisk me off somewhere. Later, around 8pm that evening, we all met in the lobby, Noel, Candy, Stas, myself and the two American ladies, and were driven to this enormous building. There were crowds and crowds of people everywhere, the men all dressed in dinner suits and bow ties, and the ladies all in evening dresses. We were shown into this enormous room, and I ended up at a table with one of the American ladies. The rest of our group were sitting elsewhere. There were at least 30 or so very big tables in the room and, on each table, was a huge bowl of fruit, piled up about three foot in the air.

The room became very quiet, and a spotlight shone up to the ceiling, which was very high. I could make out a young lady dressed in a clinging body-stocking, dancing and moving about in a huge net, which was being lowered very slowly to the floor. OK...? At this point, waiters started appearing everywhere with dishes of food. One of them came over to our table and put down three dishes of food, then another waiter come over with another couple of dishes, and then another. There was hardly any more room on our table, but another waiter came over and squeezed another few dishes on. "Thank you," I said. "Thank you. No more food please." I think they got the message, as no more waiters appeared. I don't know what we were eating, and the amount of food we left untouched was unbelievable.

All of a sudden, these guys that looked like male models appeared and started pulling out what looked like catwalks from the walls of the room. After they had finished, these lovely female models started walking up and down the catwalks. "I think we're at the wrong fucking gig," I said to my girl companion, who just started laughing. "Yeah, I think you could be right, Eric!" But, about a half hour later, Stas came up to our table. "OK, Eric, it's showtime!" I got up and followed him across the room and we went down this flight of stairs that led into a dressing room. Noel was already there with another guy who we'd never met before. Stas told us he was the drummer who would be playing with us. And he didn't speak English! There were a few guitars laying about and I picked out the one I felt comfortable with. Noel has his bass guitar on, while the drummer just looked at us a bit bewildered. "Ah, Stas," I said. "I didn't notice any amps on stage. Will they be arriving soon, as I'd like to check them out." "What do you mean, Eric? There are no amps, you're miming." I looked over at Noel, who just said, "Fuck me, matey!"

We were led onto this stage, which was the size of a football pitch, and the drum kit was set up. Then this guy appeared with something like sellotape and started covering the entire drum kit and cymbals with it. The drummer then sat behind it and waited for something to happen. At this point, another guy appeared with guitar leads, plugged one end into my guitar and the other end down a little hole in the floor of the stage, then went over to Noel and did the same. Noel, at this point, was about 20 feet away from me, but I heard him shout over, "Fuck me, matey, I think I'm fucking tripping!" The three of us just stood on stage, wondering what was going to happen next, when out of the blue, this music started coming out of speakers on stage. No count in, no nothing. "Eric, you must sing through the mic, it's for a live vocal," I heard Stas say from the side of the stage. So, not having a clue what the next song was going to be, I just tried my best up there on the stage. So, this is why we recorded those six tunes? As the last song faded out, the audience cheered and then this guy got up from one of the tables, pissed out of his head, and started singing opera. I went over to the mic and joined in with him, pretending to sing in an opera-type voice. This seemed to go down as well as our miming. I can't remember much after that, as we all had quite a few drinks and things.

Stas said he would like Noel and myself to come to his studio again the next day, and a car would be picking us up around 1pm. The next morning, I hauled myself off the bed and got ready to go down for breakfast. Like everything else, the breakfast room was huge, enormous mirrors and old paintings on the wall. I eventually found a plate, fork and knife and helped myself to the food that was out at the buffet. I was about halfway through eating, when a very dishevelled Noel Redding appeared. No socks or shoes, hair not brushed and his shirt hanging out. "Hello, matey, how's the breakfast?" and he made his way up to the buffet. He came back with his food and sat down beside me. "Man, that was one of the weirdest gigs I've played in a very long time." I definitely agreed with him on that. "OK, I think I remember there's a car to pick us up at 1pm. See you in the lobby," and off he went.

So, at 1pm, myself, Noel and Candy got into the car that was waiting. The driver looked to me to be very jerky and wired up as he started to drive through the city. I was in the back seat and Noel and Candy were in the front with the driver. I noticed there were five or six lanes of traffic on one side and the same on the other side, with a thin dividing line in between. This made the cars seem very close to each other and also the speed everyone was driving made the cars sway from side to side. I started feeling as if something was going to happen.

"Excuse me," I said to the driver. "Would you mind slowing down a bit?" "Hey," he replied. "What are you worrying about? Everybody drives like this," and he just carried on. About five minutes later, he turned the car to the left (not signalling) and then… Bang! The car behind us crashed into the back of our car. Our driver got out and started this shouting match with the other driver. I thought, fuck this, I'm off, and opened the door. There were cars everywhere, and I waited for a gap so I could get to the pavement. Our driver saw me and shouted, "Get back in the car!" "If you want to kill yourself, go ahead," I replied. "You want to learn how to drive." I made it to the pavement. I had every intention to walk back to our hotel, which was really just a straight line to get to, but by this time, Noel was out of the car. "Eric, hang about," he shouted. "Don't worry, we'll get a taxi."

Then, the strangest thing happened. Out of the blue, this huge crow flew at me, hit me on the top of my head and flew off. I was completely freaked and put my hand where the crow had just hit me. There was a little bit of blood on my fingers and the cut was smarting like hell. To this day, I can't figure out why this happened. Noel had seen what had happened. "Hey, Eric, there's a song there somewhere!" We then got into a taxi Noel had flagged down, and left our driver and his car to their own devices.

We got to Stas' studio in one piece, and I told him what had happened. He seemed very concerned and talked about firing the driver who had caused the accident. He then took us out of the studio to where the outdoor stage was. Up close, it reminded me of an old Roman amphitheatre with benches all around in a bowl shape leading to the stage. He was thinking of running some gigs in the Summer and led the way through a small corridor to an area which was underneath the stage. He knocked on a door, and it opened into a large room, where there were four or five people. They looked like the people in Britain in the 60s ,the sort of flower power look, with bell bottom jeans and flares, Afghan coats and flowered shirts. Myself and Noel and Candy sat on the floor and were given coffee. Then, Stas and one of the hippies started to tell us what it was like to live in Russia not so very long ago.

They had bands playing live music, but you had to write to the government and various people to ask permission to play rock or blues music. If you didn't and just went ahead, you were taking a very big risk. A lot of musicians were badly beaten up and some were jailed. But, things started very slowly changing, and the government became more relaxed about things, and eventually bands could play more or less what they wanted. As I write this, I saw a documentary on TV about a month ago and Stas was being interviewed about this very thing. It showed some footage and photos of musicians being beaten up and pushed into police vans. These people, who we were in the room with, were sort of catching up, reliving the 60s in their own way. It was all so very different to living in Britain. We sometimes don't know how lucky we are. I still can't believe to this day that you could get beaten up for playing music. The hippies turned out to be really nice people, doing some creative work in their rooms under the stage. One of them gave me a beautiful piece of pottery in the shape of a saucer with designs all over it. I got it back to England in one piece and still have it. A few days later, we were back to reality.

I had been home now for a month, everything quiet, and I was glad to be there with Rhona and Erik. But, a few days later, while I was in the bathroom getting washed, I happened to look out the window and saw this big, fat lady walking up the garden path of the house next to ours. She stopped and started picking up bits of wood and chair legs and bits of fridges and threw them into our garden. I froze, then went downstairs and opened the back door leading into the garden. "Excuse me," I said, "but what are you doing?" And I went over to where she was standing. "This is my garden you're throwing things in." I started to pick the rubbish up and put it back where it had been. She looked daggers at me. " You're only jealous because I'm moving into this house." I asked her what she meant, but she just said something like, "Bugger off, you silly little man", and opened the back door to her new home. Little did I know what was in store.

A few days later, the entire tribe arrived – the large lady, a very small, shrew-like man, who I think was her husband (poor sod), and about six children of various ages. Another few days passed and, as I'm sitting watching TV, I heard a door banging really loudly from next door, and it kept banging every few minutes or so. Last week there was peace… now? I put up with it for a while then, really worked up, I said to Rhona, "Fuck this, I'm gonna tell them to stop it." But Rhona didn't want any trouble, so I just sat down again and the banging kept happening.

Next day, I got the Yellow Pages and looked up various names and phone numbers, and found a contact that was supposed to help people with noisy neighbours. I spoke to someone and was told that two people would call and see me the next day. They arrived and we sat down and introduced each other. "So, what's the problem, Mr Bell?" said the young lady. I told them that the people next door had just moved in and, for some reason, are banging doors. "Well, I don't hear anything," she said. "Well, maybe they're behaving themselves because they saw you arrive," I answered. I was willing The Clumps (I started calling them this, as this was the noise the door made when they banged it) to bang a door, but all was quiet.

"Well, Mr Bell," the young lady said, and opened her briefcase and took out some forms. "I would like you to fill these forms in, what time the door bangs and what time it stops." What are these people getting paid for, I thought, the whole system that's supposed to help people is a load of bollocks. They then got up to leave. "Are you not going to talk to them about this?" I asked. "Just fill in the forms, we'll be in touch." I've always hated the way a lot of things are done. For instance, how do you get a council house? Slit your fuckin' wrists.

The banging of the door started up again and I took out one of the forms, looked at my watch and wrote down the time, then waited for the next clump. I started feeling like a right idiot, and then just made up when the door banged and stopped. Soon, I had filled in the two forms. I phoned up the so-called helpline again and told them it was still happening and that I had completed the forms. The young lady got quite angry and asked what I wanted. "I want you to stop these people ruining my life," I replied. "Very well, we'll come out again tomorrow," and she put down the phone.

So, the next day, at 2ish, the young lady and her partner called again. "I've filled in those forms," I said, handing them to her. She just looked them over quickly and put them in her case. "Right, we're going to call on your neighbours now," and they left. Fifteen minutes later, they rang the doorbell and I let them in, expecting I don't know what. "The woman is complaining that she can't sleep at night because of the noise from the fountain you have in your garden." Unreal. Rhona had a little fountain, which gave off a very quiet, soothing trickle. "You've got to be joking?" I said, and asked them to come out to the garden to hear it for themselves. They both made a big effort and came out. "How is that keeping anyone awake?" But, I could tell that the whole thing was a waste of time. "Right, Mr Bell, we've done all we can. Please don't ring us any more. If you want to take this further, you'll have to get in touch with someone else."

A few weeks later, we had a sunny spell in London and The Clumps started setting up a barbeque in their garden. Myself, Erik and Rhona went out somewhere in the car so we wouldn't hear the tribe shouting and playing this horrible disco music. Next morning, I went out to get the paper and noticed some pieces of black charred wood in the alley. Then, I saw what it was. The Clumps had burned the wooden fence down in the garden on the other side of their house. The fence was now about two foot tall. Yes, The Clumps were becoming very popular.

A few weeks passed, and I was out in the back alley cleaning the car, when one of the other neighbours came up to me. I think it was the guy whose fence had been burned down, who lived on the other side of The Clumps. He told me something about his wallet being stolen and kept on about the neighbours from hell coming into his kitchen when the door had been open and he was upstairs, and spotting a wallet that was lying on a table. He was in a real state and I told him about my experiences with them. Then, he just muttered something and walked away. But the best was yet to come.

I'm in bed around 9am, and just thinking about getting up, when I hear this voice. "One, two, testing, testing, one, two." I thought I was still asleep at one point and dreaming, but, no, I was fully awake. The voice kept on and got clearer and louder. Then, this disco music with the heavy bass drum sound started (music to build sheds to) and a female voice started to sing – or try to. I just lay there in total disbelief. These people just didn't seem to give a shit about anybody's feelings. I got up and went downstairs and Rhona was there. I wanted to do something, anything to get rid of these morons living next door, but had to be careful as Rhona's approach to it all was more laid back, relaxed. So, I just put up with it for a few days and The Clumps carried on with their disco.

I thought it through and decided people like this would carry on as it suited them, they weren't the sort of people you could try and talk to. I had to treat them the way they were treating me. So, next morning, I carried my Marshall practice amp up to the bedroom, set it up right beside the wall, got my guitar, turned up the volume to max, and waited. "One, two, testing, one, two," and the disco beat started. "Right!" I said. "Fuck this!" and hit a D chord as loud as I could, and kept on non-stop for a few minutes. Then I stopped. Total silence. My whole body was shaking with anger and frustration. Ten minutes later, they started up again, and so did I. (I was starting to feel a bit like Victor Meldrew.) Silence again. They didn't try the disco again that day, but started off again the next morning, and I gave them back what they were giving me.

When this started happening, Rhona took Erik out somewhere in the car, as she couldn't stand it. A few hours passed, then the doorbell rang. It was one of The Clumps, the granny of the tribe. "Excuse me, "she said, "but she has to practice." "We were told by the council she could sing between these hours." I butted in, "Listen, you're not living beside the council, you're living beside me. I'm a professional musician and I could blow your house away with sheer volume, but I don't. I'll keep it down." But she just repeated, "She has to practice," and walked off.

The next few days they started up again, and so did I. I knew then we were going to have to sell our house and move. I phoned Noel Redding and asked him if I could come over and stay in his place for a few days? In the middle of nowhere, peace and quiet. He said I could stay and could bring Rhona and Erik as well if I wanted. And he would try and organise a few gigs while I was there. I asked Rhona if she would like to stay in West Cork for a week or so and, to my surprise, she said yes. So, we booked the flights and a few days later, we were on the plane. At one point, I mentioned to Rhona that she would probably want to live in West Cork but she said she didn't think so.

When the plane landed, we were met by Noel and he drove us to his place. As well as his enormous house, Noel had a lovely little cottage just across the courtyard. This is where Rhona, Erik and myself would be staying. It was just the break from The Clumps and London that we needed. We drove to beaches, which were huge and mostly deserted, and stopped off at little villages and looked around. Myself and Noel and a local drummer played a few gigs, had a few free beers and made a few bob each, which would help pay for our stay. The week passed very quickly and there we were, flying back to London. I noticed Rhona was very quiet, and asked her was anything wrong? "You were right, Eric, I do want to live in West Cork."

Back in London, we prepared to put up with The Clumps again, wondering what they were going to do next. But, I'm very happy to say, they were very quiet for some reason.

I got a phone call from a friend and bass player, Tony Williams. He was from The Sunsets, and we had played together in the past. He asked would I be interested in playing a small tour in Sweden if he could set it up? I was all for it, as I now needed as much money I could get if we were moving to West Cork. Tony got in touch with a drummer called Andy Golden and we had a few rehearsals, trying out blues and rock numbers. It sounded pretty good. Tony lined up around ten gigs through a Swedish music agent, and a week later, we were playing the blues in Sweden. We went down pretty well, apart from some yobs shouting out, "The Boys Are Back In Town!" "Well, tell them to piss off then."

We were staying in a hotel that was deserted because it was a place people would stay in in the Summertime. So there was just me, Tony and Andy. Felt a bit like that movie, *The Shining*. I had gone out for a walk in a beautiful forest that was at the back of the hotel. As it was Autumn, the colours of the trees and the forest were magical. I returned to the hotel and, as I was opening the door to my room, noticed a note lying on the floor. I got the shock of my life. I don't really know how she did it, but Rhona had managed to get a message to me. In the note, I was told that Noel had been found dead in his house. She also said she had organised a flight from London to Cork and when I had landed in London, she would meet me with some clean clothes, and then I could fly to Cork to pay my respects.

Getting to Cork airport, I was met by Les Sampson, an English drummer who was living in West Cork and who had known Noel for a very long time. He drove me to Clonakilty, a small town about 40 minutes drive from the airport. When we reached it, Les parked the car and we walked through Clonakilty until we came to a funeral parlour. The man who was working there shook my hand and asked me would I like to stay and be with Noel for a little while. He took me into a room and Noel's coffin was sitting on two small, wooden tables. I couldn't see him as the lid was in place and there were beautiful wild flowers scattered on the coffin. I just sat down beside him and remained very quiet. At moments like these, the material world starts to fade and you enter a different world and realise we are all on a sort of journey. I stayed in a hotel and, a few days later,,an Irish Wake was in full swing. It was held in this pub right in the country and lots of people had turned up and everybody was enjoying the drink. Someone had set up speakers and the music of The Jimi Hendrix Experience was played non-stop all day. Then, it was time for me to fly back to London.

CHAPTER 26

I was living in Shepherd's Bush, when my cousin Davy Dunwoody got in touch. He had some time off from his job in Belfast and wanted to come over and stay in London for a week or so. But, the real reason was to buy a new Fender Stratocaster, and he wanted me to go around the music shops with him, and for me to try out some guitars. We must have tried every music shop in central London, until I picked up yet another Strat and said, "I think this might be the one, Davy." He bought it and still has the same guitar, which he played in a local Belfast blues group, Spoonful of Blues. He's a good player and I don't think he would mind if I said he should get down to practising more.

My other two cousins, Harry Lamb and Eric Dunwoody, don't play musical instruments but they are both in love with music. Harry started an R&B music festival in Belfast about eight years ago and made a great success of it. It was called The Woodstock Blues Festival and lasted around eight days. It provided all the top blues groups with gigs all around Belfast and beyond, and the audiences really enjoyed these eight days every year. Eric Dunwoody, Davy's brother, also loves his music, especially the Dublin band U2. I believe he is one of their biggest supporters.

A huge turning point came to me out of the blue. I was living in West Cork at the time and, one day, I got an email asking me would I be interested in headlining a blues gig being held in Cheshire? The guy running it was called Andy Quinn. He told me the flights and hotel and the fee would all be taken care of. So, I got in touch with the two musicians and friends I'd worked with in one of The Eric Bell Bands, Tony Williams, bass player, and Andy Golden, the drummer. They were both up for it and, in a few weeks, I got the plane to Manchester and met Andy and Tony.

We had a few hours of rehearsal and then drove to the gig. We walked into this large room that reminded me of a ballroom. I really thought we were in the wrong place, as there were about ten OAPs playing bowls at the side of the hall. Then, I met Andy Quinn, the guy running the gig. He laughed when he saw me looking at the OAPs and assured me that we were at the right place. There were another few acts with us that night and they were all young and very good players. We went down well with the audience and, as we were packing up our gear, Andy Quinn invited me for a drink in the bar at the back of the stage area. He told me he really loved early Thin Lizzy and he played guitar himself. He seemed like a really nice guy and we talked for a while, then Tony and Andy

Golden and myself said our goodbyes and headed back to our hotel.

Back in West Cork, a few weeks later I got another email from Andy Quinn, thanking me for the gig we'd played for him. Then, he asked me if I would be interested in recording an album? He would organise flights, transport, hotel and food, and the studio. Wow! What an offer. The only snag was I really hadn't got a band. I wrote songs on a little four-track mixing recorder and the demos were a bit rough, but I liked the atmosphere, the feel. I had noticed the last few albums I'd recorded with various musicians didn't somehow capture the atmosphere that was on my home demos. I asked him would he mind if I came over to the studio myself and recorded the album on my own, thinking he would tell me to take a running jump. But he was up for it and I started finishing and reworking some songs to prepare for the recording.

A few weeks later, Andy met me at Manchester Airport and Aidan O'Rourke, one of Andy's mates dropped us off at the hotel and, once checked in, drove us to Edge Recording Studios in Cheshire. When we got there, there was nobody around except this young guy who was the sound engineer, Mark Winterburn. I suddenly realised for the first time that this was it – Andy, Mark and myself. Fuck me, I thought, what have I done? I walked around the studio, trying to look confident, but deep inside I was wondering how I was going to approach this. Then I just thought, I'll pretend I'm recording on my little four-track back home. We got down to recording the first song and I played rhythm guitar to a drum machine and did rough vocal, then put on a bass guitar and lead guitar and things like tambourine and percussion. I was very pleased with the feeling of the song, and a lot of this was down to Mark's engineering and getting different sounds that I heard in my head. Andy, the producer, was very supportive throughout the whole recording and I was given complete freedom to try whatever I wished. First recording day came to an end and Aidan arrived and dropped Andy and myself back to the hotel. As we were waiting for our meal, I had a good chance to talk about things to Andy. He came across as a very positive guy, full of enthusiasm and ideas. He was like a breath of fresh air.

I'd like, at this point, to mention a few things to any young musician out there. I've been in the business a long time and experienced a lot of things. If you want to succeed in the music business, I would suggest that you work on your own thing, do your own thing, but you really have to give it everything you've got, work at it every day, day after day, so it can stand up to anything else out there. Probably just as important, I've been around lots of recording companies in the past with my little cassette of demos and it was soul destroying. Their attitude was very negative. And managers. Nearly all of these people wanted me to change, to end up doing what they wanted. It's really difficult to meet someone who honestly likes what you are doing, to accept you as an individual and work with you and what you have to offer.

That's why meeting Andy Quinn has been such a big thing for me. He has never once tried to get me to change, and he has become my friend and manager. The other person who has stuck with me through thick and thin, is my Spanish friend, Quique, who runs my website. Quique has been working on this for a very long time and I am so proud every time I view the site. It's up there with the best of them. Though we've been in touch over the airwaves for quite a while, Quique and myself have met only five or six times. Hopefully, we'll meet again in the not so distant future. Anyway, I eventually finished recording the album at Edge Studios and called it Exile. Andy and Quique promoted it, and it got some pretty good reviews and built up my confidence as a songwriter. Then, Andy offered me a chance to record a second album, and I did it the same way, on my own. I called this album, *Standing At A Bus Stop*. It has had a fair share of good reviews as well.

I am now living back in Northern Ireland for the first time since I left with The Bluebeats Showband, roughly 55 years ago. It's a small country place called Carrowdore, about 20 odd miles from Belfast. I'm still playing and writing songs and still enjoy it all.

Two of the nicest things have happened over the past few years. One was that my old school, Orangefield Boy's Secondary, got in touch with me. It was to honour some of the pupils who had made a name for themselves and, along with Van Morrison and CS Lewis, they remembered me. It was such a buzz being remembered, and I ended up playing a gig in the Girl's School building just beside the Boy's School, and Van played three gigs.vThe other thing was being included on this massive wall mural. I didn't know anything about it until, one night, my cousin Harry phoned me and said there was a mural in East Belfast and I was in it alongside George Best, CS Lewis, Gary Moore, Van Morrison and a few more famous sons. And, the funny thing is, it's just across the road from where The Belfast Ropeworks used to be.

Everyone has a story to tell, and this has been mine. I hope whoever reads it gets something from it.

All the best

Eric Bell.

ACKNOWLEDGEMENTS

Eric would like to thank Peter Healey and Sophie Wilcockson for their involvement in making his autobiography possible. He also sends a massive thank you to long standing Thin Lizzy friend and archivist, Peter Nielsen who has played such an important role in providing additional background information along with rare photos and posters.

Thank you also to photographers Aidan O'Rourke, Martin Stassen and Henrik Hildebrandt. Eric also fondly remembers Liam Quigley, whose photograph of Thin Lizzy on the road appears in this book.

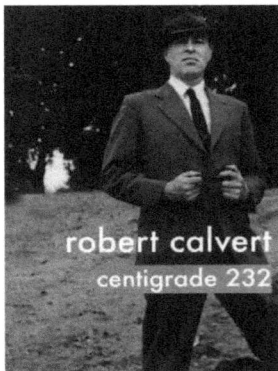

robert calvert
centigrade 232

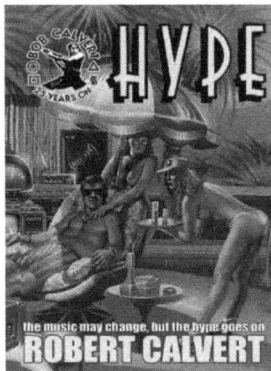

HYPE
the music may change, but the hype goes on
ROBERT CALVERT

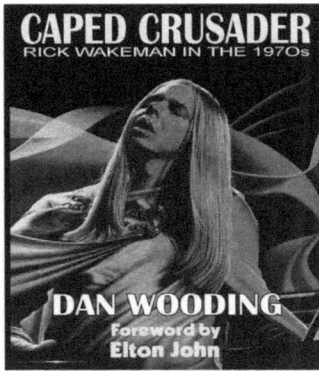

CAPED CRUSADER
RICK WAKEMAN IN THE 1970s
DAN WOODING
Foreword by
Elton John

Robert Newton Calvert: Born 9 March 1945, Died 14 August 1988 after suffering a heart attack. Contributed poetry, lyrics and vocals to legendary space rock band Hawkwind intermittently on five of their most critically acclaimed albums, including Space Ritual (1973), Quark, Strangeness & Charm (1977) and Hawklords (1978). He also recorded a number of solo albums in the mid 1970s. CENTIGRADE 232 was Robert Calvert's first collection of poems.

Hype 'And now, for all you speeding street smarties out there, the one you've all been waiting for, the one that'll pierce your laid back ears, decoke your sinuses, cut clean thru the schlock rock, MOR/crossover, techno flash mind mush. It's the new Number One with a bullet … with a bullet … It's Tom, Supernova, Mahler with a pan galactic biggie …' And the Hype goes on. And on. Hype, an amphetamine hit of a story by Hawkwind collaborator Robert Calvert. Who's been there and made it back again. The debriefing session starts here.

Rick Wakeman is the world's most unusual rock star, a genius who has pushed back the barriers of electronic rock. He has had some of the world's top orchestras perform his music, has owned eight Rolls Royces at one time, and has broken all the rules of composing and horrified his tutors at the Royal College of Music. Yet he has delighted his millions of fans. This frank book, authorised by Wakeman himself, tells the moving tale of his larger than life career.

"So many books, so little time."
Frank Zappa

THE NINE HENRYS
By Peter McAdam

TERRY DENE: BRITAIN'S FIRST ROCK & ROLL REBEL

DAN WOODING

King Squealer

MAURICE O'MAHONEY WITH DAN WOODING

There are nine Henrys, pur
ported to be the world's
first cloned cartoon charac
ter. They live in a strange
lo fi domestic surrealist
world peopled by talking
rock buns and elephants on
wobbly stilts.

They mooch around in their
minimalist universe suffer
ing from an existential
crisis with some genetically
modified humour thrown in.

Marty Wilde on Terry Dene: "Whatever
happened to Terry becomes a great deal
more comprehensible as you read of the
callous way in which he was treated by
people who should have known better
many of whom, frankly, will never know
better   of the sad little shadows of
the past who eased themselves into
Terry's life, took everything they
could get and, when it seemed that all
was lost, quietly left him … Dan Wood
ing's book tells it all."

Rick Wakeman: "There have
always been certain 'careers'
that have fascinated the
public, newspapers, and the
media in general. Such
include musicians, actors,
sportsmen, police, and not
surprisingly, the people who
give the police their employ
ment: The criminal. For the
man in the street, all these
careers have one thing in
common: they are seemingly
beyond both his reach and,
in many cases, understanding
and as such, his only associ
ation can be through the
media of newspapers or tele
vision. The police, however,
will always require the ser
vices of the grass, the
squealer, the snitch, (call
him what you will), in order
to assist in their investiga
tions and arrests; and amaz
ingly, this is the area that
seldom gets written about."

"Outside of a dog, a book is
man's best friend. Inside of a
dog it's too dark to read."
Groucho Marx

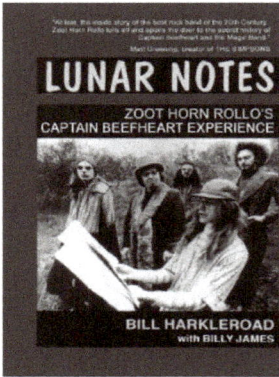

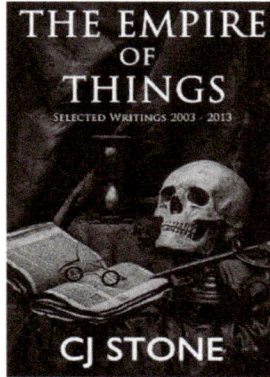

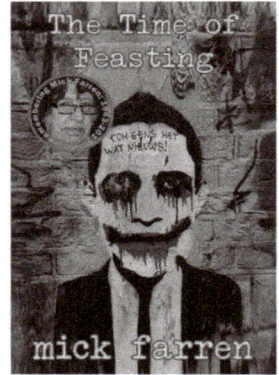

"The person, be it gentleman or lady, who has not pleasure in a good novel, must be intolerably stupid."

Jane Austen

Darklost

mick farren

STICK IT

Rock 'n Road Stories by **Corky Laing**

STRANGE BOAT

MIKE SCOTT AND THE WATERBOYS

IAN ABRAHAMS

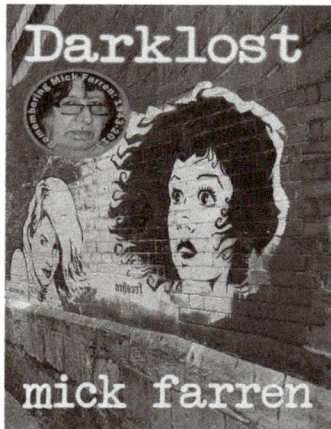

Los Angeles City of Angels, city of dreams. But sometimes the dreams become nightmares. Having fled New York, Victor Renquist and his small group of Nosferatu are striving to re establish their colony. They have become a deeper, darker part of the city's nightlife. And Hollywood's glitterati are hot on the scent of the thrill, one that outshines all others immortality. But someone, somewhere, is med dling with even darker powers, powers that even the Nosferatu fear. Someone is attempting to summon the entity of ancient evil known as Cthulhu. And Ren quist must overcome dissent in his own colony, solve the riddle of the Darklost (a being brought part way along the Nosferatu path and then abandoned) and combat powerful enemies to save the world of humans!

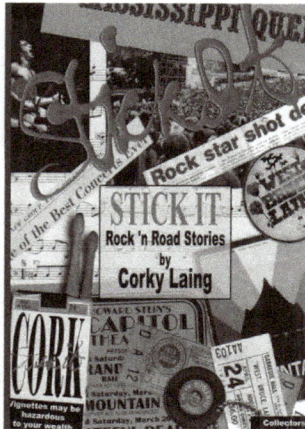

Canadian born Corky Laing is probably best known as the drummer with Mountain. Corky joined the band shortly after Mountain played at the famous Woodstock Festival, although he did receive a gold disc for sales of the soundtrack album after over dubbing drums on Ten Years After's performance. Whilst with Mountain Corky Laing recorded three studio albums with them before the band split. Follow ing the split Corky, along with Mountain gui tarist Leslie West, formed a rock three piece with former Cream bassist Jack Bruce. West, Bruce and Laing recorded two studio albums and a live album before West and Laing re formed Mountain, along with Felix Pappalardi. Since 1974 Corky and Leslie have led Mountain through various line ups and recordings, and continue to record and perform today at numer ous concerts across the world. In addition to his work with Mountain, Corky Laing has recorded one solo album and formed the band Cork with former Spin Doctors guitarist Eric Shenkman, and recorded a further two studio albums with the band, which has also featured former Jimi Hendrix bassist Noel Redding. The stories are told in an incredibly frank, engaging and amusing manner, and will appeal also to those people who may not necessarily be fans of

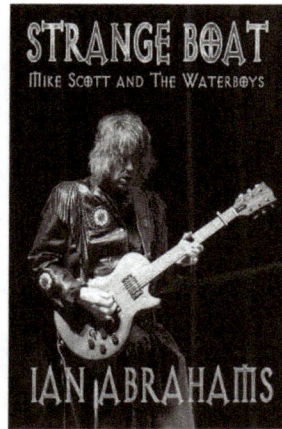

To me there's no difference between Mike Scott The Waterboys; they both mean the same thing. mean myself and whoever are my current trave ling musical companions" Mike Scott Strange B charts the twisting and meandering journey of Mike Scott, describing the literary and spiritu references that inform his songwriting and exp ing the multitude of locations and cultures in which The Waterboys have assembled and reflec in their recordings. From his early forays into music scene in Scotland at the end of the 1970s his creation of a 'Big Music' that peaked with hit single 'The Whole of the Moon' and onto t Irish adventure which spawned the classic Fish man's Blues, his constantly restless creativity led him through a myriad of changes. With his revolving cast of troubadours at his side, he' created some of the most era defining records the 1980s, reeled and jigged across the Celtic heartlands, reinvented himself as an electric rocker in New York, and sought out personal renewal in the spiritual calm of Findhorn's Sc tish highland retreat. Mike Scott's life has be tale of continual musical exploration entwined with an ever evolving spirituality. "An intrig portrait of a modern musician" (Record Collecto

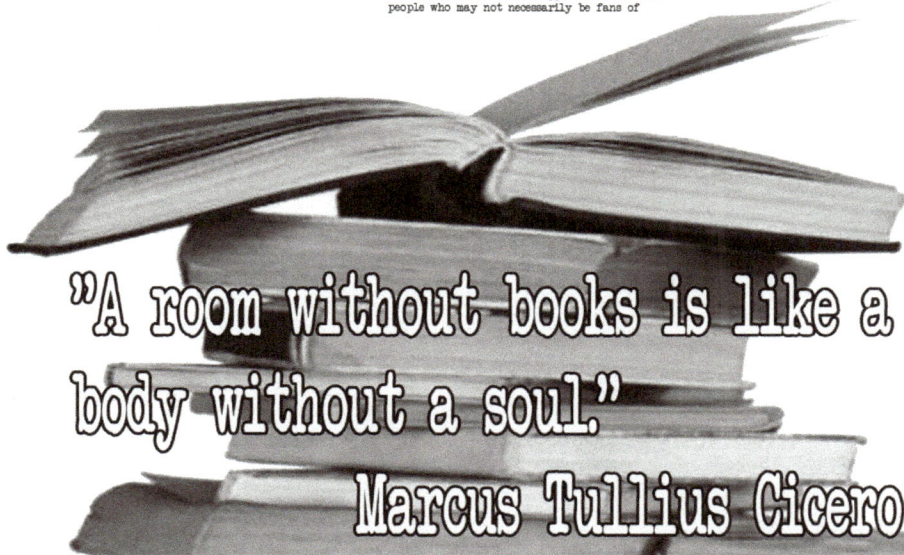

"A room without books is like a body without a soul."
Marcus Tullius Cicero

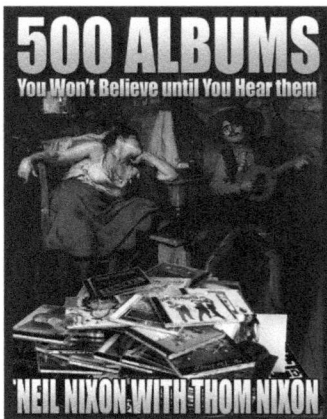

500 ALBUMS
You Won't Believe until You Hear them
'NEIL NIXON WITH THOM NIXON'

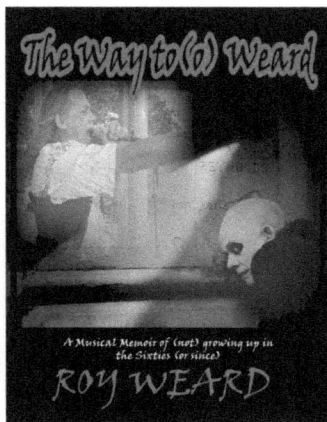

The Way to(o) Weard
A Musical Memoir of (not) growing up in the Sixties (or since)
ROY WEARD

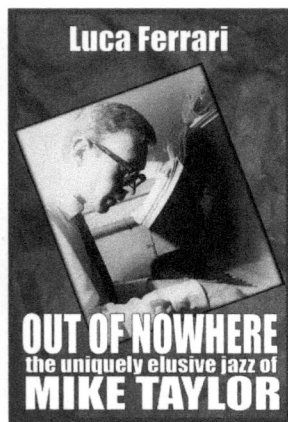

Luca Ferrari
OUT OF NOWHERE
the uniquely elusive jazz of
MIKE TAYLOR

An erudite catalogue of some of the most peculiar records ever made. We have lined up, described and put into context 500 "albums" in the expectation that those of you who can't help yourselves when it comes to finding and collecting music will benefit from these efforts in two ways. Firstly, you'll know you are not alone. Secondly, we hope that some of the work covering the following pages leads you to new discoveries, and makes your life slightly better as a result.

Roy Weard was born in Barking, then a part of Essex, in 1948. He spent most of the mid-sixties through to the mid seventies involved first in folk music and then in the psychedelic hippie scene. He toured with many bands in various capacities from T-Shirt seller to sound engineer, production manager and tour manager. He was involved in several bands of his own, played at many of the iconic free festivals, made three full length albums and two singles, wrote for music magazines, computer magazines and produced copious MySpace blogs. He has lived all over London, spent four years in Hamburg, Germany and finally settled in Brighton where he now resides. He still sings in a rock and roll band, promotes gigs, does a weekly radio show and steadfastly refuses to act his age. This is his story.

Michael Ronald Taylor (1938 - 1969) was a British jazz composer, pianist and co-songwriter for the band Cream.

Mike Taylor drowned in the River Thames near Leigh-on-Sea, Essex in January 1969, following years of heavy drug use (principally hashish and LSD). He had been homeless for three years, and his death was almost entirely unremarked. This is the first biography written about him.

"I have always imagined that Paradise will be a kind of library."
Jorge Luis Borges

THE TRIALS OF OZ

TONY PALMER

With contributions from RICHARD NEVILLE, FELIX DENNIS and JIM ANDERSON and other veterans of the OZ Obscenity Trial

40TH ANNIVERSARY EDITION

CALLING FROM A STAR

THE *Merrell Fankhauser* STORY

THE REAL PORN WARS

EXPLICIT CONTENT

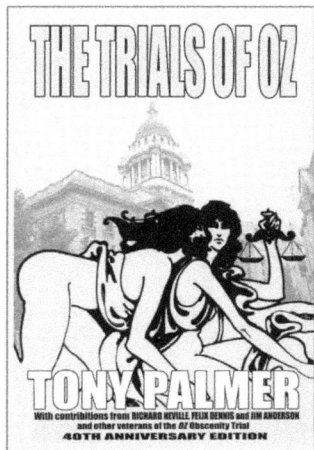

The OZ trial was the longest obscenity trial in history. It was also one of the worst reported. With minor exceptions, the Press chose to rewrite what had occurred, presumably to fit in with what seemed to them the acceptable prejudices of the times. Perhaps this was inevitable. The proceedings dragged on for nearly six weeks in the hot summer of 1971 when there were, no doubt, a great many other events more worthy of attention. Against the background of murder in Ulster, for example, the OZ affair probably fades into its proper insignificance. Even so, after the trial, when some newspapers realised that maybe something important had happened, it became more and more apparent that what was essential was for anyone who wished to be able to read what had actually been said. Trial and judgment by a badly informed press became the order of the day. This 40th Anniversary edition includes new material by all three of the original defendants, the prosecuting barrister, one of the OZ schoolkids, and even the daughters of the judge. There are also many illustrations including unseen material from Felix Dennis' own collection...

Merrell Fankhauser has led one of the most diverse and interesting careers in music. He was born in Louisville, Kentucky, and moved to California when he was 13 years old. Merrell went on to become one of the innovators of surf music and psychedelic folk rock. His travels from Hollywood to his 15 year jungle experience on the island of Maui have been documented in numerous music books and magazines in the United States and Europe. Merrell has gained legendary international status throughout the field of rock music; his credits include over 250 songs published and released. He is a multi talented singer/songwriter and unique guitar player whose sound has delighted listeners for over 35 years. This extraordinary book tells a unique story of one of the founding fathers of surf rock, who went on to play in a succession of progressive and psychedelic bands and to meet some of the greatest names in the business, including Captain Beefheart, Randy California, The Beach Boys, Jan and Dean... and there is even a run in with the notorious Manson family.

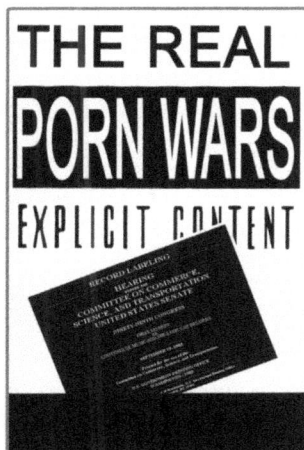

On September 19, 1985, Frank Zappa testified before the United States Senate Commerce, Technology, and Transportation committee, attacking the Parents Music Resource Center or PMRC, a music organization co founded by Tipper Gore, wife of then senator Al Gore. The PMRC consisted of many wives of politicians, including the wives of five members of the committee, and was founded to address the issue of song lyrics with sexual or satanic content. Zappa saw their activities as on a path towards censorship and called their proposal for voluntary labelling of records with explicit content "extortion" of the music industry. This is what happened.

"Good friends, good books, and a sleepy conscience: this is the ideal life." Mark Twain

Ingram Content Group UK Ltd.
Milton Keynes UK
UKHW051318110623
423250UK00016B/88

9 781908 728975